Dinner
at
Home

140 RECIPES *to* ENJOY *with*
FAMILY AND FRIENDS

JeanMarie Brownson

Chicago Tribune

S
SURREY
BOOKS

AN **AGATE** IMPRINT

CHICAGO

Chicago Tribune
Tony W. Hunter, CEO & Publisher
Gerould W. Kern, Senior Vice President, Editor
Peter Kendall, Managing Editor
Colin McMahon, Associate Editor
George Papajohn, Investigations Editor
Geoff Brown, Operations & Development Editor
Margaret Holt, Standards Editor
R. Bruce Dold, Editorial Page Editor
John P. McCormick, Deputy Editorial Page Editor
Marcia Lythcott, Commentary Editor
Amy Carr, Development Editor
Associate Managing Editors for News
    Robin Daughtridge, Photography
    Mark Jacob, Metro
    Mike Kellams, Business
    Cristi Kempf, Editing & Presentation
    Joe Knowles, Sports

Dinner at Home
ISBN 10: 1-57284-178-8
ISBN 13: 978-1-57284-178-9

Illustrations by John Burgoyne
Printed in China

Library of Congress Cataloging-in-Publication Data is on file at the Library of Congress.

10 9 8 7 6 5 4 3 2 1

Surrey Books is an imprint of Agate Publishing. Agate books are available in bulk at discount prices. For more information visit agatepublishing.com.

This book is dedicated to my mom, dad, Scott, Claire and Glen

Thank you for all your support and encouragement. Thank you for spending so much of your lives in my kitchen. And always offering to do the dishes. I love you more than I can ever say.

Thank you also to my brothers, sisters, grandparents, aunts, uncles, cousins, friends and comrades in food. Our time spent gathered at the table has been my life's greatest pleasure.

CONTENTS

From Peanut Butter Menus *to* Dinner at Home

GREW UP IN A FAMILY THAT SIMPLY LOVES to cook and eat. Food takes center stage at every event, from reunions to picnics, birthdays, baptisms and weddings. Our obsession, passion and never-ending appetite for food started with my grandparents.

My paternal grandparents grew up in Glogowacz, Austria-Hungary. They immigrated separately to the U.S. with their families nearly 100 years ago. Martin and Mary met again in Chicago and were married in 1925.

My grandmother baked, pickled and scrimped her way through nourishing eight children. My grandfather, a bricklayer, butchered and smoked

hams and sausages between gigs working on some of Chicago's most iconic buildings and churches. His brick smokehouse (tucked under the stairs in their Chicago bungalow) was my favorite spot in the house.

Martin and Mary's children cherished old-world traditions. My aunts prepared all of Gram's recipes, putting their own skill sets to good use making strudels and slaws. Her sons, including my father, still make the family sausage for our annual reunion to this very day. My generation knows the stories and recipes well, even if we don't cook them often.

Charles, my maternal grandfather, was a professional baker of Sicilian descent. To my mother's dismay, she didn't naturally inherit his skills. Instead, she took cooking classes at the local gas company. She tells tales of pie crusts gone wrong and spaghetti sauce my father wouldn't taste. Dinner parties tested her nerves. Little wonder, since she cut her cooking chops in the real *Mad Men* era. She had to not only be the perfect hostess, but look beautiful, too. *Fait accompli.*

I have two brothers and two sisters—we were five smart, willful children who tested my parents and their wallets continuously. We were always ready for dinner, but late to the table nearly every night thanks to reruns of *The Dick Van Dyke Show*.

I started paying attention to food in the fourth grade. My teacher brought avocados to the classroom after her Florida spring break and let us all taste this exotic fruit/vegetable. I was captivated by its creaminess. Then my Uncle Jake shared his *Gourmet* subscription with me (which I maintained until the magazine folded in 2009). He also bought me my first cookbook. When I complained about "hot dog night," my mom, by then an accomplished cook who prepared breakfast, lunch and dinner for 7 people every day of the week, happily passed the dinner task on to me. I consulted my new cookbook and made hot dogs stuffed with cheddar and wrapped in bacon. In middle school, I made a four-course all-peanut butter meal for my Uncle Charles, the fanciest eater I knew. Food remains a common bond.

My grandparents shared what they knew: old-world baking, pickling and smoking. Grandma Dorothy's fruit trees started my peach jam-making habit. I will never forget Grandpa Kaiser's smoky

speck or Gram's powdered sugar-coated nut and meringue-filled pillows and crescent shaped, jam-stuffed kipferls. She measured with her hands, not tools, with instinct and experience.

Little wonder that I loved chemistry in high school—after all, most experiments meant following a recipe. I pursued chemistry in college and kept cooking. By sophomore year, I had made nearly every recipe in both volumes of Julia Child's *Mastering the Art of French Cooking*—too bad I didn't have a blog or a movie deal.

My folks didn't flinch when I'd invite friends over to cook crepes at midnight. I once made chateaubriand after a Yes concert for a special friend. I paid for college by waitressing and catering parties. Dessert tables were my specialty.

Comfortable in the school kitchens, my foods and nutrition professor, Mary Abbott Hess, suggested I interview for an internship at *Cuisine Magazine*. With that, my world changed overnight from chemistry to the culinary arts.

After receiving a B.S. in foods and nutrition, I opted out of dietetics to do a chef's apprenticeship. I was the American Culinary Federation's first female apprentice in Chicago. They placed me at a high-end hotel on Michigan Avenue. I was scared.

It was the late 1970s. There was only one female chef in the kitchens. At 5 a.m. on my first day, she advised me to go out and buy a good bra and support hose to counter the physical toll 14 hours a day spent cooking takes on a body. Thirty minutes later, I cut my thumb so badly I fainted. Fortunately, my father had supplied me with a first aid kit. I pulled myself together and got back to work mincing celery for salad dressing. No one was the wiser—I think.

At *Cuisine*, we cooked dim sum, shark's fin soup and clay-baked, lotus-wrapped beggar's chicken for an article on the foods of Hong Kong. The wife of the Moroccan consul came to the test kitchens to teach us how to make bestilla and tagines for an article on the foods of Morocco. We learned about French wines and the cuisines of Spain and Thailand. We made pates, croissants, cassoulet, ice creams, sorbets, jams, jellies and more. We filled the magazine's pages with beautiful food photographs and brilliant recipes from around the world. People were cooking "gourmet" food at home, and we were there to help them.

When *Cuisine* moved New York City, I began my 16-year career at the *Chicago Tribune* as test kitchen director. Those were the glory days, when the paper had two hefty food sections, Taste and the Food Guide, helmed by editors David Dolson, Carol

 At the vegetable station, I lost the weight I gained in the pastry shop. I learned to sculpt butter, carve ice and shuck oysters fast at parties. Bone a case of quail? No problem.

I had a blast (mostly) cooking and learning in 12-hour shifts, six days a week, in the various "stations." At the vegetable station, I lost the weight I gained in the pastry shop. I learned to sculpt butter, carve ice and shuck oysters fast at parties. Bone a case of quail? No problem. I'd fall into bed with my hands smelling of garlic; cuts, nicks and burns on my arms; my heels bloody from standing. I slept soundly. I bested the male apprentices and impressed even the staunchest classically trained Swiss chefs.

When the editors at *Cuisine* offered me a full-time position in their test kitchens, I was thrilled. Hotels and restaurant kitchens were not my calling. I was getting married anyway, so the Swiss chefs stopped looking so impressive.

Haddix and Carol Rasmussen. In the fall of 1980, our food department boasted a staff of more than 10, all of whom counted on me for everything: recipe testing, recipe development, appropriate sources for articles, equipment testing, beautiful food styling. I made demi-glace so often I knew the recipe from memory. We ran recipes and stories to suit a style of elaborate, complicated cooking that few of us do any more.

I wrote weekly columns and cover stories for the Food Guide, Taste and Home sections. From 1980 to 1984, I wrote the *Sunday Magazine* food column, often bylined with editor Paul Camp. I also wrote many pieces for the *Magazine's* entertaining sections. Everyone "entertained" back then. I used to rent dishes and tablecloths and borrow albums from the library to create theme dinners.

My mother says I inherited my wanderlust from her mother. I funded many a trip by writing stories for the *Tribune's* Travel section. I started with culinary destinations and brought home recipes, techniques, tools, knives and food.

It was a heady time to be in the food business. Chefs around the world were breaking out as superstars—not just Julia, but also Jacques Pepin, Emeril, Paul Prudhomme, Paul Bocuse, Fredy Girardet, Jeremiah Towers, Daniel Boulud, Alice Waters. They came to the *Tribune* to talk food, promote their books and cook in our kitchens. The grocery business was evolving, too, carrying specialty and ethnic ingredients and pushing variety in the produce and seafood sections.

The *Tribune* food sections won multiple awards every year. We pushed the boundaries of food coverage and original food writing. Our amazing photography team proved that food could look great printed on newsprint.

Then came food on television—twenty-four hours a day on the Food Network. Would anyone watch? You know the answer: We can't turn it off. Food on TV just might be the single biggest reason for the burgeoning foodie population.

In the early 1990s, the *Tribune* launched CLTV. Our Good Eating show, hosted by Steve Dolinsky, challenged me to bring our test kitchen work to viewers' living rooms. My brightest day there was sharing the screen with Julia Child.

Speaking of Julia, she remains my biggest food hero. I had the extreme privilege of interviewing her in her Cambridge, MA home. She cooked lunch for the two of us while I peppered her with questions about her career and her latest cookbook. We ate perfectly roasted chicken and fresh corn and tomato salad at the kitchen table that is now housed in the Smithsonian. When I declined her offer of wine (I was a tiny bit pregnant with my first child, Claire), she hugged me and advised me to live a balanced life—food, yes, but family, too. It was the best advice I ever received.

In late 1996, I left the *Tribune* to push my love for food and wine in new directions. I wrote freelance pieces for magazines including *Better Homes & Gardens* and *Food & Wine Magazine*. In August of 1997 Judith Dunbar Hines and I co-chaired the annual conference for the International Association of Culinary Professionals (IACP), a four-day event that gathered more than 1,800 food and wine professionals in Chicago. I was so proud of our city and its food scene. Nearly twenty years later, Chicago remains one of the best food towns in the nation.

In 1996, I had the pleasure of co-authoring the second cookbook of celebrated chef Rick Bayless and his wife, Deann. The process was a three-year immersion in Mexican cooking, writing and testing recipes for everything from regional moles to Mexican cakes and candies. *Rick Bayless's Mexican Kitchen* won three national awards, including the IACP Julia Child Cookbook of the Year (presented to us by Julia herself), the IACP International Cookbook of the Year and a James Beard Cookbook Award. Four years later, our third cookbook together also won a James Beard Award.

With our partners Manny Valdes and Greg Keller, the Baylesses and I also built two amazing specialty food companies, Frontera Foods and Red Fork Natural Foods. I've discovered that good food manufacturing is not unlike the work I did during all those years spent in test kitchens doing recipe development. Accuracy, consistency and superior flavors are necessary for success. I thoroughly enjoy working in production kitchens, teaching methods to make food on a large scale that tastes like home cooking. I'll never cease to be amazed at the engineers who design the machinery to package food. Our team in the offices and our manufacturing partners amaze me every day with their dedication to superior quality and to our customers. We are never at a loss for ideas.

Today, thanks to international travel, food television, thousands of cookbooks and dozens of food magazines, even non-cooks know a great deal about food. In the United States, it's easy to cook with influences from beyond our borders. When my food career began more than three decades ago, I traveled all over Chicago to find such oddities as cilantro and chipotles. Now, I can cook nearly any cuisine from the supermarket down the block. I can also choose to shop online for regional or ethnic specialties, my favorite heirloom beans, imported vinegars and exotic spices. Every so often, the world comes to my door via UPS, FedEx or the USPS.

In the early 1980s, I carried an entire set of copper cookware and carbon steel knives home from Paris in my luggage. (Actually, the copper cookware ended up in my husband's backpack.) Today, top-quality pots, pans, knives and kitchen tools show up in stores all across the country.

In the United States, we cook differently in every decade. I know I do. I no longer make the classic French food I prepared in the 1970s, or the elaborate sauces and tortes of the 1980s. I had my children in the 1990s and life got more complicated, so the food on our table simplified.

Now my grill, rather than my copper pots, often saves the day. I rely on an ever-increasing supply of ready-cut salad greens, snipped herbs, diced fresh squash, top-quality bottled sauces and boneless chicken found at every supermarket. These items help me get a satisfying, healthy, delicious dinner on the table quickly.

Today, I cook more vegetables and grains and less meat. I use olive oil regularly and save butter for special occasions. I cut way back on the cream and cheese, using a fourth of what I used a decade ago.

I use Greek yogurt all the time. I buy broth and stock bases, but still grind my own spices whenever possible. I use tons of fresh herbs. I build flavor with a world of condiments, such as Korean chili paste on pork chops and miso on fish fillets.

This collection of recipes comes from my Dinner at Home column, which has appeared in the *Tribune* since 2007. The column reflects the way I cook for my family and friends. Every meal out proves to be an inspiration. Every trip to the market or grocery store motivates a dish—some new and many more familiar. I want to cook foods that nourish both body and soul. Mostly, I want my family and friends at the table with me—no matter what's on it. Cooking for friends and family ranks among my life's greatest pleasures. I wish you the same journey. I wish you dinner at home. With love.

CHAPTER 1

Notes and Tips
from a
Lifetime in the Kitchen

BELIEVE IN RECIPES. I'VE SPENT MY ENTIRE career creating, editing, testing and following recipes. I take great care in recording the activity of cooking in my kitchen—setting timers, measuring pan sizes and testing for doneness. Some recipes deserve my slavish devotion, particularly when I am baking. Others, such as grilling vegetables, simmering soup, braising stews, not so much.

That being said, nurturing your inner cook proves invaluable. It's super pleasurable to customize your cooking, to call it your own, to take pride in your creativity.

Start your cooking life by investing in equipment that you like and look forward to using. There's no better motivator for ordering take-out than hating your skillet or struggling to keep an old oven at the correct temperature. I love my little nonstick rice cooker—I'm always looking for ways to put it to use. Ditto for the vegetable knife I bought in Japan.

But don't forego cooking simply because you don't have a perfectly outfitted kitchen. I've cooked in some very sketchy places (hey, I once taught microwave cooking classes in a garage). At home, I have the pleasure of cooking on a dual-fuel six-burner Wolf range. Yet the meals we cook on a 40-year-old electric cooktop at our cabin taste just as good. It's not the stove that makes the meal delicious—it's the people who use it.

My grandmother knew exactly what a half teaspoon of salt looked like in her hand—I do not. There's no shame in measuring, only gain.

Use measuring spoons and cups. A scale, if you have it, helps. Seriously, very few of us can wing it and have success and consistency time after time. My grandmother knew exactly what a half teaspoon of salt looked like in her hand—I do not. There's no shame in measuring, only gain.

Don't make substitutions the first time you cook a recipe unless they are suggested.

Use the freshest ingredients you can afford. Fresh tastes better—it just does. Fresh ingredients in the refrigerator are great motivators to cook. Crisp, bright spinach is much more craveable than a soggy week-old mess in a bag.

Order heavy, bulky items from a delivery service if it's an option, or pick them up in a separate trip from the fresh asparagus and pork tenderloin. I lose steam for cooking when I come home with heavy laundry soaps, cleaning supplies and paper goods. By the time they're put away, all I want to do is order pizza.

Find a grocery store that's easy to navigate and has good service. If it stocks one or two items that you crave regularly, you'll be happy to make a stop there. One of my local stores always has fresh-squeezed grapefruit juice, another has more than 12 varieties of fresh Middle Eastern flatbreads, yet another has tortillas so fresh they're still warm. Once there, I always find dinner inspirations.

Use the best ingredients you can afford. I'd rather cook a great meatless recipe than use inferior meat and poultry. Look for local foods that have not traveled far to get to you; I choose organic meats, poultry and dairy when I can.

Shop at your local farmers markets. Meet the farmers. When I hand over the money to them—instead of a bunch of middlemen—I smile with deep appreciation for their hard-won skinny green

Grow what you can—start with a pot of chives on the windowsill.

beans, plump eggplants and tender carrots. Then I go home and cook their fresh eggs and taste the difference local makes in every bite.

Grow what you can—start with a pot of chives on the windowsill. The effort of watering and sustaining even one house plant will help you appreciate the farmer, the rancher, the butcher, the greengrocer.

Talk to your butcher. Skip the prepackaged meat counter. In my experience, the folks behind the butcher counter want to talk food and recipes. Engaging them may help you learn something—and at the very least will help you get the best steak or chop in the case.

Likewise, talk to the produce people in the grocery store. Ask them where the berries come from, how to select a ripe melon, how to store fresh herbs.

Let them know that you wish they stocked tri-color carrots, organic greens, fresh rosemary and pea shoots. Good food flows from conversations with growers, suppliers and cooks.

Keep a stock of pantry staples—the basics, such as balsamic vinegar, cider vinegar, olive oil, expeller-pressed canola oil for high-heat cooking, chili pastes (I like to stock Korean, Indian and Chinese-style), chicken broth, mustards, salsa, soy sauce, tomatoes, canned beans and pastas. Pepper in a few "specialty" items that motivate you to cook—red quinoa, hot chili oil, dried mushrooms, chutney, fresh horseradish, agave syrup, honey and tahini.

Arrange spices and bulk items in attractive containers. I like clear jars so I can see the contents.

A pretty jar of sweet paprika can motivate me to make a pot of goulash. Label the jars and include a date.

I have a cabinet filled with ingredients for baking—flours, sugars, leavenings, vanilla extract, chocolate of varying levels of sweetness. (I tuck whole-grain flours and nuts into the freezer to help them stay fresh.) Keeping them housed in one spot means I can gather them easily for my brownie project.

My refrigerated pantry almost always holds a carton of eggs, tubs of miso paste, organic mayonnaise, organic tofu, slender carrots, fresh herbs, peeled garlic,

Use the freezer. I store roasted farmer's market peppers, homemade herbed butter, berries, pesto starter and tomato sauces in small containers for easy thawing; they're integral to flavorful meals. In summer, a stash of frozen (homemade) crusts encourages pie. I also keep a small stash of individually portioned and packaged meats that thaw quickly, such as boneless chicken, steaks and thin chops. A brief defrost in the microwave means dinner in minutes.

I take advantage of the precut vegetables and cleaned lettuces for sale in the produce section of

 Please leave the tomatoes on the counter. Most tomatoes taste best at room temperature and in fact will ripen and sweeten further.

fresh ginger, tubes of lemongrass puree, green onions and a variety of citrus. During the peak growing season, I use a second refrigerator to briefly store baskets of peaches, berries, peppers and cucumbers until I can turn them into quick jams, pickles and condiments.

Please leave the tomatoes on the counter. I've been fighting this battle for decades. Most tomatoes taste best at room temperature and in fact will ripen and sweeten further. Only refrigerate cut tomatoes or tomatoes that are super-ripe.

Bowls of ripening tomatoes, avocados, colorful onions, garlic, winter squash, etc, on the kitchen counter signal a meal close at hand. Make pretty arrangements, then use them up.

Use dried herbs, dried chiles and spices when they are as fresh as possible. If you can, purchase whole spices and grind them yourself. Buy the smallest containers of dried spices you can find—yes, it costs more per ounce, but you'll use up the spice faster, while it's at its peak flavor.

many grocers. True, they may have lost some of their vitamin C, but having a package of shaved Brussels sprouts or diced butternut means veggies on the table tonight. Better than none, I say!

When preparing the recipes in this book, I use unsalted butter (it tastes fresher and sweeter), large eggs, freshly ground pepper and fresh garlic—not dried. I find that ordinary table salt measures more accurately than coarse salt.

Speaking of salt, I cook so my food tastes as satisfying as possible—after all, I have worked hard on the meal. That means that a recipe's salt level is designed to deliver perfectly seasoned food—not salty, but not bland either. If you are on a sodium-restricted diet, use the nutrition information provided with each recipe to determine how far you need to reduce the salt—but never eliminate the salt altogether, or your cooking efforts will be less than tasty.

Make fresh salad dressing. Just do it. You can keep it in glass jars in the fridge for a week or more.

Your salads will be transformed and you'll eliminate lots of suspect ingredients from your diet.

When grilling, cook extra for the next day. Many grilled foods taste even better the next day. Besides, what could be a more inspiring path to dinner than a piece of grilled steak? Your salads and sandwiches will thank you.

That leads me to another topic: Embrace leftovers. In fact, forget that word—embrace the "surplus" meat, veggies, rice, pasta, etc., for another day. With just a few clever tricks, your surplus fare can transform into a nearly effortless meal. Picture this: Leftover brown rice, topped with bits of cooked meat, blanched vegetables and a spoonful of chili paste from the pantry all sauteed until hot. Top it all with a fried farm-fresh egg. You get it.

Years ago, my mother advised me to always set the table first—even before starting dinner. Then, when the guests arrive, it looks like you're ready. This easy trick has saved my nerves on many occasions.

Learn to like dishwashing or fall in love with someone who does. I get into a peaceful spot when I am tidying up my favorite room in the house.

Enlist helpers. Cooking together builds bonds and makes memories. Dining together is one of life's pleasures. Do it often. Your life will be richer.

CHAPTER 2

Menus for Your Dinners
(and Other Meals)
at Home

Truth be told, most of my dinners at home spring from a craving—grilled lamb, nutty grains, comforting soup, fresh greens, a juicy burger. Weeknight dinners prove casual affairs centered on one main recipe. The rest of the meal's offerings come about after peering in the fridge—blanched broccoli, steamed fresh peas—or following an impromptu stop at the bakery for a crusty loaf.

I'm much more organized when company's coming or when we're planning a trip to the cabin with friends. When my adult children come home for the weekend, I look forward to cooking their favorites. I write up menus, complete with dates and guests expected, and tape them to the fridge. Those little notes keep me on track and ensure I don't forget to serve the salad or soften the herb butter. My helpers can refer to it, too, and set the table for the correct number of people, or help finish a dish.

I collect the menus after the guests leave and tuck them into a notebook. That notebook now contains the details of many wonderful events in our lives, from birthday dinners to graduation parties, to empty-nest celebrations.

Following are some of those menus to help get your parties started. Be flexible and swap out my suggestions with store-bought items such as breads, salads or dessert if time gets away from you. Ask for help and stay relaxed. If you find the time to enjoy the dinners you make and the guests you share them with, chances are, you'll keep cooking. And that's a good thing.

Baguette

Breakfast with Friends

Fresh grapefruit juice mimosas

Kaiserschmarren with jammy plums PAGE 267

Applewood smoked bacon

Coffee, tea

Comfort Me with Friends and Food

Red lentil soup with lamb and fresh lemon PAGE 35

Toasted flatbreads

Arugula salad with shaved parmesan and fresh lemon vinaigrette with sumac PAGE 62

Coconut mango ice cream PAGE 247

Amber beer, pinot noir

Winter Warmup Dinner

Herbed cheese spread PAGE 24

Bread sticks

Chorizo and seafood stew PAGE 44

Fresh spinach salad with red onions and homemade balsamic vinaigrette PAGE 257

Sweet apple and mincemeat tart PAGE 239

Dark beer, spiced tea

Wish We Were in Ireland Supper

Sliced smoked salmon on brown bread

Slow-cooker beef and Guinness stew PAGE 47

Green salad with homemade balsamic vinaigrette PAGE 257

White chocolate macadamia blondies PAGE 235

Guinness, of course

No Meat, No Worries

Cheese "burgers" with spicy mayo PAGE 67

Cucumber and ginger pickles PAGE 259

Barbecue sweet potato slices PAGE 150

Chocolate cherry peanut butter oatmeal cookies PAGE 249

Stiegl-Radler grapefruit beer, iced tea

We Love Lamb

Garlic and spice grilled leg of lamb PAGE 97

Cucumber yogurt sauce with garlic and herbs PAGE 256

Couscous salad with roasted cauliflower PAGE 55

Sliced heirloom tomato salad with black olives and fresh lemon vinaigrette with sumac PAGE 62

Warm flat breads

Honey and Greek yogurt spice cake PAGE 251

Pinot noir, iced tea

Summer Dining on the Deck

Brown sugar grilled salmon on cedar planks PAGE 137

Grilled asparagus

New potatoes with butter and chives

Peaches and cream trifle with ginger and bourbon PAGE 245

Iced tea and lemonade (add a splash of bourbon)

Friday Night Supper

Sweet potato pancakes PAGE 214

Kale and ham skillet PAGE 122

Latte brownies PAGE 236

Sweet tea, craft beers

Manhattan Cocktail Party

Steak and arugula crostini PAGE 23

Herbed cheese spread on endive PAGE 24

Prosciutto parmesan puffs PAGE 24

Charcuterie platter of cured meats and cheese

Assorted olives and roasted nuts

Perfect Manhattans, red wine

Saturday Lunch on the Deck

Warm black bean and rice bowl with chicken and poblanos PAGE 124

Crisp flatbreads

Sliced ripe tomatoes

Easy grapefruit granita PAGE 243

Fresh limeade

Saturday Night with Friends

Roasted chicken with tomato-olive relish PAGE 130

Smoky cheese and garlic toasts PAGE 25

Steamed broccoli

White chocolate macadamia blondies PAGE 235

Sparkling rosé

Saturday Night Beer Tasting

Assorted nuts

Herbed cheese spread and cut veggies PAGE 24

Slow-cooked choucroute garni PAGE 49

Green salad with fresh lemon vinaigrette with sumac PAGE 62

Latte brownies PAGE 236

A variety of craft beers

Sunday Brunch

Stacked boxty with smoked salmon and lemon PAGE 211

Frisee salad with sliced pears and homemade balsamic vinaigrette PAGE 257

Sparkling wine

Sunday Lunch Time

Warm grilled eggplant and prosciutto salad PAGE 59

Smoky cheese and garlic toasts PAGE 25

Lemon mascarpone panna cotta with peach and berry compote PAGE 241

Fresh lemonade

Game Day Goodness

Spicy hand-held pasties PAGE 27

Cutup veggies with lemon, cauliflower and garlic hummus PAGE 29

Meatless pumpkin and black bean chili PAGE 41

Chocolate cherry peanut butter oatmeal cookies PAGE 249

Assorted beers, sparkling cider

Dad's Birthday Dinner

Chile roasted kale PAGE 157

Assorted nuts

Roasted fish with lemon-chili relish PAGE 144

Lemon, cauliflower and garlic hummus PAGE 29

Garden fresh beans PAGE 156

Crusty bread with herbed butter

Peaches and cream trifle with ginger and bourbon PAGE 245

Saison beer, fresh lemonade

....

Come for Dessert

Lemon mascarpone panna cotta with peach and berry compote PAGE 241

Chocolate mocha cakes PAGE 233

Honey and Greek yogurt spice cake PAGE 251

Fresh strawberries and green grapes

Sparkling wine

....

It's Easy to Cook for Mom

Creamy cheesy shrimp salad on crostini PAGE 31

Butternut soup (variation on pumpkin soup) PAGE 38

Assorted crackers

Coconut mango ice cream PAGE 247

Sparkling wine

....

Ultimate Father's Day

Smoky grilled Delmonico mopped steaks PAGE 101

Grilled asparagus

Wedge salad with diced tomatoes and blue cheese and fresh lemon vinaigrette with sumac PAGE 62

Strawberry-rhubarb deep dish pie PAGE 229

Cabernet sauvignon, dark beer

....

Anniversary Dinner

Lemon, cauliflower and garlic hummus PAGE 29

Toasted pita wedges

Sauteed scallops with chermoula PAGE 139

Steamed red quinoa

Mixed green salad with fresh lemon vinaigrette with sumac PAGE 62

Easy grapefruit granita PAGE 243

Sparkling wine

....

CHAPTER 3

Party Snacks

21

WARM WEATHER GOES HAND-IN-HAND WITH A SLEW OF GRADUATION parties, baby showers and bridal celebrations. Since it's also the time of year when everyone would rather be outside playing than indoors cooking, you need a repertoire of simple, fresh ideas that taste great, can be made ahead and still impress. Homemade spreads and dips, little puffs filled with prosciutto and Parmesan and open-face steak sandwiches, or crostini, fit the bill. Make one or make them all—depending on the size of the crowd.

Steak and arugula crostini

Prep: 30 minutes | Cook: 30 minutes | Makes: About 30 pieces

These open-face sandwiches are great on Parmesan-garlic baguette, or use a regular baguette.

1 large baguette, thinly sliced

3 tablespoons olive oil, about

1 large sweet onion, halved, thinly sliced

1 tablespoon balsamic vinegar

1 to 2 teaspoons finely chopped fresh sage, optional

½ teaspoon sugar

About 1½ pounds boneless beef tenderloin, strip, rib-eye or sirloin steaks, each 1 inch thick, trimmed

1 tablespoon favorite grill rub (or salt, freshly ground black pepper to taste)

1 bag (5 ounces) arugula, chopped

Chopped fresh parsley

① Heat oven to 350 degrees. Brush bread slices lightly with oil on both sides. Arrange in single layer on baking sheets. Bake, turning once, until crisp and golden, about 20 minutes. Cool on wire rack. (Toasts can be made up to two days in advance; store in a cookie tin, and re-crisp in a hot oven.)

② Meanwhile, heat 1 tablespoon oil in a large skillet. Add onion; cook, stirring, until nicely golden, about 10 minutes. Add vinegar, sage and sugar; cook, 1 minute. Cool. (Refrigerate up to two days.)

③ Coat steaks generously with rub. Arrange on rack set over broiler pan. Broil 6 inches from heat source, turning once, until rare, about 8 minutes (or grill over direct heat). Cool to warm. Slice thinly. (Or leave steaks whole for up to 2 hours, then slice to serve.)

④ To assemble, top toasts with arugula, steak slices and a dollop of onions. Sprinkle with parsley.

Nutrition information per piece: 96 calories, 3 g fat, 1 g saturated fat, 14 mg cholesterol, 9 g carbohydrates, 7 g protein, 131 mg sodium, 0 g fiber

Herbed cheese spread

Prep: 10 minutes | Makes: about 1½ cups | Pictured on p. 22

Spread on crostini, endive spears or celery sticks.

11 ounces soft goat cheese

¼ to ½ cup whipping cream

½ teaspoon salt

Freshly ground black pepper

2 green onions, finely chopped

2 to 3 tablespoons finely chopped fresh herbs,
such as chives, parsley, tarragon

① Mash cheese in a bowl with a fork or hand mixer while adding the cream, 1 tablespoon at a time, until mixture is light and spreadable. Stir in salt, pepper, onions and herbs. Serve at room temperature. (Keeps in the refrigerator for up to three days.)

Nutrition information per serving: 44 calories, 4 g fat, 2 g saturated fat, 9 mg cholesterol, 0 g carbohydrates, 2 g protein, 97 mg sodium, 0 g fiber

Prosciutto parmesan puffs

Prep: 25 minutes | Cook: 30 minutes | Makes: About 30 puffs | Pictured on p. 22

Store cooled puffs in a cookie tin for up to two days. Pop them into a hot oven to re-crisp and warm slightly.

1 cup water

6 tablespoons unsalted butter

¾ teaspoon salt

Freshly ground black pepper

1 cup flour

4 large eggs

¼ to ⅓ cup shredded Parmesan cheese

3 ounces thin slices prosciutto, chopped

¼ teaspoon dried thyme

1 egg, beaten

Coarse (kosher) salt

① Heat oven to 425 degrees. Put water, butter, salt and pepper to taste into a medium saucepan. Heat to a boil, stirring so butter melts. Add the flour all at once; stir vigorously with a wooden spoon to make a paste. Reduce heat to low; cook, stirring (dough will be stiff), until it pulls away from side of pan, about 3 minutes.

② Remove pan from heat. Add 1 egg; beat with a hand mixer (or stir vigorously) to incorporate it into the dough. Repeat with remaining 3 eggs. Beat in cheese, prosciutto and thyme.

③ Use a pastry bag fitted with a round tip, or two spoons dipped in cold water, to form mounds 1½ inches wide and ½ inch high on two parchment-lined baking sheets. Space mounds about 2 inches apart. Brush the tops with beaten egg. Sprinkle lightly with salt, if you like.

④ Bake 10 minutes. Reduce temperature to 350 degrees; bake until golden and crisp, 15 minutes. Cool on wire racks. Serve warm.

Nutrition information per serving: 56 calories, 4 g fat, 2 g saturated fat, 44 mg cholesterol, 3 g carbohydrates, 3 g protein, 157 mg sodium, 0 g fiber

Y SON MASTERED THE ART OF GREAT GARLIC BREAD EARLY IN HIS LIFE; he could eat slabs of it at every meal. He always uses fresh garlic and sweet butter. Cheese and smoked paprika take this version over the top.

Smoky cheese and garlic toasts

Preparation time: 15 minutes | **Cooking time:** 15 minutes | **Yield:** 12 servings

You'll want to double this recipe for hearty eaters since no one can resist a second (or third) piece of this crusty cheesy garlic bread. Seek out artisanal bread loaves, with plenty of air pockets for the most interesting textures.

1 stick (½ cup) unsalted butter, melted

½ cup extra-virgin olive oil

2 cloves garlic, finely crushed

½ teaspoon salt

1 large loaf (24 ounces) crusty artisanal bread, such as Pugliese, Italian or Vienna bread, cut in half horizontally

½ cup finely shredded sharp white Cheddar cheese

½ cup shredded smoked Gouda cheese

1 teaspoon smoked or regular paprika

① Mix together butter, oil, garlic and salt in small bowl. Brush generously over cut sides of bread. Sprinkle bread with cheeses, sprinkle with paprika. (Bread can be refrigerated, well-wrapped, up to several hours.)

② Heat oven to 375 degrees. Place bread on baking sheet, cheese side up. Bake until golden and cheese begins to melt, about 15 minutes. Cut crosswise into thick pieces. Serve warm.

Nutrition information per serving: 337 calories, 21 g fat, 8 g saturated fat, 30 mg cholesterol, 29 g carbohydrates, 7 g protein, 497 mg sodium, 2 g fiber

WE LIKE ANYTHING AND EVERYTHING TUCKED INSIDE A SHORT CRUST—that flaky, tender unleavened dough used to envelop sweet fruits, spicy meat and creamy fillings. The obsession likely began with the pastry classes mom took at the gas company. She'd come home to practice, making as many as a dozen pie crusts in a day. She progressed into a peerless crust-maker. Lucky for us.

Memorable Saturday night suppers involved her flaky crust, beef stew meat and a few veggies that she'd transform into individual-size savory, rustic entrees. Seems she learned about these hand-held pies from our summer cottage neighbors who hailed from Michigan's Upper Peninsula, an area renowned for its Cornish pasties.

Mom says she never really followed a recipe; she'd simply dollop a filling of chopped lean beef, onions, carrots, turnips and spices on a small round of her pie dough.

Then she'd fold the dough over the filling to make a half-moon shaped, hand-held pasty much like the national dish of Cornwall in England. There, pasties fill the lunchboxes of the Cornish miners who brought the recipe to northern Michigan and Minnesota.

The pies can be large for big appetites or slightly smaller to suit a party spread that features other tidbits. I also make small versions for cocktail parties using a 3-inch circle of pastry. (Any leftover filling can be stirred into cooked penne or rigatoni pasta for great lunches.)

Spicy hand-held pasties

Prep: 1 hour | Cook: 40 minutes | Makes: 10 large or 16 medium-size pasties

You can substitute 1 package (22 ounces) frozen pie crusts for the pie dough. Thaw according to package directions, then cut each crust into 4 pieces. Roll each piece into a ball and chill. You'll have 8 medium-size pasties and leftover filling.

1 recipe tender pie dough (recipe follows), rolled into 10 or 16 balls, chilled

1 egg, beaten with 1 tablespoon milk

4 cups filling, about

Coarse salt

Spicy salsa

① Heat oven to 450 degrees. Roll each dough ball between two sheets of floured wax paper into ⅛-inch-thick rounds. Brush the edge with egg mixture. Using a scant ¼ cup filling for the smaller rounds and a scant ½ cup for the larger, put the filling onto one half of the dough round.

② Use the wax paper to fold the top half of the dough over the filling to enclose it, making a half-moon shape. Use your fingers to seal the dough edges together. Place on parchment-lined baking sheets. Pierce with a fork. Brush the tops with egg mixture; sprinkle with a little coarse salt.

③ Bake 15 minutes; reduce oven temperature to 350 degrees. Bake until golden, usually 10 more minutes for smaller versions and up to 25 minutes for large versions. Serve warm with salsa.

....

Nutrition information per serving (for 16 pasties with spicy beef and sweet potato filling [recipe follows]): 374 calories, 23 g fat, 7 g saturated fat, 34 mg cholesterol, 29 g carbohydrates, 35 g protein, 536 mg sodium, 1 g fiber

Tender pie dough

Makes: 10-16 hand pies

Look for trans-fat-free vegetable shortening; store it in the freezer so it is cold and easy to cut into small pieces.

- 4 cups flour
- 1 tablespoon sugar
- 1 teaspoon salt
- 1½ cups vegetable shortening, very cold
- ½ cup ice water

① Pulse together the flour, sugar and salt in a food processor until mixed. (Alternatively, mix in a large bowl.)

② Cut the shortening into small bits; add to the food processor. Pulse until mixture resembles coarse crumbs. (Or use two knives or a pastry blender to cut the shortening into the flour mixture.) Drizzle the water over the mixture; process until a ball forms.

③ Turn the dough out onto a floured board. Divide and roll the dough into balls of desired size: 10 for large hand pies or 16 for smaller pies. Wrap in wax paper; refrigerate up to 2 days.

Spicy beef and sweet potato filling

Prep: 25 minutes | Cook: 20 minutes
Makes: about 5 cups

- 1 large sweet potato
- 2 tablespoons olive oil
- 1 small onion, finely diced
- 2 or 3 cloves garlic, crushed
- 1 pound coarsely ground beef chuck
- ½ pound coarsely ground lamb (or more beef chuck)
- ½ cup chili sauce (or ketchup)
- 1½ teaspoons salt
- 1 teaspoon ground cumin
- ½ teaspoon cayenne
- 3 green onions, finely chopped
- ¼ cup chopped fresh cilantro

① Pierce sweet potato with a fork in several places. Microwave on high (100 percent power) until fork-tender, usually 6-8 minutes. Peel when cool; cut into ½-inch cubes.

② Heat oil in a large skillet. Add onion; cook over medium until golden, about 5 minutes. Stir in garlic; cook 1 minute. Add meats. Cook over high until golden, about 10 minutes. (Tip off any fat.) Stir in chili sauce, salt, cumin and cayenne. Cook and stir, 1 minute. Remove from heat. Stir in sweet potato, green onions and cilantro. Cool. Refrigerate, covered, up to 2 days.

....

Nutrition information per ¼ cup: 87 calories, 5 g fat, 2 g saturated fat, 21 mg cholesterol, 4 g carbohydrates, 32 g protein, 386 mg sodium, 0 g fiber

C AULIFLOWER, OFT CONSIDERED A BORING STAPLE, HAS THE POWER TO become a light, whipped appetizer. The trick is to boil the cauliflower in plenty of salted water, to dissipate the strong cabbage aroma. Then a quick puree in the blender with sesame oil and canned chick peas to make a kind of hummus. I save some of the tender florets to brown in oil for a golden garnish.

 This is delicious with crackers or toasted pita chips, and it can also be served as a side dish underneath roasted fish.

Lemon, cauliflower and garlic hummus

Prep: 20 minutes | Cook: 10 minutes | Makes: about 3 cups

I use light sesame oil here, not the toasty dark oil I like in stir-fries. Light, fruity olive oil makes a good substitute.

1 large head cauliflower, about 2 pounds, cored (or 24 ounces cauliflower florets)

1 can (15 ounces) garbanzo beans (chick peas), drained, rinsed

2 large cloves garlic, crushed

4 tablespoons light sesame oil or olive oil

Finely grated zest and juice of half a lemon

1 teaspoon salt

① Heat a large pot of salted water to a boil. Separate the cauliflower into small florets. You will have about 8 cups. Cook until nearly fork-tender, about 5 minutes. Use a slotted spoon to scoop out half of the florets to set aside for garnish. Cook remaining cauliflower until tender, 2-3 minutes more. Drain.

② Puree the tender cauliflower, beans and garlic in a food processor or blender until smooth. Add 2 tablespoons oil, lemon zest and juice, and salt. Puree again until smooth. Transfer to a serving bowl.

③ Heat remaining 2 tablespoons oil in large skillet over medium-high until hot. Add reserved cauliflower florets (cutting them if necessary into bite-size pieces). Cook and stir until golden, 2-3 minutes. Sprinkle over puree. Serve warm or at room temperature. (Mixture can be refrigerated covered up to 3 days; let come to room temperature before serving.)

Nutrition information per ¼-cup serving: 77 calories, 8 g fat, 0.7 g saturated fat, 0 mg cholesterol, 7 g carbohydrates, 2 g protein, 285 mg sodium, 1.5 g fiber

t's not always easy to get more fish into our diets. After all, most of us don't have fresh fish markets in the neighborhood. Mostly, I find myself at my local supermarket pondering dinner options at the seafood counter.

Admittedly, I am not a fan of most "thawed for my convenience" selections. Especially if I am not cooking the item within a few hours of buying it. So I turn to the freezer case where, hopefully, the fish has remained solidly frozen since its harvest. Then I can transport it safely home and thaw it carefully in the refrigerator.

For seafood purchases, look for key words on the package such as sustainable, wild-caught and U.S. farmed in a fully recirculating system to make wise dinner selections. For shrimp, read the packages: U.S. farmed and wild-caught shrimp are good choices. Avoid farmed imported shrimp.

Creamy cheesy shrimp salad

Prep: 10 minutes | Cook: 5 minutes | Makes: about 3 cups

The chopped shrimp salad makes a great bruschetta topping for cocktail parties or indulgent sandwich on toasted sliced brioche.

2 tablespoons butter or olive oil

2 large shallots, finely chopped

1 pound medium-size peeled, deveined raw shrimp, patted dry

2 cloves garlic, crushed

¼ cup each: softened light cream cheese, plain nonfat Greek yogurt

2 to 3 tablespoons chopped mixed fresh herbs, such as chives, dill, parsley, basil

½ teaspoon salt

Hot pepper sauce

Freshly ground black pepper

Grilled toasts

Herb sprigs for garnish

① Heat butter or oil and shallots in large nonstick skillet over medium-high heat until hot. Cook, stirring, about 1 minute. Add shrimp and garlic. Cook, stirring, just until shrimp is pink and cooked through, 2-3 minutes. Remove from heat; cool in the pan.

② Put cream cheese and yogurt into food processor; blend to mix. Add the cooled shrimp mixture. Pulse to coarsely chop shrimp. Transfer to a bowl; stir in herbs, salt, and hot sauce and pepper to taste.

③ Spoon into a serving dish. Refrigerate, covered, up to 2 days. Serve on grilled toasts. Garnish with herb sprigs.

Nutrition information per tablespoon: 17 calories, 1 g fat, 0.4 g saturated fat, 17 mg cholesterol, 1 g carbohydrates, 2 g protein, 97 mg sodium, 0 g fiber

CHAPTER 4

Soups, Stews and Salads

HEARTY, TENDER VEGETABLES, FRESH HERBS, LEGUMES AND BITS OF PRO-
tein simmered in broth assuage hunger and warm us through.

This soup features overtones of aromatic Moroccan lamb stew peppered with sweet spices and toothsome lentils. Serve the soup with a dollop of sour cream or plain yogurt laced with fresh lemon rind.

Red lentil soup with lamb and fresh lemon

Prep: 30 minutes | Cook: 1 hour, 30 minutes | Makes: About 10 cups, 8 servings

I like to accompany the soup with toasted warm whole wheat pita.

3 to 4 tablespoons olive oil

1½ pounds trimmed boneless lamb shoulder, cut into 1-inch pieces

1 large (12 ounces) yellow onion, diced

3 to 4 large cloves garlic, crushed

1½ teaspoons ground cumin

1 teaspoon turmeric

½ teaspoon each, ground: cinnamon, black pepper

⅛ teaspoon cayenne

Pinch saffron threads, crushed, optional

1 medium red bell pepper, cored, seeded, diced

1 small bulb (4 ounces) fresh fennel, trimmed, diced

8 cups chicken broth

1⅓ cups (8 ounces) red lentils or yellow split peas

1 to 1½ teaspoons salt

Grated zest of 1 lemon

1 cup light sour cream, labneh or plain yogurt

Garlic croutons

Chopped fresh cilantro or parsley

① Heat oil in large Dutch oven over medium-high heat. Add lamb, in batches, in a single uncrowded layer. Cook, turning pieces once or twice until nicely browned, 5-7 minutes. Remove with a slotted spoon; repeat to brown the remaining lamb pieces.

② Stir onion, garlic and all spices into lamb. Cook, about 5 minutes. Stir in bell pepper and fennel. Stir in broth. Partly cover the pot; simmer over low heat, stirring occasionally, until the lamb is nearly tender, about 1 hour. (Recipe can be made ahead and refrigerated, covered, up to 2 days.)

③ Reheat soup if made in advance. Stir in lentils. Simmer, stirring often, until lentils are tender, about 15 minutes (slightly longer for split peas). Season with salt.

④ Mix the grated lemon zest into the sour cream in a small bowl. (You can do this a day or 2 in advance; refrigerate.)

⑤ Serve the soup in bowls topped with a dollop of lemon sour cream, a few croutons and a generous sprinkle of cilantro.

....

Nutrition information per serving: 382 calories, 20 g fat, 7 g saturated fat, 66 mg cholesterol, 26 g carbohydrates, 25 g protein, 810 mg sodium, 8 g fiber

Homemade soup cures my November blues. It makes the house smell good and keeps me on track for healthful, lighter eating before the holiday calorie on-slaught. I can save lunch money by taking small containers to the office. All in all, it's a win-win. Especially if I'm out of the kitchen fast.

Speedy chunky vegetable black bean soup

Prep: 10 minutes | Cook: 20 minutes | Makes: 4 servings

Good broth proves the ticket for gratifying soups. I keep store-bought, low-sodium organic varieties in the pantry. When I go to the local butcher, I pick up their frozen homemade stocks. These stocks tend to be richer and stronger-flavored than packaged broth, resulting in fuller-bodied soups.

2 tablespoons olive oil

1 small leek, halved lengthwise, rinsed, thinly sliced

1 small onion, chopped

2 or 3 cloves garlic, crushed

1 can (14.5 ounces) fire-roasted diced tomatoes

3 cups vegetable or chicken broth

1 can (15 ounces) black beans, drained, rinsed

1 cup frozen shelled edamame or small lima beans

¾ teaspoon Italian seasoning

½ teaspoon salt

2 links (6 ounces total) fully cooked Italian or andouille chicken sausage, thinly sliced, optional

Extra-virgin olive oil

Shaved or shredded Parmesan cheese

① Heat 2 tablespoons oil in a 3-quart saucepan. Add leek and onion; cook until translucent, about 5 minutes. Stir in garlic and tomatoes. Simmer, 3 minutes.

② Stir in broth, black beans, edamame, seasoning and salt. Simmer, 10 minutes. Add sausage if using; simmer, 2 minutes.

③ Serve topped with a drizzle of olive oil and sprinkling of cheese.

....

Nutrition information per serving: 228 calories, 8 g fat, 1 g saturated fat, 0 mg cholesterol, 31 g carbohydrates, 10 g protein, 876 mg sodium, 10 g fiber

NOTHING DRAWS MY KIDS HOME FOR THE WEEKEND BETTER THAN THE promise of their favorite dishes. During the fall, pumpkin soup sways their plans toward our table. Same for extended family and neighbors.

This soup starts with fresh pumpkin—sugar pie pumpkins to be exact, not jack-o'-lanterns, which do not have the dense, sweet flesh of their diminutive brethren. With a couple of sharp knives, a stable cutting board and patience, we cut cubes of pumpkin to simmer with broth into melting tenderness.

Creamy pumpkin soup with roasted corn and poblanos

Prep: 45 minutes | Cook: 1 hour | Makes: 16 cups, 8 to 12 servings

Simple seasonings allow the fresh pumpkin flavor to shine. Fresh cilantro stems (use the leaves for garnish) add a great aromatic quality; so do garlic and a bit of oregano. I always include an apple in my soup; it underscores the sweet flavor of the pumpkin. Carrots and red bell pepper also add sweetness and bump up the color.

1 sugar pie pumpkin, about 3 pounds

3 tablespoons extra-virgin olive oil

1 large (12 ounces) onion, chopped

3 medium carrots, peeled, roughly chopped, about 8 ounces

1 large Golden Delicious apple, peeled, cored, chopped

1 small red bell pepper, cored, roughly chopped

5 cloves garlic, chopped

8 cups chicken broth

5 or 6 skinless chicken thighs, with bone, about 2 pounds total

Stems from 1 bunch of cilantro

1 teaspoon dried oregano

1½ teaspoons salt

¼ cup whipping cream, optional

Garnish:

2 large poblano chilies, cored, cut into ¼-inch pieces

4 ears corn, kernels removed from cobs

¼ cup chopped fresh cilantro

① Cut pumpkin into large chunks. Remove seeds and stem. Cut away the peel. Cut the flesh into roughly 1-inch chunks. You should have about 8 cups.

② Heat the oil in a very large (7- to 9-quart) Dutch oven or stockpot. Add onion, carrots, apple and bell pepper. Cook over medium-high until vegetables begin to soften, 5-10 minutes. Add garlic and pumpkin; cook and stir, 5 minutes.

③ Stir in broth, chicken thighs, cilantro stems and oregano. Simmer, partly covered, over low heat, stirring often, until pumpkin is very tender, 30-40 minutes.

Use tongs to remove chicken thighs to a cutting board. When cool enough to handle, remove meat from the bones, discarding bones. Tear meat into shreds; refrigerate, covered.

④ After removing the chicken thighs, use an immersion blender to puree soup. (Alternatively, ladle some of the soup into a blender and puree with the blender loosely covered so it doesn't overflow. Pour the pureed soup into another container and repeat to puree all of the soup.) Return the pureed soup to low heat; season with salt. Stir in the cream, if using; adjust the salt again. (At this point, the soup can be refrigerated, covered, up to 3 days).

⑤ For the garnish, heat a well-seasoned large cast-iron skillet over medium-high heat (or use a large nonstick skillet sprayed with a little oil). Add the diced poblanos; cook until lightly charred on the edges, 3-5 minutes. Transfer to a large plate. Add the corn kernels to the hot pan; cook until golden, 3-4 minutes. Add to the poblanos. When cool, stir in the cilantro.

⑥ To serve, heat the soup until hot. Stir in the shredded chicken thigh to heat it through. Ladle soup into warm bowls; top with the poblano-corn mixture.

....

Nutrition information per serving: 179 calories, 7 g fat, 1 g saturated fat, 48 mg cholesterol, 19 g carbohydrates, 12 g protein, 913 mg sodium, 3 g fiber

ON USING PUMPKIN

➤ A **3-pound pie pumpkin** yields about 2 pounds of peeled flesh, or 8 cups of 1-inch cubes, enough for this soup.

➤ **Diced raw butternut squash**, sold in most produce sections, can stand in for the pumpkin; it has a milder, less squashy flavor.

➤ In a pinch, **canned pumpkin** works in this soup too. It lacks some of the freshness but offers massive convenience. You'll need two 15-ounce cans; be sure to use the unseasoned pumpkin, not the version for pie filling.

➤ **Frozen winter squash** proves another speedy option; you'll need three 10-ounce packages.

OUR FAMILY ADORES PUMPKIN IN MANY RECIPES, SO I STOCK UP ON SMALL pumpkins. Look for sugar pumpkins or pie pumpkins for their dense, sweet flesh and manageable size. Store them whole, wrapped in paper towels in the refrigerator for up to a couple of months. Once roasted, pumpkin will keep several days in the refrigerator or in the freezer for months.

P.S. No need to despair if fresh pumpkins are unavailable: Butternut squash makes a fine substitute.

Meatless pumpkin and black bean chili

Prep: 20 minutes | Cook: 35 minutes | Makes: 4 to 6 servings

Shredded cheese is delicious as a garnish on this chili.

1 large red onion, diced

6 cloves garlic, crushed

3 tablespoons olive oil

1½ cups vegetable broth or water

1 can (15 ounces) solid-pack pumpkin

1 can (14.5 ounces) diced fire-roasted tomatoes

3 to 4 tablespoons mild chili powder, to taste

1 tablespoon pureed canned chipotle in adobo

½ teaspoon ground cumin

2 cups thinly sliced assorted bell peppers (or 1 [14-ounce] bag frozen red, green and yellow pepper strips)

2 cans (15 ounces each) black beans, drained, rinsed

½ teaspoon salt

1 or 2 cups roasted pumpkin (recipe follows), optional

For garnish: Chopped cilantro, broken tortilla chips

① Put onion, garlic and oil into a large saucepan or Dutch oven. Cook, stirring, over medium heat until onion is tender, about 10 minutes. Stir in broth, canned pumpkin, tomatoes, chili powder, chipotle and cumin. Stir in bell peppers; heat to a simmer. Cook, partly covered, over low heat, stirring often, about 20 minutes.

② Stir in black beans and salt. Simmer until heated through, about 5 minutes. Taste and adjust seasonings. Serve in soup bowls with a spoonful of roasted pumpkin, a generous sprinkling of cilantro and broken tortilla chips.

....

Nutrition information per serving (for 6 servings): 276 calories, 10 g fat, 1 g saturated fat, 1 mg cholesterol, 37 g carbohydrates, 10 g protein, 732 mg sodium, 13 g fiber

Roasted pumpkin

Prep: 20 minutes | Cook: 50 minutes

Makes: about 3 cups

Look for sugar pumpkins (also known as pie pumpkins) for cooking—they have a denser, more tasty flesh than jack-o'-lantern pumpkins. You can substitute 2½ pounds peeled, diced butternut squash.

1 small pumpkin, about 3 pounds

2 tablespoons vegetable oil or olive oil

Coarse salt

Freshly ground pepper, mild curry powder, or Moroccan or Cajun seasoning blend, optional

① Heat oven to 375 degrees. Wash exterior of pumpkin. Using a large, sharp knife, cut off tops just below stems. Then cut in half through the stem end. Scoop out the seeds and fibrous interior. Lay the pumpkin on the cutting board with the cut side down. Carefully remove all of the peel with the knife. Cut the flesh into 1-inch pieces. You'll have about 5 cups.

② Mix pumpkin and oil on a large baking sheet to coat pumpkin pieces with oil. Arrange pieces in a single uncrowded layer. Sprinkle with salt and optional spice.

③ Roast, stirring often, until tender and golden, 40-45 minutes. Turn oven to broil. Broil pumpkin 6 inches from heat source until crisped on one side, about 3 minutes. Cool.

Nutrition information per serving: 152 calories, 10 g fat, 1 g saturated fat, 0 mg cholesterol, 17 g carbohydrates, 2 g protein, 400 mg sodium, 4 g fiber

THIS RECIPE, INSPIRED BY ONE OF OUR FAVORITE SAN FRANCISCO RESTAU-
rants, Aziza, features a heady dose of honey and ras el hanout. The spice cooks with the
browned lamb and onions, increasing its aromatic powers. The sweetness from the honey
and prunes melting into the pan juices makes a perfect combination. You can make your own spice
blend and store it in a jar for several months or order it online from most spice houses.

Honeyed lamb stew with melted prunes

Prep: 30 minutes | Cook: about 2 hours | Makes: 4 to 6 servings

Select either lamb shoulder for a richer stew or leg of lamb for a leaner stew that will cook a bit faster. This stew actually improves with an overnight stay in the refrigerator. Scrape off any solidified fat from the surface of the stew before reheating. Shortly before serving, prepare the couscous.

2 pounds boneless lamb shoulder or leg, cut into
  1½-inch cubes

½ teaspoon salt

Freshly ground black pepper

2 tablespoons vegetable oil

2 small leeks or medium onions (or a
  combination), cut into 1-inch pieces

3 large cloves garlic, crushed

1¾ tablespoons ras el hanout (recipe follows)

2 cups low-sodium chicken broth

1⅓ cups (10 ounces) pitted prunes, halved

¼ cup honey

Nutty lemon couscous (see recipe on p. 167)

Chopped cilantro or flat leaf parsley

① Heat oven to 325 degrees. Pat lamb dry. Season with salt and pepper to taste. Heat oil in medium-size Dutch oven over medium heat. Cook lamb in batches until nicely browned on all sides, about 5 minutes per batch. Transfer to a plate.

② Add leeks to Dutch oven. Cook, stirring, until golden, about 3 minutes. Return the lamb to the pot. Stir in garlic and ras el hanout. Cook, stirring, 3 minutes. Stir in chicken broth, scraping up the browned bits. Cover tightly. Braise in the oven until lamb is fork-tender, about 1 to 1¼ hours.

③ Stir in prunes and honey. Season to taste with salt. Stir in a little water if the mixture seems dry. Cover; return to oven until pan juices have thickened nicely, about 20 minutes. Serve over couscous. Garnish with cilantro or parsley.

Nutrition information per serving: 545 calories, 30 g fat, 12 g saturated fat, 120 mg cholesterol, 35 g carbohydrates, 35 g protein, 365 mg sodium, 2 g fiber

Ras el hanout (Moroccan spice blend): In a small bowl, mix 1½ teaspoons each ground cinnamon, black pepper and ground coriander; 1 teaspoon each ground cumin, ginger and turmeric; ¼ teaspoon each ground allspice, nutmeg and ground red pepper; and 1/8 teaspoon ground cloves. Optional: ¼ teaspoon ground cardamom, 1/8 teaspoon ground saffron.

LOVE TO ENCOUNTER A BEAUTIFUL RESTAURANT DISH THAT INSPIRES ME TO cook at home. Stunning dish in point: a steaming bowl of clams and mussels with a chorizo-seasoned broth enjoyed at Matt's in the Market in Seattle. From the first spoonful, I knew I would be savoring this spicy, rich, yet casual entree again in many configurations.

I took notes to help me turn restaurant fare into home cooked: House-made chorizo, sparkling wine, large white beans, zesty red peppers, giant crispy croutons. This was no ordinary bowl of steamed mollusks!

To complete the menu, start with guacamole and tortilla chips, and offer a simple salad dressed with lime and chili-spiked olive oil and sweetened with a little agave. Lighten up dessert by offering a duo of sorbets and a crunchy cookie. Then celebrate home cooking!

Chorizo and seafood stew

Prep: 45 minutes | Cook: 55 minutes | Makes: 6 servings

A good-quality chorizo will not render out too much fat in the browning. If it does, drain off excess. If Mexican-style chorizo is not available, use mild or spicy Italian sausage and 2 tablespoons chili powder. You can substitute 1 can (15 ounces) large white beans, drained and rinsed, for the scallops if desired.

8 ounces hearty French bread, cut into 1-inch cubes

3 tablespoons olive oil

Sweet or smoked paprika

¾ teaspoon salt

12 ounces uncooked Mexican-style pork chorizo, removed from casing

1 small red onion, diced

1 small red bell pepper, seeded, diced

3 to 4 cloves garlic, crushed

1 cup dry white wine, dry sparkling wine or cava, or dry vermouth

½ of a 14.5 ounce can fire-roasted diced tomatoes, with liquid

2 cups chicken broth

2 pounds fresh littleneck clams, scrubbed

2 pounds fresh mussels, scrubbed, debearded

1 pound bay scallops, patted dry

Fresh cilantro, chopped

Green onions, chopped

Fresh lime wedges

① Heat oven to 375 degrees. Put bread cubes onto a large baking sheet. Drizzle with 2 tablespoons of the oil; toss well to coat. Sprinkle with paprika and ¼ teaspoon salt. Bake, stirring often, until golden and crispy about 20 minutes. Cool. (Croutons will keep a couple of days wrapped in foil.)

② Meanwhile, heat remaining 1 tablespoon oil in the bottom of a large (5- to 6-quart) Dutch oven. Add chorizo, onion and bell pepper. Cook, breaking up the chorizo into small bits with a wooden spatula,

until chorizo is cooked through and lightly browned, 12-14 minutes.

③ Stir in garlic; cook 1 minute. Stir in wine; boil to reduce it slightly, 1-2 minutes. Stir in tomatoes and broth; simmer 10 minutes. Season to taste with salt, about ½ teaspoon depending on broth.

④ Add the clams; cover the pot and cook until a few clams have opened, 3-4 minutes. Add the mussels; cover the pot and cook until a few mussels have opened, about 2 minutes. Add the scallops; cover the pot and cook until all clams and mussels are opened, usually 2 minutes more.

⑤ To serve, ladle into deep bowls (discard any clams or mussels that have refused to open) spooning plenty of the broth over all. Top with cilantro, onion and croutons. Pass lime wedges to squeeze over all.

....

Nutrition information per serving: 592 calories, 31 g fat, 10 g saturated fat, 104 mg cholesterol, 31 g carbohydrates, 44 g protein, 1420 mg sodium, 2 g fiber

Variations: The base of this chorizo and seasoned broth makes a fantastic starter for other main courses. Instead of seafood, add diced boneless skinless chicken and serve with boiled potatoes. Or pork tenderloin and cooked black beans. Or grilled eggplant, zucchini and garbanzo beans.

OUR FIRST MEAL IN DUBLIN FOREVER TRANSFORMED OUR FAMILY'S FAvorite cold-weather comfort fare: beef stew. While we battled jet lag at Madigan's Pub just off O'Connell Street, the waiter suggested we try a bowl of the classic beef with Guinness. A hearty, deeply rich and flavorful bowl of beef stew arrived beneath a cap of crisp pastry. After forks broke through the crust, all the wonderful aromas escaped. A bit of the "black stuff" was a wonderful addition to the pot.

To start this Irish-inspired dinner, serve a salad of mixed greens topped with very thinly sliced smoked salmon or trout and chives. To accompany the stew, try hearty whole-grain bread spread with softened Irish butter, such as the Kerrygold butter found at specialty markets. Or, if company's coming, serve the stew in individual dishes topped with a puff pastry crust. For dessert, baked meringue layered with whipped cream and berries is simple and light.

Slow-cooker beef and Guinness stew

Prep: 45 minutes | Cook: 3½–4 hours | Makes: 8 servings

This stew can be prepared a day or so in advance. Refrigerate it tightly covered. Remove and discard any congealed fat from the surface then reheat gently.

3 pounds boneless beef chuck, trimmed, cut into 1½-inch pieces

½ cup flour

1 teaspoon salt

½ teaspoon freshly ground black pepper

¼ cup vegetable oil

1 large (12 ounces) yellow onion, coarsely chopped

1 can (14.9 ounces) Guinness Draught beer or 1¾ cups Guinness Extra Stout

4 cloves garlic, chopped

2 cups beef broth

1 tablespoon chopped fresh parsley

2 bay leaves

2 small sprigs fresh thyme or ¼ teaspoon dried

1 pound small red boiling potatoes, halved

3 carrots, peeled, cut into 1-inch chunks

½ small rutabaga, peeled, cut into 1-inch chunks

1 package (17 ounces) frozen puff pastry, thawed according to package, optional

① Pat the beef dry with paper towels. Combine the flour, salt and pepper in a shallow dish. Add the beef; toss to coat well with the flour. Reserve the remaining seasoned flour for later.

② Heat the oil in a large non-stick skillet. Add the beef in batches in a single, uncrowded layer. Cook, turning, until browned on all sides, about 10 minutes per batch. Transfer to a slow cooker (see note). Add the onion to the skillet; cook until golden, about 5 minutes. Add the Guinness and garlic; boil 1 minute, scraping up the browned bits from the bottom of the pan. Add the mixture to the slow cooker.

③ Add the broth, parsley, bay and thyme to the slow cooker. Cover; cook on low until meat is almost tender, 2½ to 3 hours. Sprinkle in the reserved seasoned flour; stir well. Add potatoes, carrots and rutabaga. Cover; cook on high until tender, about 1 hour. Taste pan juices; adjust seasonings.

④ If serving the stew with the pastry crust, heat oven to 400 degrees. Cut pastry sheets into quarters. Place on 2 baking sheets; pierce several times with a fork. Bake until crisp and golden, about 10 minutes.

⑤ Spoon a portion of the hot stew into individual dishes. Top with a pastry square.

Nutrition information per serving: 493 calories, 28 g fat, 9 g saturated fat, 105 mg cholesterol, 22 g carbohydrates, 36 g protein, 539 mg sodium, 3 g fiber

Note: To cook stew in the oven, transfer the browned meat and onion mixture to a large Dutch oven. Proceed with the recipe as directed; cook, tightly covered, in a 325-degree oven until meat is fork-tender, about 2 hours. Add vegetables, cover the pot and return to the oven until the vegetables are tender, about 1 hour.

SEARCHING FOR THE PERFECT GUY FOOD TO SERVE AT A FOOTBALL PARTY? Think French food. Seriously. Choucroute garni, the Alsace-Lorraine one-pot specialty, couldn't be more appealing. That is, if you like a rich, satisfying amalgam of sauerkraut, simmered pork and sausages. Our updates to the classic dish include:

1. An indulgent chunk of fresh pork belly (uncured bacon). This popular pork cut adds a silky richness to the tart cabbage and smoky sausages.
2. Browning the belly and the pork country ribs. While this step may not be traditional, we enjoy the tremendous flavor the browning adds.

A confession: Sauerkraut snobbery runs in the family. Please, no tinned stuff. Only fresh, crisp kraut will do. Look for the homemade sauerkraut sold from the barrels at local German and European meat markets. Most markets offer both the "raw" kraut—crisp and briny—and a "cooked" version (ready-to- eat, seasoned with pork and spices). For this recipe, purchase the "raw" or fresh sauerkraut. In a pinch, the sauerkraut sold in bags in the refrigerated section of large grocery stores will suffice. And always do as Julia Child taught us: Rinse, rinse.

Slow-cooked choucroute garni

Prep: 30 minutes | Marinate: Overnight | Cook: 7 hours | Makes: 16 servings | Pictured on p. 51

Fresh pork belly, though not expensive, must be ordered in advance from most butchers. Lightly smoked bacon can be substituted. As for the sausages, select fully cooked varieties with varying flavors and textures—from smooth knockwurst to coarser smoky thuringer to mild veal brats with garlic. A sharp mustard and mayo dipping sauce pairs perfectly with the pork and sausages.

2½ pounds pork country ribs, cut into sections

½ pound fresh pork belly, cut into 1-inch-thick slabs

2 tablespoons coarse salt

3 pounds fresh sauerkraut

2 tablespoons bacon drippings or vegetable oil

2 large sweet onions, halved, thinly sliced

4 large cloves garlic, crushed

4 bay leaves

½ teaspoon each: caraway seeds, freshly ground black pepper

2 to 3 cups low-sodium chicken broth

1 to 2 cups dry Riesling wine

8 to 12 assorted, fully cooked sausage links, such as smoked thuringer, kielbasa, brats, knockwurst

24 small yellow potatoes, scrubbed clean

Tarragon mustard dipping sauce (recipe follows)

Crumbled cooked bacon, optional

① Rub country ribs and pork belly with salt in a glass or stainless steel bowl. Refrigerate, covered, overnight or up to 24 hours, turning occasionally. Drain and rinse.

② Put the sauerkraut into a large bowl; cover with cold water. Let stand a few minutes; drain. Repeat this step two more times. Drain well. Working with a handful at a time, squeeze excess water out of the sauerkraut.

③ Heat bacon drippings or oil in large deep skillet over medium-high heat. Pat pork ribs and belly dry. Add pork in batches to the skillet in a single uncrowded layer. Brown nicely on all sides, about 10 minutes. Transfer to a 7-quart slow cooker (see note).

④ Cook the onions in the pan drippings, stirring often, until soft and golden, about 8 minutes. Stir in sauerkraut to coat well with the drippings. Stir in the garlic and seasonings. Arrange the sauerkraut over and under the browned pork in the slow cooker. Pour in 2 cups of the broth and the wine. (Add the remaining cup of broth and/or wine if needed so sauerkraut is nicely moistened.) Cover; cook on low until pork is fork-tender, about 6 hours.

⑤ Nestle the sausages into the mixture. Cover; cook on low until heated through, about 1 hour.

Note: Mixture can be cooked in a tightly covered Dutch oven in a 325-degree oven until pork is tender, about 2 hours. Add sausages. Cook, covered, until heated, about 45 more minutes. Be sure to check liquid level periodically.

Tarragon mustard dipping sauce: Mix ½ cup mayonnaise with 3 tablespoons Dijon mustard and 1 teaspoon dried tarragon.

⑥ Meanwhile, put potatoes into a large pot; add cold water to cover. Heat to a boil; cover. Reduce heat to low; cook until tender, about 15 minutes. Drain. Keep warm.

⑦ Spoon out a portion of the sauerkraut with slotted spoon to each plate. Top with some of each of the meats and the boiled potatoes. Sprinkle with the optional bacon. Pass the sauce at the table.

Nutrition information per serving: 667 calories, 43 g fat, 14 g saturated fat, 98 mg cholesterol, 46 g carbohydrates, 24 g protein, 726 mg sodium, 6 g fiber

WITH A FEW SIMPLE TRICKS, THIS MAIN-COURSE SALAD CAN TASTE great anywhere from the picnic blanket to a neighborhood block party. It may sound counterintuitive, but using high heat for some of the salad add-ins means better flavor and varied texture. I stir-fry tender pork over high for great flavor, then sweet shallots get a light fry for a crunchy topping.

I love to sprinkle on a salad surprise just before serving. Croutons will do, but try large coconut flakes, crispy chow mein noodles, roasted nuts, toasted sunflower seeds, broken tortilla or kale chips, even cheddar popcorn.

Red curry mango and pork rice salad

Prep: 30 minutes | Cook: 35 minutes | Makes: 6 main-course servings

You can cook the pork or chicken on a medium-hot grill if preferred. Tinned French fried onions offer a time-saving alternative to the shallots.

1⅓ cups uncooked long grain brown rice

⅓ cup uncooked quinoa, red quinoa preferred

2 to 3 tablespoons Thai red curry paste, to taste

1 pound pork tenderloin or boneless, skinless chicken thighs

4 tablespoons vegetable oil

4 large shallots or ⅓ red onion, peeled, very thinly sliced and separated into rings

1 small red bell pepper, cored, seeded, diced

1 ripe mango, peeled, seeded, diced

1 cup chopped fresh cilantro

3 to 4 tablespoons chopped fresh mint

Cilantro lime dressing (recipe follows)

2 cups fresh bean sprouts

½ cup roasted flaked coconut, optional

½ cup chopped roasted salted peanuts, optional

① Put rice, quinoa, curry paste and 2¾ cups water into a medium saucepan. Heat to a boil; cover tightly. Reduce heat to very low; simmer until rice is tender but not mushy, 15-20 minutes. (Alternatively, cook the rice, quinoa, curry paste and 2⅔ cups water in a rice cooker according to manufacturer's instructions.) Remove from heat; let stand, 10 minutes. Fluff with a fork; transfer to a large bowl to cool.

② Cut pork or chicken into scant ½-inch pieces. Heat 2 tablespoons oil in large nonstick skillet over medium-high heat. Add shallots. Cook and stir until golden, about 4 minutes. Use a slotted spoon to transfer shallots to a plate.

③ Reheat the oil left in the pan. Add half of the pork or chicken. Cook, stirring occasionally, until golden, 3-4 minutes. Transfer with a slotted spoon to a plate. Repeat with another tablespoon of the oil and remaining meat. Transfer cooked meat to the plate.

④ Add remaining tablespoon oil and the red pepper to the skillet; cook until crisp-tender, about 3 minutes. Add to the meat. Stir cooked meat and red peppers into rice. Cool.

⑤ To serve, add mango, chopped cilantro and mint to rice mixture. Stir in enough of the dressing to lightly coat everything; taste and mix well. Top with bean sprouts, toss lightly. Top with coconut, peanuts and the reserved fried shallots. Serve at room temperature.

....

Nutrition information per serving (using all of the dressing): 641 calories, 34 g fat, 6 g saturated fat, 53 mg cholesterol, 58 g carbohydrates, 28 g protein, 1,305 mg sodium, 7 g fiber

Cilantro lime dressing: In a blender, put ⅓ cup vegetable oil and ¼ cup each: fresh lime juice and fish sauce. Add 2 or 3 thin slices peeled ginger, 1 clove garlic and ½ cup loosely packed fresh cilantro leaves. Process until smooth. Makes about ¾ cup. Refrigerate and use within 1 day.

I N THIS SALAD, CAULIFLOWER GETS ROASTED IN A HOT OVEN FOR GOLDEN goodness before being tossed into the bowl. I like to use bright orange, green or light purple cauliflower here when it is available at the local market.

Couscous salad with roasted cauliflower

Prep: 30 minutes | Cook: 30 minutes | Makes: 4 to 6 main-course salads

For the couscous, you can substitute 1⅔ cups (10 ounces) cracked wheat (medium-grain bulgur) soaked in 3 cups very hot water to cover in a large bowl until nearly tender, usually about 1 hour. Drain well before using.

1 medium-size cauliflower, cored, separated into small florets (total about 8 cups)

4 tablespoons expeller-pressed canola oil or olive oil

¾ teaspoon salt, about

1 box (8.8 ounces) whole wheat Israeli couscous

½ cup golden raisins

4 large ripe plum tomatoes, cored, diced

½ large seedless cucumber, peeled, cut in small dice

½ small red onion, finely diced, well rinsed

Dijon dressing (recipe follows)

4 ounces crumbled goat cheese or feta cheese

4 cups watercress, arugula or baby kale (or a combination)

¼ cup roasted and salted sunflower seeds

Balsamic glaze

① Heat oven to 400 degrees. Mix cauliflower with 3 tablespoons of the oil on a large rimmed baking sheet (or use two baking sheets). Sprinkle lightly with salt, about ¼ teaspoon. Roast cauliflower, stirring occasionally, until golden and fork-tender, 20-25 minutes. Cool.

② Meanwhile, put remaining 1 tablespoon oil into a medium saucepan. Add 3 cups water; heat to a boil.

Add couscous and ½ teaspoon salt. Reduce heat to low; cover the pot. Cook until nearly tender, about 8 minutes. Let stand a couple of minutes; drain in a colander. Transfer to a large bowl, stir in raisins and let cool.

③ Stir roasted cauliflower, tomatoes, cucumber and onion into couscous. Refrigerate covered up to 1 day.

④ Just before serving, add dressing to couscous mixture to taste. Gently mix salad. Add cheese crumbles and watercress. Toss to mix. Serve sprinkled with sunflower seeds and drizzled with a little balsamic glaze.

....

Nutrition information per serving (for 6 servings, using all of the dressing): 554 calories, 35 g fat, 5 g saturated fat, 24 mg cholesterol, 51 g carbohydrates, 12 g protein, 672 mg sodium, 6 g fiber

Dijon dressing: Mix ½ cup oil (I like to use a combination of olive oil and safflower oil), ¼ cup white wine vinegar (or white balsamic vinegar), 2 teaspoons Dijon mustard, ½ teaspoon salt and ¼ teaspoon freshly ground black pepper in a jar with a tight-fitting lid. Shake well before using. Makes about 3/4 cup. Dressing will keep in the refrigerator for a few days.

FELL IN LOVE WITH BEETS LONG BEFORE THEY APPEARED ON EVERY RESTAURANT menu. My Gram chose small specimens and pickled them lightly with a touch of sugar. Roasting them, wrapped in foil to capture steam, is super easy. Add fresh herbs, garlic, oil and vinegar to flavor them for this beautiful salad.

Roasted beet, radicchio and walnut salad

Preparation time: 30 minutes | Cooking time: 1 hour | Yield: 6 to 8 servings

Roasted walnut oil is available at specialty food stores and by mail. Pistachio oil also is delicious here. The beets can be made several days in advance; use them at room temperature. For a shortcut, buy roasted beets from the produce section and season them with the vinegar and walnut oil.

Roasted beets:

4 medium-size beets, greens and roots trimmed, quartered

3 cloves garlic, halved

3 sprigs fresh sage

½ teaspoon salt and pepper to taste

1 to 2 tablespoons olive oil

½ small red onion, very thinly sliced, rinsed

1 tablespoon each: blackberry vinegar, roasted walnut oil

Salad:

3 tablespoons each: vegetable oil, roasted walnut oil

¼ cup blackberry or raspberry vinegar

Salt to taste

Freshly ground pepper to taste

1 medium head curly endive, well rinsed, torn into pieces

1 small head radicchio, halved, thinly sliced

Coarsely chopped candied or sugared walnuts for garnish, optional

① Heat oven to 325 degrees. Arrange beets on a double thickness of heavy-duty foil cut large enough to wrap the beets well. Sprinkle the garlic, sage, seasoning and oil over the beets. Wrap the beets tightly to enclose them. Place the packet on a baking sheet. Bake until the beets are tender when pierced with a knife, about 1 hour. Let cool. Peel the beets with a small knife and slice them thinly. Toss with the onion and 1 tablespoon each of vinegar and walnut oil.

② For the salad, mix the oils, vinegar, salt and pepper in the bottom of a large bowl. Add endive and radicchio and toss well to coat. Divide among serving plates. Top each with some of the beet mixture. Sprinkle with walnuts and serve.

....

Nutrition information per serving: 172 calories, 16 g fat, 2 g saturated fat, 0 mg cholesterol, 8 g carbohydrates, 2 g protein, 213 mg sodium, 3 g fiber

COLESLAW RANKS HIGH AS ONE OF OUR FAVORITE TAKE-ALONG DISHES FOR family parties. This crunchy, refreshing version, seasoned with Asian flavors, keeps well packed in a cooler with ice.

Spicy Asian coleslaw with honey-roasted peanuts

Prep: 30 minutes | Makes: 4 to 5 servings

This recipe doubles easily. The dressing recipe makes a great marinade for flank steak and chicken breasts which make a great accompaniment to the slaw.

¼ cup rice vinegar, not seasoned

1 tablespoon each: vegetable oil, sugar, soy sauce

1½ teaspoons dark sesame oil

2 teaspoons Chinese chili paste with garlic

1 piece (½ inch long) fresh ginger root, finely grated

1 head baby bok choy, finely shredded or 1 cup thinly sliced fresh snow peas

½ small head napa cabbage, quartered, cored, very finely shredded, about 2 cups

2 cups very finely shredded red or green cabbage

¼ small white onion, finely chopped, rinsed

½ small red bell pepper, seeded, diced

2 green onions, thinly sliced

2 tablespoons each: chopped fresh cilantro, sesame seeds

⅓ to ½ cup honey-roasted peanuts, coarsely chopped

① Mix vinegar, vegetable oil, sugar, soy sauce, sesame oil, chili paste and ginger in a jar with a tight-fitting lid. Cover; refrigerate up to 2 days.

② Mix all remaining ingredients except the peanuts in a large bowl. Refrigerate covered up to 1 day. Shortly before serving, toss vegetable mixture with the dressing to coat it nicely. Serve sprinkled with peanuts.

Nutrition information per serving: 163 calories, 12 g fat, 2 g saturated fat, 0 mg cholesterol, 11 g carbohydrates, 6 g protein, 273 mg sodium, 3 g fiber

TRUE CONFESSION: I ALWAYS OVERBUY AT THE FARMERS MARKET. IF I GO with limited dollars, I find myself looking for the best bargains. A full wallet prompts stocking up—for what, I am not sure, because I will go back the following weekend and perhaps hit the downtown markets during my lunch hour. I am just happier with a full complement of vegetables in the fridge.

All this produce procurement necessitates cooking. Fine by me—especially when the grill is lit anyway. So, just as I overload the market basket, I overload the grill with onions, eggplants, squash, tomatoes, potatoes and more. Rendered tender and golden, full of smoky flavor, these vegetables inspire a host of ideas. Some get stirred into scrambled eggs, frittatas, soup and pasta. Others make phenomenal sandwich fillings and warm salads.

Warm grilled eggplant and prosciutto salad

Prep: 30 minutes | Cook: 20 minutes | Makes: 6 servings

This summer, the passel of grilled vegetables takes center stage with the luxurious addition of prosciutto and sharp cheese. To season the vegetables during the grilling, we use a gourmet-store purchase of a Tuscan-inspired grill rub made from coarse salt, dried rosemary, thyme, marjoram, fennel seed and a pinch of sugar. Bottled Italian seasoning easily stands-in; jazz it up with sea salt and a pinch of sugar to promote browning.

1 large or 2 medium (1¼ pounds total) eggplant, ends trimmed, sliced into ½-inch-thick rounds

2 large or 3 medium (1¼ pounds total) zucchini, ends trimmed, cut into ½-inch-thick slabs

3 large knob onions or 6 green onions, ends trimmed

6 tablespoons olive oil

1½ teaspoons Tuscan herb blend or Italian seasoning

1¼ teaspoons salt

Freshly ground black pepper

10 or 12 cremini mushrooms, wiped clean

1 clove garlic, crushed

5 ounces thinly sliced prosciutto, cut into matchsticks

⅓ to ½ cup mixed grated Italian cheeses (such as Parmesan, Asiago, fontina, provolone)

⅓ cup roughly chopped pitted green olives

¼ cup chopped fresh herbs, such as a combination of basil, chives and parsley

2 to 3 generous cups baby arugula or spinach leaves

Warm grilled flatbreads, for serving

① Heat a gas grill to medium-hot or prepare a charcoal fire until hot.

② Place eggplant slices, zucchini and onions on a well-oiled baking sheet. Drizzle generously with oil; sprinkle with herb blend, salt and pepper. Turn; repeat with other side. Skewer mushrooms on thin metal or wooden skewers. Brush with oil; season with herb blend, salt and pepper.

③ Grill all vegetables, turning once, until tender and golden, 6-10 minutes. Remove to a cutting board.

④ Cut eggplant and zucchini into generous ½-inch pieces. Place in large bowl. Thinly slice the grilled onions and mushrooms; add to the bowl. Add the garlic; mix gently. (Mixture can be made up 1 hour in advance; warm gently in the microwave if necessary.)

⑤ Stir in the prosciutto, cheese, olives and fresh herbs. Add arugula; toss lightly. Serve accompanied with a warm grilled flatbread.

....

Nutrition information per serving: 251 calories, 19 g fat, 4 g saturated fat, 22 mg cholesterol, 12 g carbohydrates, 13 g protein, 1,249 mg sodium, 5 g fiber

T'S EASY TO EAT PLANTS WHEN THEY'RE COVERED IN BACON AND BLUE CHEESE, which defeats the point. Same goes for salads swimming in dressing and packed with deep-fried croutons. That's why I like to make fattoush. This Middle Eastern toasted bread and vegetable salad satisfies my inner rabbit perfectly.

Fattoush vegetable and toasted flatbread salad

Prep: 25 minutes | Makes: 2 entree or 4 side salads | Pictured on p. 62–63

For fattoush, I make a lemon vinaigrette seasoned with sumac. This deep purple-red dried berry, from the sumac bushes throughout the Middle East, has a tart and fruity flavor. It's equally delicious sprinkled over salads, brown rice and roasted vegetables. Purchase it ground at spices stores or online.

1 head romaine lettuce, trimmed

1 small head Boston lettuce, halved, thinly sliced

½ cup thinly sliced fresh herbs, such as a combination of cilantro, parsley and mint

4 to 6 medium tomatoes, such as Campari, cut into eighths

3 small green onions, ends trimmed, thinly sliced

½ seedless cucumber, quartered lengthwise, thinly sliced

½ green bell pepper, seeded, chopped

4 large radishes, cut into matchsticks, about ⅓ cup

½ cup drained canned garbanzo beans

About 2 cups roughly broken crispy pita wedges or flame-toasted flatbread

2 cups shredded cooked chicken, optional

Fresh lemon vinaigrette with sumac (recipe follows)

Ground sumac, optional

Fresh lemon wedges

① Cut the romaine head lengthwise into quarters. Then slice each quarter into ½-inch-wide pieces. You should have about 6 cups. Put into a large mixing bowl along with the Boston lettuce. Add herbs and toss to mix. (Mixture can be refrigerated up to 2 days in a covered container lined with a piece of paper toweling.)

② Just before serving, add tomatoes, onions, cucumber, bell pepper, radishes and garbanzo beans to the lettuce mixture. Toss well. Add pita wedges and chicken if using, then add a couple of spoonfuls of vinaigrette (do not drench salad). Toss again to lightly coat everything with the vinaigrette.

③ Pile salad onto serving plates. Sprinkle with sumac and garnish with lemon wedges.

Nutrition information per serving (for 4 servings): 220 calories, 7 g fat, 1 g saturated fat, 0 mg cholesterol, 35 g carbohydrates, 9 g protein, 277 mg sodium, 8 g fiber

Fresh lemon vinaigrette with sumac

Prep: 5 minutes | Makes: a scant ½ cup

1 large lemon

¼ cup extra-virgin olive oil

1 small clove garlic, finely chopped or crushed

¼ to 1 teaspoon sumac to taste (or use more
   lemon rind)

¼ teaspoon salt

Freshly ground pepper to taste

① Grate the zest from the lemon into a small bowl.
Squeeze the juice and add to the zest; you should have
about ¼ cup. Stir in remaining ingredients; taste for
seasonings. Refrigerate covered up to 1 week.

Nutrition information per tablespoon: 63 calories, 7 g fat, 1 g
saturated fat, 0 mg cholesterol, 1 g carbohydrates, 0 g protein,
73 mg sodium, 0 g fiber

CHAPTER 5

Sandwiches, Pastas and Pizzas

WE COULD HAPPILY EAT A BURGER ONCE OR TWICE A WEEK. BURGERS have it all going on: great flavors and a stack of textures. Plus, most fall into a modest price range and are relatively easy to prepare. Weeknight fare, weekend celebration— you name the event and a good burger will shine.

Meatless burger patties have their merits, so we've peppered our burger rotation with them. Friends in the U.K. introduced us to their favorite meatless burger—one stuffed with a thick, slab of hot, melty halloumi cheese and sliced ripe tomato.

Cheese "burgers" with spicy mayo

Prep: 15 minutes | Cook: 5 minutes | Makes: 4 servings

Halloumi, a goat and sheep's milk cheese made with nonanimal rennet and a touch of mint, hails from Cyprus. Semifirm, the milky white cheese bronzes beautifully in a skillet. Warmed, the cheese yields a pleasantly bouncy texture with plenty of eating satisfaction—amazing tucked into a toasted bun.

14 to 16 ounces halloumi cheese, juusto, bread cheese or queso fresco

4 hearty hamburger buns, such as pretzel rolls or whole wheat buns, split

Olive oil

Spiced mayonnaise (recipe follows)

1 large ripe tomato, cut into 4 thick slices

Thinly sliced seedless cucumbers or dill pickles

Arugula sprigs or romaine leaves

① Cut the cheese into ½-inch-thick slabs slightly larger than the buns. Toast the cut sides of the buns under the broiler, watching carefully to prevent burning.

② Pat the cheese dry. Heat a large nonstick skillet over medium-high heat until hot enough to make a drop of water sizzle on contact. Add a very light film of oil; swirl it around to heat. Add the cheese slices in a single uncrowded layer. Cook, turning once, until golden on both sides, 2 or 3 minutes total. Drain on paper towels.

③ Spread the spiced mayonnaise on the bottoms of the buns. Top with a slice of the tomato. Then top with a slice of fried cheese. Top with cucumber or dill pickle slices and arugula or romaine. Put a little of the remaining mayo on the top of the buns and serve.

Nutrition information per serving: 328 calories, 15 g fat, 6 g saturated fat, 36 mg cholesterol, 33 g carbohydrates, 16 g protein, 462 mg sodium, 4 g fiber

Spiced mayonnaise: Mix ¼ cup mayonnaise with 2 tablespoons chopped fresh chives or green onion tops, 1 teaspoon za'atar, a Middle Eastern spice blend (or your favorite spice rub), and 1 pinch crushed red pepper flakes.

Two secrets to avoid soggy brown-bag sandwiches: assemble them on frozen bread slices and pack the garnishes separately. The bread thaws during transport, and a bag of lettuce, sliced tomatoes, thin cucumbers or pickles can be easily added just before eating.

Salami and cream cheese sandwich (p. 70) and Sunny carrot sandwiches (p. 71)

Summer always goes too fast. Back-to-school advertisements fill me with mixed emotions: I like the routine, I dread the monotony. A quick calculation tells me we've made more than 4,500 school lunches. Monotonous? With a modicum of imagination, no.

The biggest lesson learned? Make lunches the evening before; there's never enough time in the morning. So after the dinner dishes are done, the kitchen counter transforms into a sandwich shop, with options to customize.

With a little encouragement and trial, our kids learned to prefer whole-grain breads, and low-fat cheeses and meats on their sandwiches. My son loves to build sandwich masterpieces—his salami and cream cheese just might be his all-time favorite lunchbox sandwich; he made it at least once a week throughout high school.

Two secrets to avoid soggy brown-bag sandwiches: assemble them on frozen bread slices and pack the garnishes separately. The bread thaws during transport, and a bag of lettuce, sliced tomatoes, thin cucumbers or pickles can be easily added just before eating.

Salami and cream cheese sandwich

Prep: 10 minutes | Makes: 1 hearty sandwich | Pictured on p. 68

Sausage buns or a 5-inch section of a French baguette can be substituted for the pretzel roll.

1 oblong pretzel roll, about 5 ounces

2 to 3 tablespoons light cream cheese

1 tablespoon chopped chives or finely chopped drained giardiniera, optional

8 to 10 super-thin slices salami (peppered salami is great here)

Dijon or spicy brown mustard

2 large romaine lettuce leaves

3 or 4 thin slices of ripe tomato, optional

① Split the roll horizontally in half. Spread the cream cheese on the bottom. Top with the chives or giardiniera; press it into the cream cheese. Layer the salami over the cream cheese. Spread the mustard on the underside of the top of the roll. Close the sandwich and wrap in plastic. Refrigerate up to 1 day. Pack the lettuce leaves and tomato slices separately in small containers. Add them to the sandwich just before eating.

Nutrition information per serving: 654 calories, 13 g fat, 5 g saturated fat, 51 mg cholesterol, 102 g carbohydrates, 35 g protein, 1,609 mg sodium, 7 g fiber

Sunny carrot sandwiches

Prep: 10 minutes | Makes: 2 sandwiches | Pictured on p. 69

I like to add raisins and toasted sesame seeds to this meatless sandwich.

4 thick slices wheat or pumpernickel bread,
    toasted

2 to 4 tablespoons sunflower seed butter
    (or almond or peanut butter)

1 cup super-versatile curried carrots (recipe
    follows)

① Spread each piece of toasted bread with a smear
of the sunflower seed butter. Pile ½ cup of the carrots
on two of the pieces of bread. Top with a second piece
of bread to make a sandwich. Wrap tightly in plastic.
Refrigerate up to 1 day.

....

Nutrition information per serving: 380 calories, 15 g fat, 1 g
saturated fat, 0 mg cholesterol, 53 g carbohydrates, 13 g protein,
643 mg sodium, 6 g fiber

Super-versatile curried carrots

Prep: 5 minutes | Cook: 5 minutes

Makes: 3 generous cups

Serve these carrots as a salad or add them to sandwiches.
They also are great as a salad topping or stirred into
coleslaw or creamy tomato or butternut soup.

2 tablespoons olive oil

1 package (10 ounces) or 4 generous cups thinly
    shredded or finely julienned carrots

2 large cloves garlic, crushed

½ teaspoon curry powder

¼ teaspoon salt or to taste

2 to 4 tablespoons finely chopped fresh chives
    or parsley

① Heat oil in a large skillet over medium-high. Add
carrots; cook and stir until crisp-tender and a little
golden, about 3 minutes. Stir in garlic, curry powder
and salt. Cook and stir, about 2 minutes. Remove from
heat, stir in chives and let cool. Refrigerate covered up
to 3 days.

....

Nutrition information per serving: 123 calories, 9 g fat, 1 g
saturated fat, 0 mg cholesterol, 10 g carbohydrates, 1 g protein,
260 mg sodium, 3 g fiber.

N RECENT YEARS, THANKS TO THEIR SURGE IN POPULARITY AT UPSCALE RESTAU-rants, burgers have transitioned from a go-to weekday dinner to an indulgent night out. That's good and bad news—good because a well-made burger deserves admiration and adulation. The downside? This easy-to-cook, relatively inexpensive, unpretentious meal now often shows up dressed with expensive, indulgent and super-fattening ingredients.

For health's sake, let's dial it back a bit. And for the sanity of the home cook. I need this entree on my weekly menu—especially now when my hungry young adults gather for family dinner.

Grilled turkey burgers with kalamata olives and herbs

Prep: 20 minutes | Cook: 12 minutes | Makes: 4 servings

Lean turkey appeals when seasoned in a way that allows the flavor of the meat to shine. I like to add fresh herbs and a surprise such as kalamata olives. Proper cooking will yield juicy results.

1½ pounds ground turkey or beef chuck

¼ cup chopped, pitted kalamata or black olives

¼ cup panko breadcrumbs, optional

2 tablespoons chopped fresh parsley

2 teaspoons chopped fresh sage or ½ teaspoon dried

1 teaspoon salt

¾ teaspoon chopped fresh thyme or ⅛ teaspoon dried

½ teaspoon freshly ground black pepper

4 slices provolone or Colby cheese, optional

4 hearty whole wheat burger buns, split, toasted

Mayonnaise, optional

Thinly sliced pickles

① Put turkey, olives, breadcrumbs, parsley, sage, salt, thyme and pepper into a large bowl. Gently mix together with your hands. Shape into 4 burgers, each about ½ inch thick. Refrigerate up to an hour or so.

② Heat gas grill to medium or prepare a charcoal grill until coals are covered in gray ash.

③ Grill burgers directly over the heat, 6 minutes. Gently flip; grill until juices run clear and center of burgers is nearly firm to the touch, about 5 minutes. Top with a slice of cheese if using; grill, covered, 1 minute.

④ Serve on toasted buns spread with mayonnaise and topped with a pile of the pickles.

Nutrition information per serving: 410 calories, 19 g fat, 5 g saturated fat, 123 mg cholesterol, 23 g carbohydrates, 37 g protein, 990 mg sodium, 4 g fiber

TIPS FOR BURGERS

➤ Buy wisely: Fresh, coarsely ground meat tastes best, so skip the meat case and go to a butcher who knows the pedigree of the meat being sold. For ground turkey, use a combination of breast and dark meat for best flavor and texture. Look for all-natural meats and turkey without seasonings or additives.

➤ Season the meat before shaping into burgers—that way it will taste great through and through—not just on the exterior.

➤ Chill seasoned burgers up to 1 hour before cooking to let the seasonings mellow.

➤ Cook on natural, hardwood charcoal for optimal flavor; use a gas grill for speed (adding a packet of soaked wood chips to the grill will boost smoke and flavor). Indoors, heat a nonstick ridged grill pan until very hot; add the burgers and sear one side. Flip and finish in a 400 degree oven.

➤ Test meat and poultry burgers for doneness by pressing on the center of the burger—it should barely yield indicating medium-rare to medium doneness. Do not pierce the meat or press on it during cooking or juices will escape.

➤ Add cheese during the last minute of cooking; any earlier in the process will just mean the cheese melts off. Don't over-cheese or you'll overpower the meat. Mild cheeses on mild poultry burgers—stronger cheeses such as blues, smoked and goat cheeses with bison, lamb and beef burgers.

➤ Choose complementary breads—mild-tasting turkey burgers taste great on crispy, toasted, whole grain breads. Heartier beef burgers are delicious on less complex breads.

➤ Control the condiments—let the flavor of the meat and bread shine through.

LOVE LAMB BURGERS—GREEK-STYLE WITH FRESH HERBS, THICK YOGURT AND a zesty tomato ketchup. Most butchers will grind lamb shoulder to order, yielding a juicy burger with just enough fat for flavor and moistness. If lamb doesn't sit well with your crowd, try using a combination of lean ground beef and lamb. This recipe works well with beef and pork, too.

Grilled lamb burgers with eggplant and yogurt

Prep: 45 minutes | Chill: 1 hour | Cook: 20 minutes | Makes: 4 servings

You can double this recipe for a crowd.

½ small onion

1 to 1¼ pounds ground lamb (or beef, or a combination of the two)

1½ tablespoons each chopped fresh parsley, mint (or 1½ teaspoons each dried)

1 clove garlic, crushed

½ teaspoon salt, plus more for sprinkling

¼ teaspoon freshly ground black pepper or grains of paradise

Pinch each ground cinnamon, allspice

1 medium-size (12-ounce) eggplant, scrubbed, ends trimmed, cut into 8 round slices

1½ tablespoons olive oil

4 thick pita breads with pockets or hearty buns

Zesty tomato ketchup (recipe follows)

About ¼ cup plain Greek-style yogurt

① Coarsely grate the onion using the largest holes on a four-sided grater into a large bowl. Stir in meat, herbs, garlic, ½ teaspoon of the salt, pepper, cinnamon and allspice. Refrigerate covered, 1 hour.

② Shape meat into four burgers, each about ½ inch thick. Brush eggplant slices on both sides generously with olive oil; sprinkle with salt to taste.

③ Prepare a charcoal grill or heat a gas grill to medium-hot. Arrange eggplant slices on grill. Grill,

turning once, until nicely golden on both sides, about 8 minutes total. Remove to a plate.

④ Grill burgers, turning only once, until medium, about 10 minutes. Near the end of the cooking, place buns on edge of grill to toast lightly.

⑤ To assemble burgers, place 1 eggplant slice into each pita or on each bun bottom. Top with burgers, then a generous spoonful of the tomato ketchup and a dollop of yogurt. Top with another eggplant slice (add bun top if using).

Nutrition information per serving: 400 calories, 22 g fat, 7 g saturated fat, 77 mg cholesterol, 25 g carbohydrates, 25 g protein, 649 mg sodium, 3 g fiber

Zesty tomato ketchup: Saute 1 crushed clove garlic in 1 tablespoon olive oil until golden, about 1 minute. Stir in 1 can (28 ounces) crushed tomatoes, 1 tablespoon red wine vinegar, 1 teaspoon sugar, pinch of ground red pepper and salt to taste. Simmer, stirring often, until thickened, about 15 minutes. Let cool. Use at room temperature. Store leftovers in refrigerator.

We happily spent endless Saturdays on the sidelines at soccer fields, football fields and in the waiting rooms at indoor tennis facilities and piano studios. Now, the kids live away from home. Saturdays offer a world of new possibilities. So we think about exercising and then plan leisurely lunches with fellow empty-nesters.

On one such Saturday, we swooned over a crispy BLT fish sandwich at a local restaurant. Unforgettable layers of spicy catfish, smoky bacon, sweet tomatoes and crunchy lettuce piled on a rich egg bun slathered with spicy mayo. The garlicky slaw served alongside likewise captivated. The combo delivered a clear missive: Make this at home. And often.

Wisconsin cabin lunches with my family taught me that fish and bacon fat enjoy a natural partnership. The sweet taste of most fish and the rich smoke of bacon complement each other beautifully.

I'm sure the cabin's stock of cast-iron pans contributed to the marriage—lending stunning texture to the northern pike and walleye my father snagged. Even the kids' blue gill catch benefited from the smoky fat and hot pan.

For my version of those memorable BLT fish sandwiches, I enjoy wild-caught Alaskan cod or farmed catfish. Sprinkle the fish generously with a spicy Cajun seasoning before it goes into the hot bacon-fatted pan. Then turn on the exhaust fan so you can cook with plenty of heat to create a rich, golden char. When pressed for time, breaded fish fillets from the fish counter or the freezer aisle taste terrific in this sandwich. Simply swap out the skillet for a superhot oven to crisp the fish.

Crispy fish BLT sandwiches with sriracha mayonnaise

Prep: 40 minutes | Marinate: 30 minutes | Cook: 20 minutes | Makes: 4 servings

You'll need to be a bit of a short-order cook to coordinate the sandwich assembly so the bread is hot and crusty and the fish perfectly cooked. Be sure to have all the sandwich fixings near the work surface for speedy assembly as soon as the fish is cooked.

4 skinless thick fish fillets, such as wild-caught Alaskan cod, each about 6 ounces

1 to 2 tablespoons Cajun seasoning blend (recipe follows)

4 thin slices applewood smoked bacon, cut in half

4 slices brick or Monterey jack cheese

4 sandwich buns (such as brioche)

2 tablespoons sriracha mayonnaise (recipe follows)

8 thick slices ripe tomato, such as Campari tomatoes

4 thin slices large dill pickle, optional

8 small romaine leaves

① Rinse fish fillets; pat dry with paper towels. Place on a baking sheet. Generously sprinkle Cajun seasoning on both sides. Let stand at room temperature, up to 30 minutes, or refrigerate for several hours.

② Meanwhile, cook bacon in large, well-seasoned, cast-iron skillet (or nonstick skillet) over medium heat, turning, until crisp, about 10 minutes. Transfer to a plate; reserve the pan drippings.

③ Heat the skillet with the drippings over medium-high heat. Add fillets in a single, uncrowded layer (in batches if necessary). Cook without turning until darkly golden, about 5 minutes. Carefully flip; brown the second side, about 2 minutes. Top with a slice of cheese; remove from the heat.

④ Meanwhile, toast the buns in a toaster oven or on a grill pan until golden. Spread sriracha mayonnaise over the insides of the buns.

⑤ Build each sandwich with 1 fillet, 2 tomato slices, 1 pickle slice if using, 2 half-pieces bacon and lettuce leaves on the bottom of the bun. Put the top of the bun in place and serve right away.

....

Nutrition information per serving: 540 calories, 19 g fat, 9 g saturated fat, 104 mg cholesterol, 47 g carbohydrates, 43 g protein, 1,285 mg sodium, 3 g fiber

Cajun spice mixture: Mix 1 teaspoon each salt, freshly ground black pepper, paprika and oregano with ¼ teaspoon each cayenne and dried thyme.

Sriracha mayonnaise: Mix ¼ cup mayonnaise with 2 tablespoons sriracha hot sauce and 1 or 2 tablespoons chopped fresh cilantro. Refrigerate covered up to several days.

WORK FULL TIME IN THE FOOD BUSINESS. FOR MORE THAN THREE DECADES, MY days have centered on food—from wrangling recipes and groceries, to ingredient research, to tastings in a test kitchen. So when the kids ask what I want for Mother's Day, the answer is simple: Cook for me. Nothing exotic, I tell them, and if you search the pantry and freezer, you won't even need to shop. Start with pasta. Keep things healthy. Use your imagination.

First, pair the pasta shape to complement the sauce/toppings. Pick hollow pasta such as rigatoni for saucy toppings such as cream sauces or marinara. Choose flat pastas, such as linguine and fettuccine, for sauteed or chunky toppings such as diced vegetables, shredded meats or fish. Coordinate the size of the pasta with the size of the add-ins; tiny orzo goes well with cooked peas, and penne pairs nicely with broccoli florets.

We usually have some type of fully cooked protein in the fridge or freezer that lends itself to a speedy meal. These treasures, such as fully cooked sausages, require little more than heating and cutting to mix with pasta. A piece of cooked pot roast or pork shoulder can be shredded and mixed with marinara sauce for a very simple rendition of a homemade ragu we enjoy over wide egg noodles.

My daughter pairs good-quality canned tuna with toothsome bucatini pasta (long, fat strands with a hole running down the length) and plenty of fresh lemon and parsley. She adds the olives and capers for me.

Bucatini with lemon, tuna and capers

Prep: 20 minutes | Cook: 20 minutes | Makes: 4 servings | Pictured on p. 78

You can use either oil-packed or water-packed tuna here. Or substitute 1 pound cooked small shrimp or 3 cups shredded cooked chicken.

½ cup coarse breadcrumbs or panko crumbs

¼ cup olive oil

1 large red bell pepper, cored, diced

½ large lemon

½ cup sliced or chopped pitted manzanilla, Kalamata or Castelvetrano olives

2 tablespoons drained capers, optional

½ pound bucatini or spaghetti

2 cans (12 ounces each) solid albacore tuna, drained

¼ cup chopped fresh parsley

Freshly ground black pepper

① Place breadcrumbs in a large nonstick skillet over medium heat. Toast, stirring constantly (do not walk away), until crisp and golden, 3-4 minutes. Transfer to a plate to cool.

② Heat a large pot of salted water to a boil. Meanwhile, heat olive oil in a large skillet over medium heat. Add red pepper; cook until tender, 3-4 minutes. Remove from heat. Grate the zest of the lemon into the peppers, then squeeze in the lemon juice. Stir in olives and capers.

③ Add the pasta to the boiling water. Cook, stirring occasionally, until al dente, 8-10 minutes. Drain well.

④ Turn the heat on under the skillet; add the tuna, parsley and black pepper to taste. Heat briefly, breaking tuna into large chunks. Stir in hot pasta. Serve sprinkled generously with the crisp breadcrumbs.

....

Nutrition information per serving: 561 calories, 19 g fat, 2 g saturated fat, 61 mg cholesterol, 55 g carbohydrates, 43 g protein, 567 mg sodium, 4 g fiber

MORE TOPPINGS

Here are some more combinations to toss with cooked pasta:

➤ Cooked green vegetables such as sauteed zucchini or diced green beans, feta chunks and pitted Kalamata olives.

➤ Canned garbanzo beans, diced bottled roasted peppers and shredded cheese.

➤ Diced peppered salami, sauteed radicchio and little lumps of cream cheese.

➤ Toasted breadcrumbs, nuts, garlic and hot pepper flakes.

➤ Small shrimp, sauteed onions and baby kale or spinach.

➤ Halved cherry tomatoes with refrigerated pesto.

➤ Shredded roast chicken, spicy salsa and diced queso fresco.

➤ Diced ham, cooked peas and butter and cheese.

MY FAVORITE FOODS OF SUMMER—RIPE TOMATOES, MEATY EGGPLANT, skinny green beans, toothsome wax beans and tender squash never cease to inspire. I buy them nearly every week at one farmers market or another. Then I blanch, steam, grill or chop them in readiness for a shower of garden fresh herbs for side dishes, salads and amazing meatless mains.

To keep things interesting, I'll add an intriguing pantry ingredient to my market standbys—like fregola pasta. A specialty of Sardinia, fregola's toasted, nutty flavor and toothsome texture pairs beautifully with summer vegetables. Cookbook author Claudia Roden posits that these semolina granules, sometimes called fregula sarda, made by moistening the grain and rolling it gently with the fingertips (similar to couscous), were introduced to Sardinia by the Romans. The pasta, about the size and shape of peppercorns, is gaining favor in this country. Look for it in stores with a good selection of imported Italian pastas. I order the Rustichella D'Abruzzo brand online from Amazon. It cooks beautifully. Grandanina pasta (sometimes called couscous) imported from Italy is another online option.

Serve the hearty meatless pasta salad warm with crusty grilled bread that's been topped with sliced tomatoes and olive oil. For meat lovers, I like to stir in slices of grilled Italian sausage, medium-rare steak or shredded chicken. Chunks of grilled or broiled meaty fish also taste great here.

Fregola salad with green beans, raisins and mint

Prep: 30 minutes | Cook: 15 minutes | Makes: 8 servings

Leave skinny green beans whole for an attractive salad. Cut larger beans in half.

¼ cup pine nuts, sliced almonds or chopped pecans

2 lemons

6 tablespoons extra-virgin olive oil

3 cloves garlic, crushed

1½ teaspoons salt

12 ounces skinny green beans, wax beans or haricots verts, ends trimmed

1 pound fregola pasta, Israeli couscous or whole wheat orzo

1 cup small raisins or currants

1 pint fresh shelled peas or 2 cups thawed frozen tiny peas

⅔ cup chopped fresh chives

½ cup packed freshly sliced mint

① Put the nuts into a small nonstick skillet. Cook over medium heat, stirring and watching them closely, until barely golden, 1 or 2 minutes. Transfer to a plate to cool.

② Finely grate the zest from the lemons into a small bowl. Juice the lemons into the bowl. Stir in the olive oil, garlic and salt.

③ Heat two large pots of salted water to a boil. Add the beans to one of the pots; boil uncovered until tender-crisp and bright, about 5 minutes. Drain; let cool. Add the fregola to the other pot; boil, stirring often, until al dente, about 10 minutes. (Alternatively, cook couscous or orzo according to package directions.)

④ Meanwhile, put raisins and peas in bottom of a large mixing bowl. Drain the pasta well when it's done; pour it over the raisins and peas. Let stand a few minutes without stirring to let the heat of the pasta warm the raisins and peas.

⑤ Pour the lemon juice dressing over the pasta; toss well to mix. Stir in the cooked beans and herbs. Toss to mix. Sprinkle with the toasted nuts. Serve while still warm.

....

Nutrition information per serving: 438 calories, 14 g fat, 2 g saturated fat, 0 mg cholesterol, 70 g carbohydrates, 11 g protein, 483 mg sodium, 7 g fiber

GOOD NEWS. TODAY'S WHOLE WHEAT AND WHOLE GRAIN PASTAS TASTE A heck of a lot better balanced than the pasty, overly grassy varieties available a decade or so ago. I've come to enjoy the slightly nutty flavor of most whole wheat pastas and now use them in all my standard pasta recipes.

The deep, rich, pleasantly earthy flavor of pasta made with whole grains pair best with amped-up toppings. Think bacon, deeply flavored kale, tangy creme fraiche and fresh herbs. Bold cheeses such as goat, blue or aged sharp cheddars likewise make a better team.

The only real downside to any pasta dinner is the number of pans needed—a large deep kettle to boil the pasta water and at least one more to cook toppings. If you choose to add a hearty green such as kale, you'll need a third pan to blanch it to near-tenderness.

The penne recipe here features lots of bold flavors and makes a totally satisfying main dish. For the ultimate convenience, I purchase bagged prewashed and cut kale.

Penne with caramelized onions, kale, bacon and goat cheese

Prep: 25 minutes | Cook: 25 minutes | Makes: 6 main-course servings

Smoked turkey bacon is good here, too, but it won't crisp like pork bacon. If you like, add 1 to 1½ cups diced smoky ham or smoked turkey along with the garlic in step 3.

2 or 3 thick slices smoky bacon, diced

¼ cup extra-virgin olive oil

1 very large sweet onion, cut in half, then cut into thin wedges

1 large or 2 small leeks, ends trimmed, halved, rinsed, thinly sliced

2 cloves garlic, crushed

3 tablespoons balsamic vinegar

¾ to 1 teaspoon salt

Freshly ground black pepper

1 pound whole wheat penne or whole grain rotini

1 package (10 ounces) chopped kale or 6 cups sliced, trimmed kale leaves

6 ounces crumbled goat cheese or blue cheese

⅓ cup toasted pine nuts or chopped walnuts, optional

① Heat two large pots of salted water to a boil over high heat.

② Cook bacon in very large (12- to 14-inch) nonstick skillet until bacon is crispy, about 5 minutes. Remove crisp bacon with slotted spoon; set aside. Add oil, onion and leek to pan drippings. Cook over medium-high heat, stirring often, until nicely browned, 10 to 12 minutes. Add garlic, balsamic, salt and pepper to taste; cook, 1 minute. Remove from heat. (You can do this step up to an hour in advance.)

③ Meanwhile, cook penne in one of the pots of boiling water until al dente (a little toothsome at the center), about 10 minutes. Reserve ½ cup cooking water; drain pasta well. Return to pan.

④ Meanwhile, add kale to the other pot of boiling water. Boil gently, stirring once or twice, 4 minutes; drain well.

⑤ Stir drained kale into onion mixture; heat through. Toss with drained pasta adding a little of the reserved water for moistness. Sprinkle with bacon, cheese and pine nuts. Toss and serve.

Nutrition information per serving: 426 calories, 9 g fat, 1 g saturated fat, 49 mg cholesterol, 63 g carbohydrates, 21 g protein, 498 mg sodium, 6 g fiber

'LL BE THE FIRST TO ADMIT IT: MY WEEKDAY COOKING OFTEN SLIPS INTO A rut. Most nights the options look familiar: chicken or pork on the grill, pasta with red sauce, steamed veggies and tossed salads. Nothing too exciting, but always healthier than fast food.

So when my daughter requests meatless mains every now and then, I'm happy for the challenge. Plus, eliminating some animal proteins and fats might be the simplest way to achieve our healthy eating goals and cut calories.

One mainstay in our meatless repertoire combines whole grain pasta, beans, cheese and tomatoes. The recipe that follows will remind you of pizza—at least one made with super-ripe tomatoes, fresh basil, sharp cheese and a generous topping of arugula salad.

Penne with garbanzo beans, arugula and spicy tomatoes

Prep: 25 minutes | Cook: 10 minutes | Makes: 6 servings

Take note: Leftovers make great lunches.

1 can (15 ounces) garbanzo beans, drained

4 large ripe plum tomatoes diced

½ large seedless cucumber, diced

⅓ cup finely diced red onion, well rinsed

Roasted tomato vinaigrette (recipe follows)

12 ounces whole wheat penne pasta

½ to ¾ cup shredded Italian four cheese blend
    (Parmesan, Asiago, fontina, provolone)

2 cups baby arugula leaves

½ cup finely sliced fresh basil leaves

① Heat a large pot of salted water to a boil over high heat. Meanwhile, mix beans, tomatoes, cucumber and onion in a large bowl. Add vinaigrette; toss to mix well.

② When water is boiling, add pasta. Cook, stirring occasionally, until al dente (a little toothsome to the bite), about 10 minutes. Drain pasta. Add to bowl with bean mixture; toss to mix well.

③ Stir in cheese, arugula and basil. Serve warm.

Nutrition information per serving: 574 calories, 19 g fat, 4 g saturated fat, 10 mg cholesterol, 84 g carbohydrates, 22 g protein, 782 mg sodium, 12 g fiber

Roasted tomato vinaigrette: Put ¼ cup olive oil, half of a 14.5-ounce can fire-roasted tomatoes, 2 tablespoons red wine vinegar, ½ teaspoon salt and ¼ to ½ teaspoon crushed red pepper flakes into a blender. Process until smooth.

T HIS MEATLESS WHOLE WHEAT PASTA DISH SHOWS UP OFTEN AT OUR WEEK-
day suppers. For homemade bread crumbs, purchase a loaf of artisanal-style hearty French
or Italian bread and leave it uncovered on the counter overnight. The next day, cut it into
large cubes. Put a few handfuls of cubes at a time in the food processor fitted with the metal blade.
Pulse on/off to make crumbs about the size of oatmeal flakes. Put the crumbs into a freezer bag
and store in the freezer for up to several months.

Homemade meals let us eat better and save money. Now there's a credo we can live by.

Whole wheat pasta with herbed crumbs

Prep: 15 minutes | Cook: 15 minutes | Makes: 5 servings

*The key to success with this recipe is great breadcrumbs—make your own, purchase some from the local bakery or
substitute panko crumbs. The breadcrumb mixture can be made 2 days in advance; cover and refrigerate it then reheat
before using.*

3 cups coarse, homemade breadcrumbs

¼ cup extra-virgin olive oil

¼ cup minced fresh parsley, chives or a
combination

1 large shallot, finely chopped

2 large cloves garlic, finely chopped

1 teaspoon sweet or smoked paprika

½ teaspoon salt

¼ teaspoon ground red pepper, optional

1 pound whole wheat spaghetti or other
pasta shape

① Heat a large pot of salted water to the boil.
Meanwhile, mix everything except the pasta in a large
nonstick skillet. Cook, stirring, over medium heat until
the crumbs are golden, 3-4 minutes. Remove from heat.

② Cook the pasta in the boiling water until al dente,
about 10 minutes. Drain. Return it to the pan. Add the
toasted crumbs; toss well. Serve hot.

Nutrition information per serving: 625 calories, 20 g fat, 2 g
saturated fat, 1 mg cholesterol, 102 g carbohydrates, 15 g protein,
243 mg sodium, 9 g fiber

A GOOD FRIEND MADE A SINCERE PLEA AT A TRENDY RESTAURANT DINNER recently: Please leave the bacon out of the dessert. Keep it savory, and keep it away from chocolate. We agree. Treating bacon as a novelty ingredient needs to stop. Bacon deserves our respect. Plus, we don't want just hints of bacon. We want BACON.

We are not alone. Lots of friends, from vegetarians to meat lovers of all ages, happily forgo diets and endure days of self-denial to indulge. Favorite recipes get passed around—memories of intriguing dishes shared. From bacon-topped burgers to macaroni and cheese with bacon to chili infused with bacon.

Bacon-topped pizza means pulling out the stops, including the grill and homemade dough. We make the dough in the food processor the night before, then refrigerate it in a large plastic food bag leaving room for the dough to rise. Refrigerated dough from the store makes a fine substitute. Sometimes the local pizza parlor will sell you freshly made dough.

Grilled pizzas with bacon and goat cheese

Prep: 45 minutes | Rise: 45 minutes | Cook: 20 minutes | Makes: 8 small pizzas | Pictured on p. 89

A little bacon fat brushed over the dough ups the satisfaction quotient. Don't worry if your pizza-dough-shaping technique proves less than perfect—we've never met anyone who'll turn down the practice pizzas. You can top the pizzas with whatever you like; we're partial to caramelized onions and goat cheese.

2 pounds pizza dough (recipe follows), or
    purchase refrigerated

6 strips thickly sliced bacon, sliced into ⅛-inch-
    wide matchsticks

1 medium-size red onion, halved, thinly sliced

1 or 2 small cloves garlic, crushed

1 can (28 ounces) crushed tomatoes

11 ounces soft goat cheese

1 cup shredded Parmesan or Romano cheese
    (or a combination)

Sliced fresh basil leaves, or chopped

① Make pizza dough. When it has risen, divide into 8 equal portions; roll into balls. Let stand covered with a towel on the work surface.

② Cook bacon in large nonstick skillet until crisp and golden, about 10 minutes. Remove with slotted spoon to a paper-towel-lined plate. Add onion to pan drippings. Cook until tender and nicely browned, about 10 minutes. Add garlic; cook 1 minute. Remove with a slotted spoon to a plate. Reserve pan drippings.

③ Prepare a grill for medium-hot, indirect heat. Have the bacon, onions, tomatoes and cheeses at hand. (Alternately, heat oven to 400 degrees; bake prepared pizzas on a baking sheet until dough is crisp.)

④ Roll or gently stretch dough balls into 7-inch rounds on a floured work surface. Brush each lightly with bacon drippings (or olive oil). Place a few dough circles on the cooking grate directly over the heat until they brown lightly on one side, about 1 minute. Remove from grill.

⑤ Spoon a layer of crushed tomatoes on the cooked side of the pizza circles. Put onions, bacon and several dollops of goat cheese over tomatoes. Sprinkle with Parmesan. Return to grill; cook until toppings are warm and bubbly, about 2 minutes. Serve sprinkled with a little chopped fresh herbs, if desired. Repeat with remaining dough circles.

....

Nutrition information per pizza: 486 calories, 19 g fat, 10 g saturated fat, 37 mg cholesterol, 57 g carbohydrates, 23 g protein, 937 mg sodium, 5 g fiber

Pizza dough: Put 3½ cups all-purpose flour, ½ cup whole wheat flour and 1 teaspoon salt into food processor or mixer bowl fitted with a dough hook. Pulse several times to mix well. Mix 1⅓ cups warm (105 to 115 degrees) water, 1 envelope active dry yeast and a pinch of sugar in small bowl; let stand until foamy. Add to flour along with 2 tablespoons of bacon drippings (or use olive oil). Process or mix until the mixture forms a ball. If it is sticky, add a couple of tablespoons of flour and pulse until incorporated. Transfer to a lightly oiled bowl, cover with plastic wrap. Let rise in a warm place until doubled, about 45 minutes to 1½ hours. Punch down dough; turn out onto a lightly floured board. Knead several times to expel air before using.

CHAPTER 6
The Main Dish

PORTOBELLOS TAKE WELL TO GRILLING. I LIKE TO STUFF THE CAPS WITH their own grilled and seasoned stems. Topped with a gently grill-warmed tomato and a wedge of unctuous burrata cheese, they make a stunning first-course. For a meatless main, accompany the caps with pasta.

The grill and summer vegetables: A match made in heaven.

Lemon-garlic grilled portobellos with burrata and tomatoes

Prep: 25 minutes | Cook: 15 minutes | Makes: 6

Ricotta makes a nice substitute for the burrata; you'll need 2 tablespoons per mushroom cap.

¼ cup olive oil

Grated zest and juice from 1 small lemon

2 teaspoons Dijon mustard

½ teaspoon salt

6 large (about 1½ pounds total) portobello mushrooms, each 4 inches in diameter

1 medium red onion, cut into 4 thick slices

3 medium-size ripe yellow or red tomatoes

Half of an 8-ounce container burrata cheese

3 to 4 tablespoons chopped fresh basil and fresh chives

① Prepare a charcoal grill or heat a gas grill to medium heat. Mix oil, lemon zest and juice, mustard and salt in a small bowl.

② Gently twist the mushroom stems off the caps. Lightly brush the caps, stems and onion slices with the oil mixture. Grill stems and onion slices directly over the heat, turning once, until golden and tender, about 10 minutes. Transfer to a cutting board.

③ Add caps to a cooler section of the grill, gill side down. Cook, 2 minutes. Flip; brush with oil mixture. Add tomatoes to grill. Grill until smooth side of mushroom caps are golden and tomatoes are warmed and softened a bit, about 3 minutes. Remove from grill; place mushroom caps on a serving platter. Use a small serrated knife to cut the tomatoes in slices.

④ Chop grilled stems and onion; put into a small bowl. Season with a teaspoon or two of the remaining oil mixture. Divide the filling among the mushrooms caps. Top with a portion of the burrata and two tomato slices. Sprinkle generously with fresh basil and chives. Serve while warm or at room temperature.

Nutrition information per grilled portobello mushroom:
186 calories, 14 g fat, 4 g saturated fat, 16 mg cholesterol, 12 g carbohydrates, 7 g protein, 275 mg sodium, 3 g fiber

MY MOM HAS COOK'S INTUITIONS IN SPADES, SOMEHOW COOKING NEW recipes for a hungry family of seven on a shoestring budget. Veal shanks were cheap when she was a young cook; we had them often. Today, thick shank slices (labeled osso buco) in the meat case typically sell for $16 a pound and even more from a specialty butcher.

I usually opt for my butcher's version because he sells center-cut veal shanks from the hind shank, which yields a higher meat-to-bone ratio than those cut from the foreshank or narrower part of the leg. Most recipes say a slice of shank serves one, but that depends on the person. At our house, four 2- to 2½-inch-thick shank slices, weighing about 4 pounds total, with plenty of vegetables added, serve six.

As with most braises, browning the meat builds the first level of flavor. I add a light coating of seasoned flour to aid in the browning. Next come the aromatics—in this case, I like the look and texture you get from using whole small shallots, chunks of carrots and halved mushrooms. Prepared this way, the vegetables remain intact throughout the braise.

White wine traditionally deglazes the pan in classic osso buco. Red wine makes a richer dish; broth can stand in if you prefer. I like to enhance the pan juices with a small amount of intensely flavored dried porcini mushrooms. They can be omitted, or you can use less expensive dried mushrooms.

For the cleanest ripe tomato flavor, I prefer to use tomatoes that are canned without citric acid and calcium chloride. Look for imported Italian brands, such as Pomi, and read the labels. I found beautiful canned cherry tomatoes (by the Mutti brand from Parma, Italy) packed in tomato puree that looked and tasted great. Diced canned or plum tomatoes will work too.

I use an enameled cast-iron Dutch oven for almost all of my braising. It cooks so evenly that the meat is uniformly tender. The tight lid allows just the right amount of evaporation to make delicious pan juices. If you use a stainless steel Dutch oven, check the meat during cooking to be sure the moisture level is right. If you choose to use a slow cooker, don't skip the browning steps as they are key to the finished flavors. Set the slow cooker to low (never high) for delicate meat like veal, and allow six to eight hours.

Veal osso buco with porcini, kale, white beans and gremolata crunch

Prep: 40 minutes | Cook: 2½ hours | Makes: 4 to 6 servings

While I'm cooking this dish, I recall the scent of bay laurel trees in Northern California, the first porcini I tasted in Positano, Italy, and the cooking classes I so enjoyed in southern France where I first learned to braise. Poof, there go the winter blues. Here comes dinner.

4 center-cut veal shanks, each about 2-2½ inches thick, total weight 4¼ pounds

¼ cup flour

½ teaspoon salt

¼ teaspoon pepper

2 tablespoons each: olive oil, butter

10 to 12 small whole shallots (1 pound total), peeled

4 medium carrots (½ pound total), peeled, cut into thirds

½ pound baby bellas or button mushrooms, halved

¾ cup dry red or white wine (or more broth)

1 can (15 ounces) cherry tomatoes packed in tomato puree (or diced tomatoes)

¼ cup (½ ounce) dried porcini mushroom pieces or other dried mushrooms

2 bay leaves

½ teaspoon dried rosemary

1 cup homemade or canned low-sodium chicken broth

Gremolata crunch:

Finely grated zest of 2 lemons

½ cup very thinly sliced parsley

4 large cloves garlic, finely chopped

Half of a 2-ounce can anchovy fillets, patted dry, finely chopped, optional

1 or 2 tablespoons olive oil

¾ cup panko breadcrumbs or coarse homemade dry breadcrumbs

Finishing:

1 bunch (10 ounces) lacinato kale, tough stems removed, leaves cut into 1-inch pieces

1 can (15 ounces) cannellini beans, drained, rinsed

① Heat oven to 300 degrees. Pat veal dry. Mix flour, salt and pepper on a plate. Dredge veal shanks in the flour mixture.

② Heat a large Dutch oven or deep heavy-bottomed pan until hot. Add oil and butter; when they are hot and the butter has melted, add floured shanks in a single, uncrowded layer. Cook until golden brown, about 5 minutes. Turn and brown the second side, 5 minutes. Transfer to a plate.

③ Stir shallots, carrots and mushrooms into pan. Cook and stir until shallots are golden, about 5 minutes. Stir in wine; heat to a boil, scraping up browned bits. Boil to reduce the wine by half, about 2 minutes. Stir in tomatoes, porcini, bay leaves and rosemary. Boil hard, 2 minutes, then stir in broth.

④ Nestle shanks down into the mixture in the pan. Put a piece of parchment paper directly over the veal to protect it and capture any condensation. Cover pan tightly with lid. Slide into the oven; cook checking for adequate moisture every 30 minutes, until meat is fork-tender, about 2 hours. (If your lid is tight, you will not need to add any extra liquid.). You can also simmer the dish over low heat on the stovetop.

⑤ Meanwhile for gremolata, mix lemon zest, parsley, garlic and anchovies in a bowl. When veal is done, sprinkle half of this mixture over it; cook, 15 minutes.

⑥ Heat 1 tablespoon oil in a large skillet over medium heat. Add breadcrumbs; cook just until golden, 1-2 minutes. Remove from heat; stir in remaining gremolata mixture. Transfer to a serving bowl.

⑦ Use tongs and a spatula to gently transfer veal to a large, deep serving platter (or individual deep plates). Cover with foil to keep warm. Stir kale and beans into the mixture remaining in the pot. Simmer over medium heat until kale is tender and pan juices are thickened enough to lightly coat a spoon, about 5 minutes. Taste and adjust seasoning with salt, usually about ½ teaspoon.

> **Chicken osso buco:** Substitute 4 whole chicken legs, separated into thighs and drumsticks, for the veal. Brown chicken, and cook as directed, but reduce the oven time to 1 hour in Step 4. Finish as directed.

⑧ Spoon the vegetables and pan juices over the meat. Pass crispy gremolata for guests to add as they wish.

Nutrition information per serving: 577 calories, 18 g fat, 5 g saturated fat, 220 mg cholesterol, 39 g carbohydrates, 64 g protein, 732 mg sodium, 8 g fiber

LAMB COMES FROM SHEEP LESS THAN 1 YEAR OLD, MEANING ALMOST ALL OF the meat is tender. I look for lamb with a fine grain, bright red color and pinkish (not gray) bones that look moist. I prefer a little marbling on the meat, so I opt for leaving a thin fat coating, which adds tremendous flavor while grilling.

Whenever possible, I buy meat that was raised right: Fed a vegetarian diet (preferably grass for the best flavor), allowed to range and not given antibiotics or hormones. Buying lamb from the farmer at a local farmers market proves satisfying because the money goes directly to the folks responsible for the care of the animal. A boneless leg of lamb from these animals will be about 6 pounds, just right for a group of 8 to 10, with some leftovers.

I love to grill boneless leg of lamb because it's speedy—cooking time is less than 30 minutes—and carving is a breeze. Most butchers will remove the leg bones for you with advance notice. If you do purchase a bone-in leg of lamb, removing the bones proves easier than it sounds: Simply keep your knife as close to the bones as possible while you gently loosen the meat from around them. Once loosened, simply twist out the bones. After boning, I cut the meat into two equal-size pieces for easier handling on the grill.

Garlic and spice grilled leg of lamb

Prep: 15 minutes | Chill: 8 hours to 3 days | Cook: 25 minutes | Makes: 10 servings with leftovers | Pictured on p. 99

I like to serve the grilled lamb with a condiment made of shredded cucumber and plain yogurt. Labneh, the Middle Eastern yogurt, tastes especially rich and satisfying. The combo reminds us of gyros, so we serve it with flatbreads, toasted until warm on the grill.

1 boneless leg of lamb, 6 to 8 pounds

3 to 5 large cloves garlic, cut into thin slivers

2 teaspoons each: ground coriander, ground cumin, salt

1 teaspoon each, ground: cinnamon, black pepper

1 teaspoon crushed fennel seeds, optional

½ teaspoon ground cardamom, optional

2 cups cherry or apple wood chips, optional

Extra-virgin olive oil

Cucumber yogurt sauce with garlic and herbs (see recipe on p. 256)

① Cut the boneless leg of lamb into two even pieces. Use a very sharp small knife to cut small slits in the lamb at regular intervals; insert a sliver of garlic into each slit as you go. Combine all the spices in a small dish. Rub the spices into the lamb on all sides. The lamb can be refrigerated in a glass dish, covered lightly with butcher paper, for 8 hours or up to 3 days.

② Prepare a charcoal grill or heat a gas grill to medium hot. If using, soak wood chips in water to cover, about 30 minutes. Then drain and periodically sprinkle the chips over the hot coals. (If using a gas grill, set the chips on a piece of foil and place the packet over the heat source.)

③ Spray or brush lamb on all sides with olive oil. Place the lamb directly over the heat source. Cover the grill; cook, 12 minutes. Turn lamb over. Cover grill; continue grilling until a meat thermometer registers 140 degrees when inserted in the thickest portion, 11-13 minutes more. Transfer lamb to a cutting board. Cover loosely with foil; let stand, 10-15 minutes.

④ Use a very sharp knife to slice the lamb thinly. Serve with the cucumber sauce.

....

Nutrition information per serving: 445 calories, 16 g fat, 6 g saturated fat, 213 mg cholesterol, 1 g carbohydrates, 69 g protein, 627 mg sodium, 0.5 g fiber

THE NEW CROP OF YOUNG RESTAURANT CHEFS REALLY PUSHES THE CULI-nary envelope. They are way into all aspects of their craft, from growing the food to making everything from butter to vinegar to pickles. I'm especially fond of the homemade char-cuterie—salamis, cured hams and pates—offered at many new-American restaurants.

While I'm not about to cure a ham at home, I can easily make the classic American pate known as meatloaf! Lower in fat and labor than fancy baked French terrines, galantines and smooth liver mousse, a well-made meatloaf equally satisfies.

Glazed porcini and bacon meatloaf

Prep: 30 minutes | Cook: 1½ hours | Makes: 8 servings

If using grass-fed beef, I like to increase the eggs to three.

¾ ounce dried porcini or other dried mixed mushrooms

¼ cup dry red wine or beef broth

3 ounces (4 thick strips) smoky bacon, finely chopped

2 small ribs celery, finely chopped

1 small leek, halved, rinsed, finely chopped (white and 2 inches of green)

2 large eggs, lightly beaten

1 cup panko or other dry coarse breadcrumbs

2 tablespoons Dijon mustard

1 teaspoon each: salt, dried leaf thyme

½ teaspoon each: freshly ground black pepper, oregano

2 pounds ground beefchuck or sirloin

Glaze:

½ cup chili sauce (such as Bennet's) or mild barbecue sauce

1 tablespoon Dijon mustard

① Heat oven to 350 degrees. Soak mushrooms in wine until tender, about 15 minutes. Strain wine into a large bowl; finely chop mushrooms; add to the bowl.

② Cook bacon in a large skillet over medium heat until it starts to soften, about 5 minutes. Stir in celery and leek. Cook until tender, about 6 minutes. Stir mixture into mushrooms. Cool.

③ Stir in eggs, breadcrumbs, mustard, salt, thyme, pepper and oregano. Mix well. Add the meat; use clean hands to gently incorporate the seasonings into the meat. Gently pack the mixture into a 9-by-5-inch loaf pan, pressing down a bit to remove any air pockets.

④ Bake 1 hour. For the glaze, mix the chili sauce and mustard. Generously coat the loaf with the glaze; con-tinue baking until the internal temperature registers 150 degrees on an instant read thermometer, about 20 minutes more. Let rest 15 minutes before slicing.

Nutrition information per serving: 310 calories, 15 g fat, 5 g satu-rated fat, 120 mg cholesterol, 17 g carbohydrates, 25 g protein, 1,073 mg sodium, 1 g fiber

Delmonico steak, made famous by the original Delmonico's restaurant in New York City, always makes me swoon when it's offered on menus. I know I'll get a generous portion of a rich piece of beef. There's some debate about which cut of steak makes a Delmonico, but we're opting for a bone-in rib steak for its shape, ease of cooking and decadent texture from lots of marbling.

To cook steaks properly, don't go too thick or too thin. In our experience, 1- to 1¼-inch-thick steaks cook beautifully everywhere from the grill to the broiler to a hot skillet. This thickness also takes well to aggressive seasoning on the exterior yet leaves you with a definite steak sensation in the center. Don't trim the fat too closely—you'll want to leave a little to keep the cooking moist and so it chars nicely, which adds flavor.

Whenever possible, buy choice or prime steaks for the best flavor and most marbling, which means more foolproof cooking. Steaks graded "select" are very lean and supereasy to render dry and tough. Grass-fed steaks sold at natural grocery stores and online prove worth the added cost for the lessened environmental impact and rich flavor.

I take a two-step approach to seasoning these thick steaks: First, a simple rub applied a couple of hours in advance. Second, the mop with a smoky barbecue-inspired steak sauce. Our sauce recipe cooks in just 10 minutes and will keep a couple of weeks in the refrigerator.

Good steaks deserve high-heat cooking and the flavor of hardwood charcoal. After all, that's what we get when we go to our favorite steak joints. Select natural charcoal so the meat doesn't taste like chemicals. Alternatively, for gas-grilling, soak natural wood chips in water, then make a foil packet of them (pierced with holes) and place it over the heat source to add smoke.

Smoky grilled Delmonico mopped steaks

Prep: 10 minutes | Cook: 10 minutes | Makes: 4 generous servings | Pictured on p. 103

Other steak choices good here include top loin strip steak, T-bone and porterhouse. Top sirloin and flat-iron steaks also work; just be sure to cook them no more than medium-rare so they stay moist.

4 beef rib steaks on the bone, each about 1 inch thick and weighing about 14 ounces

1 recipe Simple steak rub (see recipe on p 264)

½ cup smoky barbecue steak sauce (recipe follows)

① Place steaks on a platter. Sprinkle each with about 1 teaspoon of the steak rub. Flip the steaks and sprinkle the other side with the rub. Refrigerate uncovered while you prepare the grill (or better yet, for 3 to 4 hours).

Smoky barbecue steak sauce

Prep: 5 minutes | Cook: 10 minutes

Makes: about 1½ cups

1 cup ketchup

⅓ cup each: apple cider vinegar, dark brown sugar

2 tablespoons Worcestershire sauce

1 tablespoon bacon fat, optional

1½ teaspoons pureed chipotle in adobo or 1 teaspoon chipotle chili powder

1 teaspoon smoked paprika

½ teaspoon salt

¼ teaspoon ground allspice

② Prepare a charcoal grill or heat a gas grill to medium high. Put the steaks directly over the heat source. Cover; cook, 6 minutes. Flip the steaks; baste with some of the sauce. Cover the grill; cook 2 minutes. Flip the steaks again; baste the other side with sauce. Grill, covered, until medium-rare, 1-2 minutes.

③ Transfer the steaks to a board; let rest a couple of minutes before serving.

① Mix all ingredients in a small saucepan. Simmer over low heat, about 10 minutes. Cool; store in a jar in the refrigerator up to a couple of weeks.

Nutrition information per serving: 783 calories, 43 g fat, 17 g saturated fat, 257 mg cholesterol, 15 g carbohydrates, 80 g protein, 1,019 mg sodium, 2 g fiber

Nutrition information per tablespoon: 26 calories, 0 g fat, 0 g saturated fat, 0 mg cholesterol, 6 g carbohydrates, 0 g protein, 169 mg sodium, 0 g fiber

Y WOK INCITES A KITCHEN CONUNDRUM: IT LOOKS LIKE HELL, BUT IT cooks like an angel. My husband says our wok is a beautiful thing; I hide it away from the shiny stove-of-my-dreams for months at a time. Then we start cooking in the wok and wonder why we ever tuck it out of sight. Seafood and bits of meat emerge perfectly browned, and vegetables cook to crisp-tender. Fast.

Made from rolled steel, the wok sports a nonstick patina that comes from decades of use and proper cleaning with hot water (no soap). That, along with the wok's concave shape, means I can cook with high heat and a minimum of oil to make amazing one-pot dinners.

Lately we've been on a fried rice kick. Stir-frying all kinds of leftover cooked rice with tidbits of flavorful add-ins. Traditionally, seafood and veggies with soy sauce, but rich steak and teriyaki sauce please, too. When the fridge offers them up, we combine roasted poblano chilies, corn and cilantro with some red chili sauce or mix basmati rice with roasted eggplant and an Indian curry sauce.

Asparagus and teriyaki steak fried rice

Prep: 30 minutes | Cook: 15 minutes | Makes: 4 servings

You'll want to work with high heat for the steak fried rice. Then everything will take on golden flavors and great textures. It makes a great one-pot meal, especially piled over a bed of baby spinach or arugula for a stunning main course.

¼ cup teriyaki sauce

½ to 1 teaspoon wasabi paste or powder, optional

8 ounces skirt steak (or other tender steak)

2 large eggs

1 teaspoon dark sesame oil

¼ teaspoon salt

4 tablespoons expeller-pressed canola oil, safflower oil or peanut oil

1 small red onion, halved, cut into thin wedges

½ teaspoon sugar

½ bunch skinny asparagus, ends trimmed, cut into 2-inch lengths

½ green bell pepper, cut into ¼ inch pieces

2 cloves garlic, finely chopped

4 cups chilled, cooked brown or white rice

Chopped fresh cilantro

① Mix teriyaki sauce and wasabi in small bowl for serving.

② Cut steak into 3-inch-wide pieces. Turn the pieces so you can cut the steak against the grain into super-thin slices. Beat eggs with sesame oil and a pinch of salt in a small bowl. Put all ingredients near cooking surface.

③ Heat a well-seasoned wok (or large deep-sided nonstick skillet) over high heat until a drop of water evaporates on contact. Add 1 tablespoon oil, then add onion. Stir-fry over high heat, 2 minutes. Sprinkle with sugar and a pinch of salt. Stir-fry until nicely caramelized, about 3 minutes. With a slotted spoon, transfer onion to a large plate.

④ Add 1 tablespoon oil to wok; add asparagus and bell pepper. Stir-fry until crisp-tender, about 2 minutes. Stir in garlic; cook, 30 seconds. Transfer to plate.

⑤ Add 1 tablespoon oil to wok; add sliced steak. Stir-fry until medium-rare, 2-3 minutes. Transfer to plate.

⑥ Add remaining 1 tablespoon oil to wok. When hot, add egg mixture; stir-fry with a spatula until lightly scrambled. Add the rice; stir-fry until very hot, about 3 minutes. Stir in all ingredients from plate. Stir-fry until heated through, 2-3 minutes. Drizzle with teriyaki sauce. Serve garnished with cilantro.

....

Nutrition information per serving: 553 calories, 25 g fat, 4 g saturated fat, 132 mg cholesterol, 61 g carbohydrates, 22 g protein, 782 mg sodium, 5 g fiber

*Fresh herbs
and freshly
ground spices
are worth
the trouble.*
Always.

Herbed meatballs with creamy
dill sauce (p. 108)

MEATBALLS EMBRACE THE BEST MERITS OF GROUND MEAT. THEY ARE ECOnomical per pound, easy to portion and play well with others, especially bold flavors such as fresh herbs, spices and cheese. In our house, we welcome highly seasoned versions as well as those cooked golden and sauced creamily.

Herbed meatballs with creamy dill sauce

Prep: 30 minutes | Chill: 1 hour or more | Cook: 25 minutes | Makes: 26 meatballs, serving 6 | Pictured on p. 106-107

I like to serve these meatballs over buttered spaetzle or egg noodles. Or, stir smaller meatballs with their sauce into cooked whole wheat rotini pasta.

4 slices home-style white bread (about 3.5 ounces), torn into small pieces

½ cup milk or half-and-half

1 large egg, lightly beaten

¼ cup thinly sliced fresh chives (or 4 green onions, trimmed, thinly sliced)

2 tablespoons finely chopped fresh dill

1 teaspoon salt

½ teaspoon freshly ground black pepper

¼ teaspoon freshly ground allspice

1 pound ground beef chuck or sirloin

1 pound ground pork

Expeller-pressed canola oil for high heat cooking

Sauce:

1 tablespoon soft butter

2 tablespoons flour

2 cups chicken broth

2 tablespoons creme fraiche or whipping cream

2 tablespoons chopped fresh dill

Salt

① Mix bread and milk in bottom of large bowl. Let stand until bread has absorbed all of the liquid, about 5 minutes. Stir in the egg, chives, dill, salt, pepper and allspice. Add the meats. Use clean hands to mix lightly until combined.

② Shape mixture into 1½-inch diameter meatballs; place on a parchment paper-lined baking sheet. Cover with plastic wrap. Refrigerate at least 1 hour or up to 24 hours.

③ Heat oven to 200 degrees. Heat a large nonstick skillet over medium-high heat. Film the pan lightly with oil. Add the meatballs in a single, uncrowded layer (work in batches, if necessary). Cook, turning occasionally, until golden brown on all sides and nearly firm when pressed, 8-10 minutes. Remove the meatballs as they are done to a serving dish; keep warm in the oven until all are cooked.

④ For the sauce, mix the butter and flour in a small dish. Tip off all but 1 tablespoon fat from the meatball skillet. Stir in the flour mixture; cook over medium heat, 1 minute. Gradually whisk in the broth. Cook, stirring constantly, until smooth and thickened, 3-4 minutes. Stir in cream and 1 tablespoon dill. Season to taste with salt.

⑤ Spoon the sauce over the meatballs. Sprinkle with remaining 1 tablespoon dill. Serve.

Nutrition information per serving: 458 calories, 30 g fat, 11 g saturated fat, 143 mg cholesterol, 17 g carbohydrates, 33 g protein, 932 mg sodium, 1 g fiber

TIPS

➤ Always use the freshest ground meat available: Check the dates on packaged meat, or ask the butcher to grind it to order. Request a fine grind for delicate meatballs and a coarser grind for hearty specimens such as those destined to simmer in sauce or stews.

➤ Fresh herbs and freshly ground spices are worth the trouble. Always.

➤ Use bread to add a light texture and to bind the meat for easy shaping. Soaking the bread in liquid allows it to incorporate completely into the meat.

➤ Do not overwork the meat mixture, or the meatballs will be tough; use clean, wet hands and work gently to mix the seasonings into the meat.

➤ Check for proper seasoning by tasting a little of it before shaping the meatballs: Fry a dollop quickly in a small skillet and then taste it, and adjust the main mixture accordingly.

➤ Shape the meatballs in advance, then chill an hour or more, so the seasonings meld into the meat and they'll keep their shape during cooking.

➤ Cook the meatballs in a nonstick (or well-seasoned cast-iron) skillet, so you can use a minimum of fat and have easy cleanup.

➤ Cook meatballs in oil suited for high-heat cooking, such as expeller-pressed canola oil or peanut oil.

➤ Work in uncrowded batches in the pan to get maximum browning, which adds flavor.

➤ Use a thin, heat-proof spatula to loosen the meatballs from the pan, then turn them with tongs as they brown.

➤ A splatter guard will help keep the cooktop clean.

➤ Completely cooked and cooled, meatballs can be refrigerated up to several days or frozen for several months.

➤ Rewarm meatballs in a moderate oven (300 degrees) or in the microwave on medium (50 percent) power.

Chalk it up to goulash. A bowl full of my grandmother's simple goodness ignited a passion for spice that never wanes. She peppered chicken or beef with the freshest Hungarian paprika possible. The rusty red powder smelled sweet and tasted lush, nearly intense. A far cry from those cans of bland, pale red dust often used to garnish potato salad.

My grandparents favored intensely red, sweet paprika imported from Hungary and sold in bulk at their local meat markets. Fresh paprika has a full rich red pepper flavor with almost no heat. Occasionally they'd used half-sharp Hungarian paprika, which is spicier than the sweet version, adding a nice kick to the pot, which I enjoy immensely.

Some recipes call for adding wine or beer to their goulash. Gram was very traditional and used only water. I make a light homemade chicken broth from simmering the neck, giblets and wing tips in water. This adds a little more body and flavor.

Grandma served her goulash in wide soup bowls with fall-apart tender potatoes. Often, bowls of egg noodles or dumplings were proffered. I also enjoy spaetzle to soak up the delicious paprika-flavored broth.

Spicy beef goulash with bacon and potatoes

Prep: 25 minutes | Chill: 1 hour | Cook: 2 hours | Makes: 6 servings

If you are not using half-sharp Hungarian paprika you can substitute sweet Hungarian paprika and spice it up with cayenne, usually ⅛ to ¼ teaspoon.

2½ pounds boneless beef chuck, cut into 1-inch pieces

1 teaspoon salt

6 thin slices (3 ounces total) smoked bacon or salt pork, diced

2 medium (12 ounces total) yellow onions, halved, sliced

2 to 3 cloves garlic, minced

3 to 4 tablespoons half-sharp Hungarian paprika

6 medium (2 pounds total) yellow potatoes, peeled, cut into eighths

Chopped fresh parsley

Cooked egg noodles or spaetzle

Sour cream, optional

① Sprinkle beef pieces with salt. Place in a covered baking dish or bowl. Refrigerate 1 hour or up to 1 day.

② Cook diced bacon and onions in bottom of a heavy 6-quart saucepan or Dutch oven over medium-low heat until lightly browned, about 15 minutes. Add garlic; cook, 1 minute. Transfer with a slotted spoon to a bowl.

③ Pat beef dry; add to pan in a single, uncrowded layer. (Do this in batches if necessary.) Cook until beef is nicely browned on all sides, about 10 minutes.

④ Return all beef to the pan; sprinkle the paprika over all. Add bacon and onions. Stir in 3 cups water. Heat to a simmer. Reduce heat to very low. Cover pan tightly; simmer until beef is nearly fork tender, about 1 hour. Add potatoes; cook until beef and potatoes are tender, 20-30 minutes.

⑤ Sprinkle with parsley. Serve with noodles and a dollop of sour cream.

....

Nutrition information per serving: 406 calories, 10 g fat, 4 g saturated fat, 115 mg cholesterol, 35 g carbohydrates, 42 g protein, 439 mg sodium, 4 g fiber

ON BUYING PAPRIKA

I use the excellent Hungarian paprika bought online from TheSpiceHouse.com. It sells a high-quality sweet paprika from the Kalocsa region of Hungary as well as the spicy half-sharp paprika. The red can of Hungarian sweet paprika from Pride of Szeged sold at many grocery stores also tastes delicious. One tip: Buy paprika only in quantities that you'll use fairly quickly—in months, not years—as it stales and pales quickly. I buy fresh paprika for every batch of goulash for optimal flavor.

Please note: As much as I love Spanish paprika, it does not work in this dish— different chilies make it taste different from Hungarian sweet paprika. Certainly do not use smoked paprika (aka pimenton) if you want anything close to the Old World version.

Because my daughter is more prone to vegetarian dishes, she needed tips for cooking for a self-proclaimed meat-lover. The eggplant Parmesan she loves so easily morphs into a meaty dish with the addition of browned Italian sausage to the tomato sauce and thin slices of lean, tender pork tenderloin in place of the eggplant.

We reviewed the three-step breading process she'd be using for the pork, assuring her it's not as difficult as it sounds. The only real downside is three dirty plates from the flour mixture, the egg mixture and the crumbs. On the plus side, the breaded pork or eggplant benefits from chilling in the refrigerator while the kitchen gets tidied up. (My not-so-subtle reminder that a neat cook is always a welcome cook.)

Three cheese pork (or eggplant) Parmesan

Prep: 1 hour | Chill: 20 minutes or more | Cook: 30 minutes | Makes: 4 to 6 servings

For frying, choose an expeller-pressed canola oil or grapeseed oil.

1 pound pork tenderloin or 1 large eggplant (1¼ pounds)

⅓ cup cornstarch

½ teaspoon salt

¼ teaspoon freshly ground black pepper

2 large eggs

3 tablespoons milk or half-and-half

2 cups panko crumbs or coarse breadcrumbs

Expeller-pressed canola oil for high heat cooking

3 cups Italian herbs and sausage tomato sauce (recipe follows)

¼ cup fat free ricotta cheese or soft goat cheese

½ cup shredded part-skim mozzarella cheese

¼ cup shredded Parmesan cheese

① Cut pork on an angle into thin slices not quite ½ inch thick. If using eggplant, trim off the ends and cut into ½-inch-thick rounds.

② Mix cornstarch, salt and pepper in a shallow dish. Beat eggs with milk in a second shallow dish. Put panko crumbs into a third dish.

③ Dip each pork (or eggplant) slice into the cornstarch mixture to coat it on both sides; shake off excess. Dip each slice into the egg mixture to coat; dredge into the crumbs to coat well. Set slices on a rack set over a baking sheet. Refrigerate uncovered at least 20 minutes or up to several hours.

④ Heat oven to 350 degrees. Pour a thin layer of oil (about ⅛ inch deep) into a large, nonstick skillet. Heat over medium until hot. (Dip an edge of the coated pork into the oil; it should sizzle vigorously.) Add slices of pork (or eggplant) in an uncrowded layer. Cook, turning once, until golden on both sides, 3 to 5 minutes.

Remove with tongs to a paper-towel-lined plate. Repeat to cook all slices, adding more oil if needed.

⑤ Pour about half of the tomato sauce over the bottom of a 13-by-9-inch baking dish. Layer the pork (or eggplant) over the sauce. Top with remaining sauce. Dollop the ricotta over the sauce. Sprinkle with mozzarella and Parmesan. Bake until cheese is melted and sauce is bubbly hot, about 20 minutes. Serve.

Variation: You can bake the pork or eggplant instead of frying, if you like. Put the coated slices on an oiled baking sheet. Bake at 425 degrees until golden and crisp, turning once, 15-20 minutes.

Nutrition information per serving: 319 calories, 11 g fat, 4 g saturated fat, 129 mg cholesterol, 26 g carbohydrates, 28 g protein, 1,149 mg sodium, 3 g fiber

Italian herbs and sausage tomato sauce

Prep: 10 minutes | Cook: 30 minutes

Makes: about 4 cups

Gourmet Garden makes an Italian herb blend from fresh herbs and sold in a squeeze tube that takes the waste out of buying fresh herbs. Look for it in the refrigerated section of the produce department at large supermarkets.

- 1 pound mild or spicy Italian sausage
- 1 jar (26 to 28 ounces) marinara or other tomato sauce
- 2 tablespoons refrigerated Italian herb blend or chopped fresh herbs such as basil, rosemary, parsley or 1 teaspoon dried Italian seasoning

① If sausage is in a casing, remove it by slicing it open and pushing it into a large saucepan. Cook over medium heat, breaking the sausage into small pieces with a wooden spatula, until cooked through and golden, about 12 minutes. Transfer to a paper towel-lined plate to soak up the fat.

② Return the sausage to the pan. Stir in tomato sauce, herbs and ½ cup water. Simmer over very low heat, stirring often, about 20 minutes. Taste and adjust seasonings, adding salt if needed. Refrigerate covered up to 3 or 4 days.

....

Nutrition information per ¼ cup serving (for 6 servings): 90 calories, 5 g fat, 2 g saturated fat, 9 mg cholesterol, 7 g carbohydrates, 4 g protein, 363 mg sodium, 1 g fiber.

WANT TO WIN PRAISE FOR YOUR GRILLING? SIMPLE. MIX UP THIS SWEET, spicy, salty, intriguing red chili glaze and slather it over just about any cut of pork. Seriously. My brother-in-law declared this pork so "bad" he just had to clean his plate. My husband proclaimed it the best pork roast of his life. High praise indeed.

To help less-tender or super-lean cuts of pork retain moisture on the grill, I like to brine them first in water flavored with sugar, salt, vinegar, garlic and fresh orange. Pork shoulder, country-style ribs and pork loin especially benefit from brining. The shoulder should be brined overnight or up to two days in the refrigerator. Country-style pork ribs and pork loin need only a few hours.

Red chili-glazed slow-grilled pork shoulder

Prep: 30 minutes | Brine: Overnight | Marinate: Several hours | Cook: 3 hours | Makes: 8 to 10 servings
Pictured on p. 116–117

Leftovers make great sandwiches on toasted buns.

½ cup each: granulated sugar, coarse salt

¼ cup distilled white vinegar

6 cloves garlic, crushed

Grated zest of 1 orange

1 large (about 5 pounds) bone-in pork shoulder blade roast

1 to 2 cups Sweet and spicy red chili grilling glaze (see recipe on p. 262)

2 cups hickory wood chips, optional

① Mix 2 quarts lukewarm water, sugar, salt, vinegar, garlic and orange zest in very large non-aluminum bowl or stockpot. Stir until sugar and salt dissolve. Add the pork roast. Cover; refrigerate overnight or up to 2 days.

② Remove pork from the brine, discarding brine. Put pork into a glass dish. Coat well on all sides with some of the red chili glaze. Cover; refrigerate several hours or up to 1 day.

③ Soak wood chips in a large bowl of water for at least 1 hour.

④ Prepare a charcoal grill or heat a gas grill to medium-hot. For indirect cooking, arrange coals on two sides of the grill or turn off burners in center of gas grill. Place the cooking grate in place; let it heat a few minutes.

⑤ Put the pork roast in the center of the grill (not directly over the heat). Add a small handful of the wood chips to the coals. (For gas grilling, wrap the soaked chips in a foil pouch, pierce it with several small holes and place directly over the heat source.) Cover the grill; cook on medium-low (about 275 degrees if you have an oven thermometer), basting frequently with some of the red chili glaze, until an instant-read thermometer registers 160 degrees, 2½ to 3 hours or so. The roast should be very nicely burnished red with some crispy edges.

⑥ Let pork rest on cutting board about 20 minutes. Slice very thinly. Serve.

Nutrition information per serving for 10 servings: 210 calories, 8 g fat, 2 g saturated fat, 69 mg cholesterol, 10 g carbohydrates, 22 g protein, 1,254 mg sodium, 0 g fiber

Sweet and spicy crispy pork packed with smoky flavor from the grill. What more could you want?

Red chili-glazed slow-grilled pork shoulder (p. 115)

Dining out inspires dinner at home. Especially when the restaurant meal features seasonal ingredients with easy to re-create preparations. After a day of bicycling in Austria, a stunning skillet of golden pork chops smothered in Pfifferling mushrooms proved splendid inspiration.

Perfect timing, too, since all manner of mushrooms populate most markets in the fall. Golden-hued, funnel-shaped Pfifferlinge, aka chanterelles, appear in generous portions on all manner of dishes in Germany and Austria. Little wonder, with their subtle peppery taste, rich flavor and pleasing, toothsome texture. Here, fresh chanterelles can be found at farmers markets, produce stores and specialty stores. They also can be ordered online, fresh or dried. Both are quite pricey, but a little goes a long way.

Most mushrooms taste best when sauteed over high heat with a hint of aromatic seasonings. I like to combine several varieties to keep costs low and to take advantage of their individual textures. My favorite medley includes thinly sliced shiitake caps with chunks of oyster mushrooms and a small handful of those colorful chanterelles. Or course, a couple of morel mushrooms elevate any dish they grace. If button or cremini mushrooms prove the only fresh option, I enhance their subtle flavor with the complexity of dried mushrooms.

At home, I bring out the cast-iron skillet and crank the heat—both stove top and in the oven. I like to briefly brown the chops in a single uncrowded layer in oil suitable for high-heat cooking and then finish their cooking in a very hot oven using the convection option for speed. This two-step cooking captures moisture in even the leanest of chops.

Pan-fried pork chops with sauteed mushrooms

Prep: 25 minutes | Cook: 20 minutes | Makes: 6 servings

You can substitute ¼ cup dried mushrooms (rehydrated in warm water, then drained and chopped) for ¼ pound of the fresh.

1 pound assorted fresh mushrooms, such as chanterelles, shiitake, oyster, button, cremini

6 center-cut, bone-in pork chops, each a scant ¾ inch thick, about 3 pounds total

¾ teaspoon salt

Freshly ground black pepper

1 large tropea onion or 1 small red onion or 2 shallots

2 cloves garlic

½ teaspoon minced fresh thyme or ⅛ teaspoon dried

2 or 3 tablespoons chopped fresh parsley or chives

2 to 3 tablespoons safflower, sunflower or expeller-pressed canola oil

2 tablespoons butter

① Clean mushrooms: Discard stems from shiitake mushrooms, trim stems of other mushrooms. Wipe caps clean. Cleaned mushrooms can be stored in the refrigerator in a paper bag for a day or two. Before using, cut large mushrooms into 1 inch slices or chunks.

② Pat pork chops dry. Sprinkle generously on both sides with salt and pepper. Let stand at room temperature up to 1 hour or refrigerate up to 24 hours.

③ Heat oven to 375 degrees on convection or 400 degrees on conventional oven setting. Finely chop the onion or shallots and garlic. Have the herbs ready. Set all ingredients near the stove.

④ When the oven is hot, heat 1 large or 2 medium well-seasoned cast-iron skillet(s) over medium-high heat until drops of water sizzle vigorously when added to the pan. Swirl a film of oil in the bottom of the pan or pans. Add the chops in a single uncrowded layer. Cook on medium-high until the bottoms are golden, 3 to 4 minutes. Use tongs to flip the chops and brown the other side, 2 minutes more. Carefully slide the skillet or skillets with the chops into the oven to finish the cooking, 3-4 minutes. Pan juices should run clear and chops will be almost firm (but not hard) to the touch.

⑤ Transfer the chops to a wire rack set over a tray to collect the juices. Tent the chops with foil to keep them warm.

⑥ Put the skillet from the chops over medium-high heat; swirl in half of the butter. Add half of the mushrooms, onion and garlic; cook until golden, 3-4 minutes. Transfer to a plate. Repeat with remaining mushrooms, onion and garlic. Combine all the mushrooms in the skillet; tip in any of the juices from the chops. Stir in the thyme.

⑦ Arrange the chops on a warm platter; spoon the mushrooms over the chops. Sprinkle with the parsley or chives; serve.

....

Nutrition information per serving: 312 calories, 17 g fat, 5 g saturated fat, 110 mg cholesterol, 4 g carbohydrates, 34 g protein, 364 mg sodium, 1 g fiber

THIS RECIPE'S MARINADE SPORTS A PLEASING TARTNESS FROM TAMARIND fruit—those pale brown pods found in Latin and Asian markets. Inside the pods you'll find a dark brown, jamlike flesh that tastes deeply of citrus. For ease, I stock bottled tamarind. I'm particularly fond of Neera's tamarind concentrate—it's available on Amazon. I use it in salad dressings, salsas, barbecue sauces and just about any place that I want pure pucker. It also makes a great citrus juice substitute and keeps in the refrigerator for months. Stir a little into sparkling water or iced tea for a refreshing beverage.

Sweet and tangy grilled pork tenderloin

Prep: 15 minutes | Marinate: 30 minutes or up to 4 hours | Cook: 20 minutes | Makes: 4 to 6 servings

Serve the pork with sauteed greens and jasmine rice or mashed potatoes.

½ recipe Sweet and tangy ginger-soy marinade (recipe follows)

2 pieces, about 1 pound each, trimmed pork tenderloin

Cilantro sprigs

① Put marinade into a plastic food bag or shallow baking dish. Add pork to the marinade; turn to coat. Refrigerate covered at least 30 minutes or up to 4 hours.

② Prepare a charcoal grill or heat a gas grill to medium heat. Remove pork from marinade; place on grill directly over heat source. Cover grill; cook, 10 minutes. Turn tenderloin; move to a cooler section of the grill. Continue grilling until an instant-read thermometer registers 135 degrees in the thickest portion, usually 10-15 minutes more.

③ Remove to a cutting board; let rest 10 minutes. Serve thinly sliced and garnished with cilantro.

Nutrition information per serving (for 6 servings): 224 calories, 9 g fat, 3 g saturated fat, 103 mg cholesterol, 1 g carbohydrates, 33 g protein, 187 mg sodium, 0 g fiber

Sweet and tangy ginger-soy marinade

Prep: 10 minutes | Makes: a generous ½ cup

2 large shallots, finely chopped

4 cloves garlic, finely chopped

¼ cup soy sauce

2 tablespoons tamarind pulp or ¼ cup fresh lemon juice

2 tablespoons grated fresh ginger or refrigerated ginger puree

2 teaspoons each: ground coriander, sugar

1 teaspoon each: salt, ground cumin

½ teaspoon cayenne, optional

① Mix all ingredients in a jar with a tight-fitting lid. Refrigerate covered up to 2 weeks.

FIFTEEN MINUTE DINNERS PROVE WORTH THEIR WEIGHT IN GOLD. SLICED ham and bags of chopped kale make this skillet dinner super quick. I especially enjoy the chopped lacinato kale (aka Tuscan kale) that's recently hit the produce section. No rinsing or trimming needed.

Serve this homey dish straight from the skillet with plenty of hot sauce and cornbread or biscuits. I love to add a fried egg to each portion. The mixture also makes a great topping for flapjacks or sweet potato pancakes.

Kale and ham skillet

Prep: 10 minutes | Cook: 15 minutes | Makes: 4 to 6 servings

Fresh peas are a real treat; fortunately many stores now sell them shucked in the produce section. I love the texture of frozen lima beans, seriously. Shelled edamame works, too.

2 tablespoons extra-virgin olive oil or safflower oil

1 medium-size onion, halved, thinly sliced

1 bag cut lacinato (Tuscan) kale, about 10 ounces

1 ham steak (about 1 pound), trimmed, diced, about 3 cups

3 cloves garlic, finely chopped

1 cup fresh or thawed frozen sweet peas or lima beans

Salt to taste

⅛ to ¼ teaspoon crushed red pepper flakes, to taste

Red pepper hot sauce, plain Greek yogurt

① Heat oil in large skillet over medium-high heat. Add onion; cook until golden, about 5 minutes. Stir in kale; cover. Cook over medium, stirring occasionally, until kale is wilted, 4-5 minutes. Stir in ham, garlic and peas. Cook and stir until hot, 3-4 minutes.

② Season to taste with salt and pepper flakes. Serve with hot sauce and a dollop of yogurt, if you like.

Nutrition information per serving (for 6 servings): 197 calories, 8 g fat, 2 g saturated fat, 34 mg cholesterol, 13 g carbohydrates, 18 g protein, 1,052 mg sodium, 3 g fiber

HAVE FRIENDS AND FAMILY WHO EAT OUT ALMOST EVERY MEAL. I JUST CAN'T do it — I enjoy cooking, but mostly I covet control of my food dollars and my nourishment. For most weeknight dinners and lunches, I rely on a well-stocked pantry.

Canned beans save the day on many occasions. But when I take the time to cook dried beans, the flavor and textural differences prove astounding. All you need is a saucepan, water and 2 hours of largely unattended cooking to upgrade this inexpensive protein powerhouse. No need to soak beans; in fact, you'll retain color and flavor if you skip soaking.

Here's my favorite basic cooked beans method: Put 2 cups dried (rinsed) beans in a large saucepan. Add 2 quarts water and 2 tablespoons olive oil (or bacon fat if you dare). Cook over low heat, stirring often, until beans are nearly tender to the bite, about 1½ hours. Stir in 1 teaspoon salt and simmer until fully tender, another 10 to 20 minutes. Cool.

Warm black bean and rice bowl with chicken and poblanos

Prep: 40 minutes | Cook: 15 minutes | Makes: 6 servings

Black rice, like the Heirloom Forbidden Rice by Lotus Foods, makes this dish look super dramatic. Easiest rice ever? Cook 2 cups rice with 2⅔ cups water in a rice cooker. Turn cooked rice out onto a baking sheet to cool so you can pack it in small containers. I love to eat my portion topped with a fried egg.

1 medium zucchini, halved lengthwise, sliced ¼ inch thick

Olive oil

Salt

2 medium poblano peppers

2 cups canned crushed tomatoes or 1 can (14.5 ounces) small diced tomatoes

2 tablespoons chili powder

2 cups drained, cooked black beans or 1 can (15 ounces) black beans, rinsed, drained

1½ cups cooked rice (such as black rice or long grain brown rice)

1 cup corn kernels, thawed

1 medium-size red bell pepper, seeded, cut into small dice

4 green onions, trimmed, thinly sliced

2 cups shredded cooked or rotisserie chicken

¼ cup thinly sliced fresh cilantro

Crumbled queso fresco, mild goat cheese or farmer's cheese

① Heat oven to 400 degrees. Put sliced zucchini on a baking sheet. Add 1 or 2 tablespoons oil; toss to coat it with the oil. Sprinkle lightly with salt. Bake, stirring once or twice, until tender and slightly golden, about 20 minutes. Cool.

② Meanwhile, set poblanos directly over a gas flame or under the broiler. Cook, turning occasionally, until peppers are lightly charred on all sides, 2 to 5 minutes. Set on a plate and cover with a towel; let rest until cool enough to handle. Rub off the charred skin, remove the seeds and pith. Cut peppers into ½-inch pieces.

③ Mix poblanos and tomatoes in bottom of a large microwave-safe bowl. Stir in chili powder and 1 teaspoon salt; mix well. Stir in beans, rice, corn, bell pepper and green onions. Mix well. Microwave on high, stirring once or twice, until everything is warmed through, 2 to 4 minutes. Gently stir in zucchini and chicken. Taste and adjust salt as needed.

④ Spoon into warm serving bowls. Sprinkle with cilantro and cheese. Serve warm.

....

Nutrition information per serving: 297 calories, 6 g fat, 1 g saturated fat, 40 mg cholesterol, 41 g carbohydrates, 24 g protein, 789 mg sodium, 10 g fiber

V ARIETY PROVES THE SECRET TO SATISFYING MAIN-COURSE SALADS AND lunches. I frequently cook a couple of items specifically designated for these meal occasions. Chicken thighs taste great here and stay moist; shorten the cooking time if using ultra-lean chicken tenders. Serve over couscous or brown rice.

Balsamic-glazed chicken

Prep: 5 minutes | Cook: 8 minutes | Makes: 4 servings

Pack small containers of this cooked chicken to add to salads or sandwiches.

1 pound boneless skinless chicken thighs or chicken breast tenders

½ teaspoon each: thyme leaves, salt

¼ teaspoon freshly ground black pepper

2 tablespoons olive oil

½ medium red onion, cut into ½-inch pieces

3 tablespoons balsamic vinegar

① Cut chicken into 1-inch pieces. Pat dry; sprinkle with thyme, salt and pepper. Heat oil in large skillet over medium-high heat. Add onion; cook until golden, about 4 minutes. Add chicken in a single uncrowded layer. Cook, stirring once or twice, until golden and cooked through, 4-5 minutes for tenders, or 6-7 minutes for thighs. Stir in vinegar during the last minute of cooking. Cool; refrigerate covered up to 3 days.

Nutrition information per serving: 215 calories, 13 g fat, 3 g saturated fat, 106 mg cholesterol, 3 g carbohydrates, 19 g protein, 508 mg sodium, 0 g fiber

EVERY WEEK, I BUY A PACKAGE OF BONELESS, SKINLESS CHICKEN BREASTS. The intention: simple, lower-fat meals in quick order. Truth be told: Half the time they end up in the freezer. "Boring!" the kids announce.

A better plan is needed. Since boneless, skinless chicken breasts are by nature irregularly shaped, pounding them uniformly flat proves an excellent method for foolproof cooking. With just a few minutes of preparation time and effort, this ubiquitous cut of poultry transforms from boring to fabulous. Seriously. The chicken remains moist and the seasonings penetrate every bite.

Boneless, skinless chicken thighs also take kindly to a little pounding. I usually plan on two small thighs per serving.

Once we adopted the pound-before-cooking method, we discovered all kinds of ways to enjoy lean boneless, skinless chicken, which we dubbed golden chicken. Serve it simply cooked and thinly sliced with a side of brown rice and steamed broccoli.

Golden chicken breasts with tomato-avocado-chili relish

Prep: 30 minutes | Cook: 20 minutes | Makes: 4 servings

A zesty fresh relish adds another layer of flavors and textures that everyone will love.

4 medium-size boneless, skinless chicken breast halves, about 1½ pounds total

¾ teaspoon salt

Freshly ground black pepper

3 to 4 medium ripe tomatoes, cut into ¼-inch dice

1 small hot chili, seeded, finely chopped

Juice of ½ fresh lime

2 to 4 tablespoons chopped fresh cilantro, chives or basil

1 or 2 small ripe avocados, halved, pitted, diced

1 or 2 tablespoons extra-virgin olive oil

3 to 4 shallots or green onions, finely chopped

1 cup dry white wine, dry vermouth or chicken broth

3 to 4 tablespoons unsalted butter

Cilantro sprigs for garnish

① Heat oven to 200 degrees. Slide an ovenproof serving platter into the oven to heat.

② Put each chicken breast between 2 sheets of heavy plastic wrap. Use the flat side of a meat mallet or the bottom of a heavy skillet to pound the chicken until uniformly ½ inch thick. Repeat to pound all the chicken pieces. Season on both sides with ¼ teaspoon salt and pepper to taste.

③ For the relish, mix tomatoes, chili, lime juice and cilantro in a small bowl. Gently stir in avocado. Season with remaining ½ teaspoon salt.

④ Heat olive oil in a large, nonstick skillet over medium heat. Add shallots; cook until golden, 1 or 2 minutes. Move shallots to one side of pan. Add chicken in a single, uncrowded layer. (Work in batches if chicken does not fit comfortably.) Cook without turning over on medium to medium-high heat until golden, about 4 minutes. Flip chicken; cook until golden on second side, 2 to 3 minutes. Remove chicken to the heated platter.

⑤ Add wine to skillet; heat to a boil. Scrape all the browned bits up off the bottom of the pan. Boil gently until mixture has reduced to about 2 tablespoons liquid, about 2 minutes. Carefully add any accumulated juice from chicken platter to the skillet. Working over low heat, whisk in butter until smooth (do not boil the sauce). Taste for seasoning.

⑥ Pour pan sauce over chicken; top with relish. Garnish with cilantro sprigs.

....

Nutritional information per serving: 315 calories, 15 g fat, 3 g saturated fat, 94 mg cholesterol, 9 g carbohydrates, 36 g protein, 528 g sodium, 5 g fiber

TIPS

➤ Seek out best-quality chicken such as brands clearly marked antibiotic free or organic.

➤ Use fresh, never frozen chicken breasts for the best texture.

➤ Select small breasts for proper portion control.

➤ Trim off any fat or white tendons before pounding.

➤ Pound the chicken between two sheets of heavy plastic. I like to use a zippered food bag cut apart at the seams because it holds up to the pounding.

➤ Pounded chicken breasts can be refrigerated up to 1 day if tightly wrapped.

Sources tell us that the average American eats about 80 pounds of chicken per year. Too bad so much of that will be dry and uninteresting. The challenges of chicken? Keeping it moist and purchasing the right chicken.

These days, widely available commodity chicken is so affordable that we are tempted to stock up. However, chicken raised in crowded factory farms, with nasty chemicals and feed filled with who-knows-what, stifles our appetite. A better choice: Chickens that have been allowed to roam around, fed an organic or vegetarian diet and raised without the use of antibiotics.

Roasted chicken with tomato-olive relish

Prep: 25 minutes | Marinate: 30 minutes | Cook: 25 minutes | Makes: 4 servings

Cherry tomatoes and a bed of arugula add unexpected color and freshness to the platter of chicken. This recipe doubles easily for a crowd.

1 lemons
2 tablespoons extra-virgin olive oil
½ teaspoon salt
¼ teaspoon dried thyme
Freshly ground pepper
4 bone-in chicken breast halves, skin removed
¼ teaspoon sweet paprika
½ cup assorted pitted olives, chopped
1 cup cherry or grape tomatoes, roughly chopped
1 or 2 tablespoons each, chopped fresh: basil,
    chives (or 2 teaspoons each dried)
1 bag (5 ounces) arugula

① Remove zest from lemon with a rasp grater or citrus zester. Set aside.

② Squeeze juice from lemons into a large baking dish. Add 1½ tablespoons olive oil, salt, thyme and pepper to taste. Mix well. Add chicken; turn to coat each piece. Let stand at room temperature, up to 30 minutes. (Or, refrigerate, covered, up to 1 day; remove from refrigerator 30 minutes before cooking.)

③ Heat oven to 375 degrees. Arrange chicken on an oiled rimmed baking sheet. Pour any marinating juices over the chicken. Sprinkle with paprika. Bake until juices run clear when a knife is inserted in the thickest part, about 25 minutes.

④ Meanwhile, mix reserved lemon zest with remaining 1 tablespoon olive oil, chopped olives, tomatoes, basil and chives. Season to taste with salt and pepper. (The relish can be refrigerated, up to 1 day. Leave the fresh herbs out of the mixture until right before serving. Serve at room temperature.)

⑤ Arrange arugula on a serving platter. Top with hot chicken. Spoon relish over everything.

Nutrition information per serving: 238 calories, 12 g fat, 2 g saturated fat, 73 mg cholesterol, 6 g carbohydrates, 28 g protein, 363 mg sodium, 3 g fiber.

CHICKEN BRAISED IN TOMATO SAUCE GRACED OUR CHILDHOOD DINNER table on a regular basis. Chicken cacciatore and similar dishes proved to be no-fuss, low-cost dinner options that easily served a large family. My mother always made it look easy: Brown chicken pieces, add some homemade tomato sauce, a few vegetables from the produce bin and pop the skillet in the oven. I like to salt the chicken and refrigerate it for a few hours before cooking; the finished dish will be better for the trouble.

Chicken cacciatore with red and yellow peppers

Prep: 30 minutes | Cook: 1 hour, 20 minutes | Makes: 6 servings | Pictured on p. 90

My mother's "fast" dinner option now is "slow food" for us, reserved for weekend cooking. It's a satisfying cold-weather pleaser with bone-in chicken beautifully browned in olive oil.

1 whole chicken, 3 pounds, cut up

2½ teaspoons salt

¼ cup olive oil

½ pound sliced mushrooms

1 small onion, chopped

1 large each, cored, cut into 1-inch pieces: red bell pepper, yellow bell pepper

4 cloves garlic, crushed

1 cup dry white wine

1 can (28 ounces) crushed tomatoes

½ cup water

2 bay leaves

1 sprig rosemary

¼ cup minced flat leaf parsley

¼ teaspoon freshly ground black pepper

① Season chicken with 2 teaspoons of salt; refrigerate up to 12 hours.

② Heat oven to 375 degrees. Pat the chicken pieces very dry and remove excess salt. Heat the oil in a deep 12-inch (or larger) skillet over medium heat. Add the chicken, in batches if necessary, skin side down, in a single, uncrowded layer. Brown the chicken on all sides, adjusting heat if necessary, about 10 minutes. Transfer to a large platter.

③ Add the mushrooms to the pan; cook until golden on all sides, about 5 minutes. Remove with slotted spoon to the platter. Add onion and peppers to the skillet; cook until onion is golden, about 6 minutes. Add garlic; cook 1 minute.

④ Add the wine; heat to a boil; stirring to scrape up browned bits. Boil to reduce the wine to almost nothing, about 5 minutes. Add the tomatoes, water, bay leaves, rosemary and half of the parsley. Season with ½ teaspoon of the salt and pepper. Return the chicken and mushrooms to the pan, nestling everything into the sauce.

⑤ Partly cover the pan; bake in the oven until the chicken juices run clear, about 40 minutes. (If sauce is too thin, remove chicken and vegetables to a platter; boil the sauce over medium-high heat until desired thickness.) Sprinkle with remaining parsley.

....

Nutrition information per serving: 411 calories, 25 g fat, 6 g saturated fat, 89 mg cholesterol, 13 g carbohydrates, 32 g protein, 658 mg sodium, 3 g fiber

THE NO. 1 TRICK TO ROASTING CHICKEN: HEAT. FOR PERFECTLY GOLDEN SKIN, turn on the convection setting on the oven, if you have one, or fully heat the oven to 400 degrees. For moistness, let the chicken swim first in a briny solution of water, sugar and salt for a few hours before roasting. Then, for a wonderful aroma and subtle flavor, tuck some paper-thin slices of fresh lemon between the skin and flesh and add a handful of cilantro to the cavity.

Since the chicken takes a long time in the oven, I figure I have time to roast vegetables, too.

Lemony roast chicken with caramelized fennel

Prep: 30 minutes | Brine: Several hours | Cook: 1½ hours | Makes: 6 servings

To accompany the rich roasted chicken and vegetables, I offer plain broccoli florets, gently blanched or steamed until bright green and crisp-tender. Pass sliced whole-grain baguette to mop up every bit of the lemony chicken flavor.

¼ cup each: salt, sugar

1 whole roasting chicken, about 5 pounds, giblets and neck removed

¼ cup extra-virgin olive oil

2 large leeks with most of the green, split lengthwise, well rinsed, cut into ½-inch pieces

2 large or 3 small fennel bulbs, fronds reserved, bulbs chopped into ½-inch pieces

2 small thin-skinned lemons, very thinly sliced, seeded

1 handful fresh cilantro

1 teaspoon each: salt, dried oregano

½ teaspoon freshly ground black pepper

① Dissolve ¼ cup each salt and sugar in 2 quarts of warm water in a large bowl or pot. Add the chicken and additional cool water if necessary to completely submerge the chicken. Refrigerate covered at least 2 hours or up to overnight. Drain; rinse chicken; pat dry.

② Heat oven to 375 degrees on convection or 400 degrees conventional. Pour 3 tablespoons oil into a large roasting pan. Add leeks and fennel; mix well to coat with the oil.

③ Use your hands to gently loosen the skin away from the flesh of the chicken. Slip the lemon slices under the skin on the back and front of the chicken. Tuck the cilantro into the chicken cavity. Sprinkle the salt, oregano and pepper on all sides of the chicken. Place the chicken on top of the vegetables in the pan. Drizzle with remaining 1 tablespoon oil.

④ Roast the chicken in the oven, stirring the vegetables around in the pan juices every 20 minutes or so, until the chicken is golden and the juices run clear when the thigh is pierced, 1¼ to 1½ hours. An instant-read thermometer inserted in the thickest part of the thigh should register about 165 degrees.

⑤ Gently transfer the chicken to a cutting board; tent with foil. Let rest, 10 minutes. Meanwhile, skim and discard most of the fat from pan juices. Transfer pan juices and vegetables to a serving bowl; season with salt, if needed.

⑥ Carve the chicken into serving portions. Serve each with a generous spoonful of the vegetables.

Nutrition information per serving: 568 calories, 34 g fat, 8 g saturated fat, 158 mg cholesterol, 14 g carbohydrates, 51 g protein, 828 mg sodium, 4 g fiber

LIKE MOST SEAFOOD, MUSSELS ARE HIGHLY PERISHABLE. I TRANSPORT THEM from store to home in a small cooler. Don't seal the plastic bag the mussels are sold in; they need to breathe. I usually allow about 12 to 18 mussels per serving depending on their size. At home, refrigerate them covered with a damp towel on a rack set over a tray of ice. (Don't put them into the ice; it's too cold.)

To clean mussels, use a small brush on the exterior and kitchen shears to snip any "beard" off the opening. Then give them a quick rinse under cold water just before cooking. Their shells should clamp tightly closed.

Beer-steamed mussels with smoked ham

Prep: 25 minutes | Cook: 15 minutes | Makes: 4 main-course or 6 hearty appetizer servings

Mussels steam to tenderness in five minutes. To add flavor, I make a highly seasoned base in advance. Just minutes before serving, I reheat the base, add a steaming liquid such as beer and broth, then add the mussels and steam away. (Discard any mussels that don't open during cooking.)

3 tablespoons extra-virgin olive oil

2 small leeks, halved lengthwise, well rinsed, thinly sliced

3 large ripe tomatoes, cored, diced

4 cloves garlic, crushed

½ pound smoked ham or Canadian bacon, diced

Salt to taste

¼ teaspoon black pepper

⅛ teaspoon cayenne pepper

6 tablespoons olive oil or regular mayonnaise

6 to 8 thick slices crusty sourdough or peasant bread, toasted

¾ cup each: pale ale beer, chicken broth

3 pounds fresh mussels, shells scrubbed clean

1 tablespoon each chopped fresh: tarragon, parsley

① Heat olive oil in deep 4-quart saucepan or Dutch oven over medium heat. Cook leeks in the oil until tender, about 10 minutes. Stir in tomatoes and garlic. Cook, stirring, until reduced to a thick concentrated mixture, about 4 minutes. Stir in smoked meat, salt, black pepper and cayenne. Set aside or refrigerate covered up to 1 day.

② Heat broiler. Spread mayonnaise over one side of toasted bread slices. Put onto baking sheet.

③ Shortly before serving, heat tomato mixture until hot. Add beer and broth. Heat to a boil over medium-high heat. Add mussels; cover pot tightly. Steam just until mussels open, usually 4-5 minutes.

④ Meanwhile, broil bread just until mayonnaise is golden, 30-40 seconds.

⑤ Remove mussels with slotted spoon to 4 or 6 deep serving bowls. Taste pan juices; adjust seasonings. Pour over mussels. Sprinkle each lightly with the chopped herbs. Serve with the hot bread.

Nutrition information per serving (for 4 servings): 778 calories, 42 g fat, 6 g saturated fat, 154 mg cholesterol, 55 g carbohydrates, 42 g protein, 1,500 mg sodium, 4 g fiber

L IKE MANY FATHERS, MY DAD BELIEVES IN THE FLAVOR OF WOOD PAIRED with the crisp, clean flavors of seafood. He cooks on hardwood charcoal only; we usually follow suit. However, this dish tastes fantastic on the gas grill as well. Especially when cooking on wood grilling planks, readily available at Whole Foods, Williams-Sonoma and most specialty cookware shops.

Brown sugar grilled salmon on cedar planks

Prep: 10 minutes | **Soak:** 30 minutes or more | **Cook:** 12 minutes | **Makes:** 4 servings

I like to serve this recipe with a side salad of lime-dressed watercress and grill-roasted potatoes.

2 wood grilling planks, such as cedar, alder, maple

½ cup packed dark brown sugar

2 tablespoons whole-grain Dijon mustard

1½ teaspoons chili powder

¼ teaspoon salt

4 wild-caught salmon fillets, about 8 ounces each, rinsed, patted dry

Fresh herbs

① Soak planks in water, at least 30 minutes or up to 4 hours.

② Heat a gas grill to medium-high heat or prepare a charcoal grill.

③ Thoroughly mix sugar, mustard, chili powder and salt in a small bowl.

④ Remove the planks from the water and place fish on them, leaving a little space between each piece of fish. Spread sugar mixture thickly over the top of the fillets. Place on the grill. Cover the grill; cook without turning the fish, until the fish almost flakes, 10-12 minutes. Remove planks from grill. Carefully transfer fish to heated serving plates. Garnish with some fresh herbs; serve immediately.

Nutrition information per serving: 437 calories, 15 g fat, 2 g saturated fat, 125 mg cholesterol, 29 g carbohydrates, 45 g protein, 449 mg sodium, 0 g fiber

MY HUSBAND ADORES SCALLOPS, ESPECIALLY LARGE, MEATY SEA SCALLOPS. They're speedy to cook—you want them slightly "rare" in the center, so the texture stays pleasingly bouncy, not chewy. A simple sauce of fresh herbs and lemon makes an elegant presentation.

Seek out scallops that are "dry-packed"—that is, with no additives such as sodium tripolyphosate (which is used to unnaturally plump them and imparts a metallic aftertaste). A reputable seafood store will steer you in the right direction. Thaw frozen scallops gently (wrapped in paper and set on a bed of ice) in the refrigerator.

Sauteed scallops with chermoula

Prep: 20 minutes | Cook: 5 minutes | Makes: 4 servings

Leftover chermoula makes a fantastic dressing for romaine, chicken or shrimp salad. Bottled preserved lemons make a quick substitute for homemade.

Chermoula sauce:

- ¾ cup olive oil
- ½ cup each: parsley leaves, cilantro leaves
- ⅓ cup fresh lemon juice
- 4 cloves garlic
- 1 teaspoon ground cumin
- 1 teaspoon sweet or smoked paprika
- ¾ teaspoon salt
- ¼ teaspoon ground red pepper

Scallops:

- 1¼ pounds large sea scallops
- ¼ teaspoon salt
- Freshly ground pepper
- 2 tablespoons olive oil
- Easy preserved lemons (recipe follows), optional
- Parsley sprigs

① For chermoula sauce, process oil, parsley, cilantro, lemon juice, garlic, cumin, paprika, salt and ground red pepper in a blender until garlic and herbs are finely chopped. Taste; adjust seasonings. (Chermoula will keep up to 2 days covered in the refrigerator; use at room temperature.)

② Pat scallops dry. Season with the salt and pepper to taste. Heat oil in large nonstick skillet until hot. Add the scallops in a single, uncrowded layer. Sear over medium-high heat until golden, about 3 minutes. Turn; sear the other side, about 1 ½ minutes.

③ Transfer scallops and pan juices to 4 heated serving plates. Pour about 2 tablespoons chermoula over and around each serving. Sprinkle preserved lemon over all. Garnish with parsley sprigs.

Nutrition information per serving: 309 calories, 21 g fat, 3 g saturated fat, 47 mg cholesterol, 5 g carbohydrates, 24 g protein, 521 mg sodium, 0 g fiber

Easy preserved lemons

Prep: 10 minutes

Marinate: 9 days

Meyer lemons are good here—they are sweet and tender. Look for them at Trader Joe's and large specialty markets.

2 whole lemons, scrubbed clean

Coarse (kosher) salt

¼ to ½ cup fresh lemon juice

① Cut each lemon into wedges, leaving them attached at the stem end. Coat with a generous amount of salt. Place in a small glass jar; sprinkle with more salt. Repeat with the other lemon, packing it tightly into the jar. Add lemon juice to come about halfway up the lemons. Put the lid on the jar.

② Let stand at room temperature a couple of days, shaking the jar every day. Refrigerate about 1 week. Lemons will keep 3 months or more in the refrigerator and the skins will get softer. Rinse off salt before using.

A COUPLE OF TIMES A MONTH, WE GIVE IN TO POWERFUL SHRIMP CRAVINGS. Our favorite indulgence: Salt-and-pepper shrimp from a local Chinese takeout restaurant. Large pink shrimp, fried just so, tossed with lots of salt, pepper and green chili. Irresistible as a nibble or as a main-course feast piled on rice. We could go for it right now.

As with any dish that captures our hearts, we knew we had to learn to make this at home. But a few rules applied to the finished dish before we would declare success: Better than takeout. Worth the dirty dishes. Less expensive.

For the seasonings, we opted for ordinary fresh black pepper (some recipes use Sichuan pepper), fine salt and a little sugar. Plenty of shallots and fresh jalapeno add crunch and a pleasant burn.

We're so enamored of the shrimp from this technique we created a sweet version with fresh pineapple, perfect for those who have grown out of the sweet and gloppy Asian main dishes we enjoyed as kids.

Salt-and-pepper shrimp with jalapeno

Prep: 20 minutes | **Cook:** 5 minutes | **Makes:** 4 servings | **Pictured on p. 142**

Anaheim, poblano or green bell pepper can be substituted for the jalapeno to reduce the kick.

1 teaspoon fine salt

½ teaspoon each: sugar, freshly ground black pepper

1 large or 2 small shallots, peeled, finely chopped (or 4 green onions)

2 large cloves garlic, finely chopped

2 to 3 jalapeno peppers, stemmed, halved lengthwise, seeded, thinly sliced

1 pound colossal-size shrimp, 13 to 15 pieces, peeled, tail intact, deveined

1½ tablespoons cornstarch

1 cup vegetable oil or expeller-pressed canola oil

① Mix salt, sugar and pepper in a small bowl. Mix shallots, garlic and jalapenos in another small bowl. Pat shrimp very dry with towel. Toss lightly in a bowl with the cornstarch.

② Heat oil in a heavy-bottomed wok or small saucepan over medium-high heat until hot. (Dip the edge of a shrimp in the oil; it should bubble vigorously.) Add a quarter of the shrimp; continuously move them around in the oil with metal tongs or a wire strainer, until they turn pink, about 40 seconds. Remove to a plate to drain; repeat with remaining shrimp.

③ Very carefully pour the oil off into a heatproof container. Return 1½ tablespoons of the oil to the wok (or a large nonstick skillet). Heat over medium-high.

Add the salt mixture; stir-fry 10 seconds. Add the shallot mixture; stir-fry 10 seconds. Add all the shrimp; stir-fry just until shrimp are tender, about 1 minute. Immediately remove from wok to serving platter. Serve hot.

Nutrition information per serving: 221 calories, 11 g fat, 1 g saturated fat, 172 mg cholesterol, 6 g carbohydrates, 24 g protein, 752 mg sodium, 1 g fiber

Red chili pineapple shrimp: Substitute 1 teaspoon crushed red pepper flakes for the jalapeno and add it along with 1 cup fresh pineapple (cut into ½-inch dice) to the shallot-garlic mixture in step 1. Sprinkle finished dish with chopped fresh cilantro.

BUYING TIPS

Some shrimp may come from places that are overfished or raised in ways that they are harmful to the environment.

➤ When possible, **buy shrimp farmed in the United States** because we enforce strict environmental laws for the farmers that other countries do not. The Monterey Bay Aquarium tells us that some U.S. shrimp farmers have even further reduced their impact on the environment by raising shrimp in fully recirculating systems or inland ponds, away from sensitive coastal habitats.

➤ The easiest way to purchase shrimp responsibly is to **shop at stores that provide origin information**. Avoid shrimp that is not labeled adequately.

➤ All shrimp are sold by size—how many shrimp per pound—even if they have a name such as colossal or jumbo. For a terrific treat in the recipe below, **use the impressive 13 to 15 per pound shrimp**. When using smaller shrimp, such as jumbos (16 to 20 per pound), or extra large (22 to 24 per pound), decrease the cooking time to prevent overcooking.

'M PARTIAL TO MEATY FILLETS, SUCH AS WILD-CAUGHT SWORDFISH OR SEA bass. Halibut works too. Here, I'm seasoning the thick fish fillets with sweet spices and herbs. A drizzle of olive oil just before cooking will ensure moist results.

I usually prefer to grill fish rather than cook it indoors. But a superhot broiler drastically reduces the timeline to dinner. Simply turn the broiler to high and let it heat. Then turn on the exhaust fan before you slide the fish 6 inches from the heating element.

A lemon-chili relish, made from grated lemon rind, lemon juice, hot green chili, chopped parsley, garlic and salt, gives the finished fish easy restaurant sophistication. Serve with sauteed greens, toasted pita and a romaine lettuce salad.

Roasted fish with lemon-chili relish

Prep: 25 minutes | Cook: 15 minutes | Makes: 4 servings

Boneless skinless chicken cutlets (made by slicing boneless chicken breasts horizontally in half) make a fine substitute for the fish. So do scallops; reduce cooking time to a total of 4 minutes.

4 portions of meaty, boneless fish, such as
    swordfish, sea bass or halibut, each piece
    8 to 10 ounces and 1 to 1¼ inches thick

1 teaspoon each, dried: oregano, marjoram

½ teaspoon each: cinnamon, allspice, salt

¼ teaspoon freshly ground black pepper

Lemon-chili relish:

¼ cup chopped fresh parsley

1 small serrano chili, stemmed, halved, seeded,
    very finely chopped

Finely grated zest and juice of half a lemon

1 large clove garlic, crushed

½ teaspoon salt

Olive oil for drizzling

Lemon, cauliflower and garlic hummus
    (see recipe on p. 29)

Parsley sprigs

① Rinse fish; pat dry. Mix oregano, marjoram, cinnamon, allspice, salt and pepper in a small bowl. Coat fish on all sides with mixture. Let stand at room temperature, about 30 minutes. (Or refrigerate covered for a couple of hours.)

② Meanwhile, for lemon-chili relish, mix parsley, chili, lemon zest and juice, garlic and salt in a small bowl.

③ Heat broiler to high. Place fish on broiler pan or wire rack set over a drip pan. Drizzle fish lightly with olive oil. Broil fish, 6 inches from heat source, turning once, until fish nearly flakes, usually about 8 minutes total.

④ Divide cauliflower hummus among 4 serving plates. Make a well in center of hummus. Top each with a portion of fish. Spread with lemon-chili relish. Garnish with sauteed cauliflower and parsley sprigs.

Nutrition information per serving: 322 calories, 17 g fat, 4 g saturated fat, 129 mg cholesterol, 2 g carbohydrates, 39 g protein, 745 mg sodium, 1 g fiber

CHAPTER 7

Vegetables and Other Sides

147

TWO SECRETS COME TO MIND FOR SUCCESSFUL VEGGIE GRILLING: KEEP 'EM moist; season highly. Since grills offer dry heat, a light coating of oil seals in moisture when grilling cut vegetables. Alternatively, I trap moisture by wrapping firm veggies such as potatoes, beets, turnips and carrots in foil. Sweet potatoes: We thickly slice and then sprinkle ours with a "barbecue" seasoning. A medium grill will soften the hard potatoes and char their natural sugars beautifully. My family sneaks them right off the grill. They think I don't know. Instead, I cook double the quantity so we have a great accompaniment to grilled steak, pork chops and ribs.

Barbecue sweet potatoes with chickpeas and arugula

Prep: 20 minutes | Cook: 5 minutes | Makes: 4 main-course servings

Roasted and salted, smoked or candied pecans make a great substitute for the toasted pecans here. Crumbled goat cheese tastes great in place of the sour cream, too.

¼ cup pecan halves

2 tablespoons smoky barbecue sauce

1 tablespoon each: olive oil, red wine vinegar

½ cup drained canned chickpeas

5 ounces baby arugula or baby kale or 4 cups roughly chopped frisee leaves

Salt, optional

Barbecue sweet potato slices (recipe follows)

A few tablespoons thin sour cream or plain yogurt, optional

Chopped fresh chives or very thinly sliced green onions

① Place pecans in a small nonstick skillet. Cook over medium heat, stirring constantly, until fragrant and lightly browned, 1-2 minutes. Cool, then chop roughly.

② Mix barbecue sauce, oil and vinegar in a small bowl. Add chickpeas; toss to coat. Arrange greens on a large platter. Sprinkle lightly with salt if desired.

③ Cut potato slices into 1-inch chunks. Put into a large bowl. Cover with plastic wrap vented at one corner. Microwave on high until potatoes are warm, 2 to 3 minutes.

④ Add warm potatoes and chickpea mixture to salad greens. Toss lightly to coat everything with the dressing. Sprinkle with pecans. Drizzle with sour cream if using. Serve sprinkled with chives.

Nutrition information per serving: 304 calories, 16 g fat, 2 g saturated fat, 0 mg cholesterol, 37 g carbohydrates, 6 g protein, 305 mg sodium, 5 g fiber

Barbecue sweet potato slices

Prep: 15 minutes | Cook: 20 minutes
Makes: 4 to 6 servings

Make extra; these potato planks taste great the next day.

1 tablespoon chili powder

1½ teaspoons sugar

2 to 3 large sweet potatoes (1½ to 2 pounds total), peeled if desired

2 tablespoons extra-virgin olive oil

Coarse (kosher) salt

① Prepare a charcoal grill or heat a gas grill to medium heat. Mix chili powder and sugar together in a small dish.

② Cut potatoes lengthwise into slabs about ½ inch thick. Place in a single layer on 1 large well-oiled baking sheet. Turn potatoes to coat with the oil.

③ Sprinkle the potatoes generously on all sides with the chili mixture; sprinkle lightly with salt.

④ Arrange potatoes on the grill in a single un-crowded layer. Cover grill; cook, 10 minutes. Use a pancake flipper to carefully turn potato slices over. Grill the second side until potatoes are tender when pierced with a fork and edges are slightly charred, 8-10 minutes. Serve hot.

ROASTED BRUSSELS SPROUTS GRACE OUR FALL TABLES FOR ENTERTAINING AS well as weekday meals. The trick is to select the smallest, deepest green sprouts you can find—they'll prove less bitter and cook more quickly than their large yellowy brothers. I trim the bottoms (where they were attached to the stalk) and then cut them lengthwise in half. Gather any leaves that fall off during the process and roast those as well—they'll crisp so nicely the cook will likely eat them up the minute they come out of the oven. The crispy sprouts can be seasoned simply with salt, pepper and Parmesan shreds. The recipe here glazes them with a spicy-sweet combination of soy, rice vinegar, sugar and sriracha. Addictive even cold in a lunchbox the next day.

Sweet and spicy roasted Brussels sprouts

Prep: 15 minutes | Cooks: 30 minutes | Makes: 6 servings

Use organic soy sauce to avoid preservatives. Add the glaze to the roasted sprouts to taste; we like to use it all, but you can save some for another batch or to drizzle over roasted cauliflower or steamed broccoli.

2¼ pounds small Brussels sprouts, about 60

¼ cup expeller-pressed canola oil, rice bran oil or safflower oil

½ cup organic soy sauce or all natural light soy

¼ cup unsweetened rice vinegar

¼ cup sugar

1 to 2 tablespoons all-natural sriracha or 1 to 2 teaspoons crushed red pepper flakes

1 teaspoon dark Asian sesame oil

2 to 4 tablespoons each, chopped: cilantro, green onions

Sesame seeds

① Heat oven to 375 degrees on convection or 400 degrees conventional. Use a small paring knife to trim the stem ends of the Brussels sprouts. Cut each in half through the stem end. Put the halves and any loose leaves onto a large nonstick baking sheet. (Use 2 sheets if necessary so the sprouts are in a single uncrowded layer.) Drizzle the oil over the sprouts; toss well to coat evenly.

② Roast the Brussels sprouts, stirring them every 10 minutes, until a knife inserted in the end comes out easily, the exteriors are golden and edges are crispy, 20 to 30 minutes.

③ Meanwhile, put soy sauce, vinegar and sugar into a small saucepan. Heat to a boil over medium heat. Boil gently until mixture is reduced and slightly thickened, about 5 minutes. Remove from heat; add sriracha or chili flakes to taste. Stir in sesame oil.

④ Toss the hot crispy Brussels sprouts with enough sauce to coat them generously. Pile sprouts onto a warm serving platter. Sprinkle with cilantro, green onions and sesame seeds. Serve right away.

Nutrition information per serving: 176 calories, 10 g fat, 1 g saturated fat, 0 mg cholesterol, 19 g carbohydrates, 6 g protein, 812 mg sodium, 6 g fiber

Nothing takes the chill out of winter like a house filled with the aroma of slow-cooking goodness. In our house, that aroma frequently includes a touch of curry spice on roasting veggies.

In some parts of the world, curry means a dish of seasoned food. Around here when we talk about curry, we're thinking of spice jars filled with intriguing flavors and aromas. Most commercial curry powders, made from a blend of spices, taste similar. I seek out special curry powders from my local spice seller.

Roasted curried vegetables

Prep: 25 minutes | Cook: 30-40 minutes | Makes: 6 to 8 servings

Cubes of winter squash or root vegetables taste great with curry, too. Cooking time will be slightly longer for denser vegetables.

4 medium zucchini, yellow squash or a
  combination of the two, trimmed

1 or 2 small chayote squash, halved, seeded

2 medium red bell peppers, cored, seeded

6 to 8 medium tomatillos, husked

1 large (1 pound) yellow onion, quartered, thinly
  sliced

4 to 6 tablespoons olive oil

1½ teaspoons curry powder

1 teaspoon salt

Chopped fresh cilantro

① Heat oven to 425 degrees. Cut the zucchini and yellow squash lengthwise in half. Cut the halves into ½-inch-thick slices. Cut the chayote and bell peppers into ½-inch pieces. Cut the tomatillos into quarters.

② Combine all the vegetables in a large bowl. Toss with 4 tablespoons of the oil, curry powder and salt to coat everything nicely. Divide mixture among 2 oiled baking sheets so the vegetables are in a single layer.

③ Roast, stirring once or twice, until tender and lightly browned on the edges, 30-40 minutes. Serve sprinkled with cilantro.

Nutrition information per serving: 105 calories, 7 g fat, 1 g saturated fat, 0 mg cholesterol, 10 g carbohydrates, 1 g protein, 295 mg sodium, 3 g fiber

LOVE OF PARSNIPS IS INHERITED FROM MY FATHER. HE ALWAYS SNEAKS MORE than his share out of the stewpot or roasting pan. I posit that his sweet tooth gets the better of him, for this pale golden root proves incredibly sweet—especially when slow-roasted or braised. They also make a fabulous mash. (I like to pair them 50/50 with carrots.) Leftover mashed can be transformed into fried fritters. Here, I've braised them in apple cider and gilded the dish with bacon.

Bacon braised parsnips

Prep: 25 minutes | Cook: 10 minutes | Makes: 6 servings

Totally irresistible—even for the uninitiated.

3 slices apple-wood-smoked bacon, diced
1 pound fresh parsnips, trimmed, peeled
1 cup unfiltered apple cider
1 to 2 tablespoons agave syrup or honey
½ teaspoon salt
Freshly ground black pepper
Minced fresh thyme or rosemary, optional

① Cook bacon in large skillet over medium heat until crisp, about 10 minutes. Remove and reserve crisp bacon.

② Meanwhile, cut parsnips into sticks about 2 inches long and ¼-by-¼ inch. Add parsnip sticks to bacon fat in skillet. Cook, stirring, over medium-high heat until parsnips are golden brown, about 5 minutes. Add cider and syrup. Boil hard over high heat until pan juices reduce to a glaze, about 4 minutes.

③ Season with salt and pepper to taste. Serve garnished with crisp bacon and herbs.

....

Nutrition information per serving: 102 calories, 2 g fat, 0 g saturated fat, 3 mg cholesterol, 21 g carbohydrates, 2 g protein, 275 mg sodium, 3 g fiber

D URING GREEN BEAN SEASON, NOTHING SATISFIES MORE THAN PLUNGING into the bins of slender green beans and sunshine-yellow wax beans and filling a bag to the brim. With beans this fresh, no need to waste time picking through every bean in the bin—do that when you trim the ends. If the green and wax beans are roughly the same diameter they can be cooked together in the same pot—the combination of colors and slightly different flavors are great.

Garden fresh beans, two ways

Prep: 25 minutes | Cook: 25 minutes | Makes: 8 servings

These beans can be served without the sauce in step 3. For zest and variety, continue on and add the spicy glaze.

2 pounds fresh small green beans, wax beans, or a combination, trimmed

3 tablespoons vegetable oil

1 large sweet onion, halved, thinly sliced

½ pound assorted mushrooms, trimmed, thinly sliced

4 cloves garlic, finely chopped

½ teaspoon salt

Optional sauce:

⅓ cup ketchup

2 tablespoons each: pureed chipotle chilies in adobo, balsamic vinegar

① Heat a large saucepan of salted water to a boil. Add beans; cook, uncovered, until crisp-tender, 8-10 minutes. Drain; rinse under cold water. Drain.

② Heat the oil in a large non-stick skillet. Add the onion and mushrooms. Cook, stirring often, until the onions are golden, about 8 minutes. Add the garlic; cook 1 minute. Add the beans; cook to heat through, about 4 minutes. Season with salt.

③ For sauce, mix all the ingredients in a small bowl. Stir the sauce into the beans; heat through to glaze the beans, about 2 minutes.

Nutrition information per serving, with sauce: 106 calories, 6 g fat, 0 g saturated fat, 0 mg cholesterol, 13 g carbohydrates, 3 g protein, 291 mg sodium, 5 g fiber

O N A RECENT FALL HIKE, FRIENDS TALKED FAVORITE WAYS WITH KALE for a half mile. Consensus among the hikers: Use baby kale raw in salads, slaws and on hearty roast turkey or pork sandwiches. Roast medium-size leaves for a great snack. Braise larger leaves with rich broth for a comforting side with not too many calories. Think I'll share that idea with my exercise teacher—perhaps she'll ease up on our push-ups.

Chile roasted kale

Prep: 10 minutes | Cook: 10 minutes | Makes: 4 servings

I like the bright spiciness of guajillo chili powder here, but everyday chili powder tastes great too. If the kale leaves are small and tender, they taste good raw simply coated with the oil, chili and salt.

2 bunches (14 ounces total) medium kale leaves, such as lacinato (Tuscan) kale, rinsed, dried

3 tablespoons extra-virgin olive oil

½ to ¾ teaspoon chili powder, such as guajillo powder

About ½ teaspoon coarse (kosher) salt

① Heat oven to 400 degrees. Trim kale stems; cut leaves into 2-inch pieces. Put into large bowl. Add oil, half of the chili powder and half of the salt. Use clean hands to toss and work the oil and seasonings into the leaves.

② Divide the kale among 2 large baking sheets. Sprinkle with the remaining chili powder and salt. Roast, stirring often, until crisp with some browned edges, about 10 minutes. Serve hot.

Nutrition information per serving: 120 calories, 11 g fat, 1 g saturated fat, 0 mg cholesterol, 6 g carbohydrates, 2 g protein, 270 mg sodium, 2 g fiber

KOHLRABI AND CHAYOTE—TWO VEGETABLES I'M PRONE TO OVERLOOK. LONG, slow roasting draws out their sweetness. Topped with crumbled cheese and nuts, they satisfy deeply as a main or hearty side.

Roasted kohlrabi and chayote with feta and pistachios

Prep: 20 minutes | Cook: 40 minutes | Makes: 4 main-course servings, more as a side

Kohlrabi, a member of the cabbage family, has a mild sweet taste not unlike broccoli stems. Most are about the size of a small baseball. Often, larger varieties like the Gigante can be found at farmers markets and are easier to peel. Kohlrabi is delicious eaten raw or shredded for use in salads and stir-fries. It takes well to roasting, which brings out its natural sweetness.

2 pounds kohlrabi, peeled, cut into 1-inch pieces

2 chayote squash, peeled, halved, pitted, cut into 1-inch pieces

1 medium red onion, cut into 1-inch pieces

3 to 4 tablespoons olive oil

½ teaspoon each: salt, dried Italian seasoning (or a combination of dried basil, oregano and thyme)

Freshly ground black pepper

Several handfuls baby arugula or spinach

1 cup crumbled feta or goat cheese

¼ to ⅓ cup chopped nuts, like pistachios

Chopped fresh parsley and chives

① Heat oven to 400 degrees. Mix kohlrabi, chayote squash and onion on a large, rimmed baking sheet in a single uncrowded layer. Drizzle with olive oil, then sprinkle with salt, Italian seasoning and pepper to taste. Mix well.

② Roast, stirring every 10 minutes, until vegetables are fork-tender and golden brown, 30 to 40 minutes.

③ Taste and season again with salt. Stir in arugula or spinach. Spoon into a wide, deep serving bowl. Top with cheese and nuts. Sprinkle with the fresh herbs. Serve hot.

Nutrition information per serving: 293 calories, 22 g fat, 7 g saturated fat, 33 mg cholesterol, 18 g carbohydrates, 10 g protein, 662 mg sodium, 7 g fiber

MOST SUMMER FOODS LEND THEMSELVES TO COOKING OUTDOORS. BAKED beans not so much. The quintessential summer side tastes best with a long, slow simmer. Why bother heating up the kitchen when there's such a huge assortment of canned baked beans in stores? My family cooks them for several reasons: pleasure, personalized flavor and accolades. No two recipes are alike. All summer long, we attend parties with someone's rendition. One thing in common: I like them all!

I am especially fond of my late brother-in-law Dave's vegetarian slow-cooker version for its simplicity and ease. Then again, there's my late mother-in-law Mickey's recipe, jampacked with bacon and brown sugar. She'd wrap the hot bean pot, crusty with caramelized bits, in large beach towels to stay warm on their trek to family picnics.

Mickey's bacon baked beans

Prep: 25 minutes | Cook: 2 hours, 30 minutes | Makes: 10 servings

These taste even better when reheated.

1 pound lean bacon strips, such as apple-wood-smoked

1 sweet or Vidalia onion, diced

1 cup water

1 can (15½ ounces) each, drained: kidney beans, butter beans

1½ cups frozen lima beans

1 can (28 ounces) pork and beans (do not drain)

1 cup packed dark brown sugar

① Heat oven to 350 degrees. Cut bacon into small pieces. Cook in large Dutch oven, stirring often, until crisped. Drain off most of the fat, leaving a little for flavor.

② Stir in onion and water. Heat to a boil; simmer, 10 minutes. Add all the beans and the sugar. Cover tightly; bake, stirring occasionally, 1½ hours. Uncover; bake until the top is crusty and the liquid thick and reduced, about 1 hour or so.

....

Nutrition information per serving: 331 calories, 7 g fat, 2 g saturated fat, 16 mg cholesterol, 56 g carbohydrates, 16 g protein, 952 mg sodium, 9 g fiber

Pictured: Top left, Mickey's bacon baked beans; bottom left, Dave's veggie baked beans (p. 162)

Dave's veggie baked beans

Prep: 10 minutes | Cook: 3-8 hours | Makes: 8 servings

A slow cooker helps keeps the kitchen cool while the flavors simmer together.

1 can (15 ounces) chili beans in mild chili sauce

1 can (15½ ounces) each, drained: light kidney beans, butter beans

2 cups (about half of a 16-ounce bag) frozen corn kernels

1 small onion, chopped

2 celery ribs, chopped

¾ cup packed light brown sugar

⅓ cup barbecue sauce

1 teaspoon yellow mustard

① Mix all ingredients in a medium-size slow cooker. Cover; cook, stirring occasionally, until flavors are blended and liquid slightly thickened, 3 to 4 hours on high setting or 8 hours on low.

....

Nutrition information per serving: 244 calories, 1 g fat, 0 g saturated fat, 0 mg cholesterol, 54 g carbohydrates, 9 g protein, 673 mg sodium, 8 g fiber

T ANGY, BUTTERY SOFT RED CABBAGE ALWAYS GRACES OUR HOLIDAY TABLES—especially when roast goose is on the menu. But if goose isn't on your menu, don't fear—this wintry mix pairs well with any roast poultry or pork.

Curried red cabbage with chestnuts

Prep: 25 minutes | Cook: 30 minutes | Makes: 8 servings

Leftovers reheat beautifully. Substitute chopped dried apricots or raisins for the chestnuts, if desired.

2 slices thick bacon, diced

1 large red onion, halved, thinly sliced

1 head (about 2 pounds) red cabbage, quartered, thinly sliced

1 tablespoon minced fresh ginger root

1 cup chicken broth

1 teaspoon curry powder

½ teaspoon salt

1 cup bottled roasted chestnuts, coarsely chopped

Chopped fresh cilantro or parsley

① Cook bacon in large Dutch oven until golden, about 5 minutes. Add onion; cook, stirring, until tender, about 5 minutes. Stir in cabbage and ginger; cook 2 minutes.

② Stir in broth, curry powder and salt. Cover; cook, stirring occasionally, until cabbage is fork-tender, about 20 minutes. Stir in chestnuts. Adjust seasonings. Garnish with cilantro.

....

Nutrition information per serving: 91 calories, 1 g fat, 0 g saturated fat, 2 mg cholesterol, 18 g carbohydrates, 3 g protein, 330 mg sodium, 3 g fiber

F YOU ARE NEW TO STIR-FRYING, START WITH THIS SIMPLE FRIED RICE. THE RECIPE is manageable and can be done over medium-high heat. The dish is great alongside grilled salmon or roasted pork tenderloin. I also enjoy it reheated for lunch with the addition of shredded chicken or tuna.

Simple fried rice

Prep: 10 minutes | Cook: 10 minutes | Makes: 3 or 4 servings

Be sure to use cold cooked rice for the best-textured fried rice.

2 large eggs

1 teaspoon dark sesame oil or garlic oil

⅛ teaspoon salt

2 tablespoons expeller-pressed canola oil, safflower oil or peanut oil

3 cups chilled, cooked brown or white rice

4 green onions, thinly sliced

2 or 3 tablespoons chopped fresh cilantro

Tamari or light soy sauce

① Beat eggs with sesame oil and salt in a small bowl. Place all ingredients near the cooking surface.

② Heat a well-seasoned wok (or large nonstick skillet) over medium-high heat until a drop of water evaporates on contact.

③ Add canola oil; heat until hot but not smoking. Add the eggs; swirl with a heatproof rubber spatula until nearly set, about 30 seconds. Immediately add the rice; stir to coat it with the oil and mix in the egg. Keep stir-frying, breaking up any clumps, until the rice is very hot, 2-3 minutes. Stir in onions and cilantro. Serve with a little tamari.

Nutrition information per serving (for 4 servings): 276 calories, 12 g fat, 2 g saturated fat, 93 mg cholesterol, 36 g carbohydrates, 7 g protein, 112 mg sodium, 3 g fiber

TIPS

➤ **The better the rice, the better the stir-fry.** I like jasmine rice for its fragrance when adding simple vegetables; brown rice works well with hearty add-ins such as beef; toothsome medium grain rice counters bouncy bites of shrimp nicely.

➤ Start with **cooled rice**—using warm rice will stir-fry into sogginess.

➤ **Break up any clumps** in the rice so each grain can be fried quickly and easily.

➤ Stir-fry with **oils that like high temperatures** such as expeller-pressed canola oil, safflower oil or peanut oil. Do not stir-fry with regular canola oil or olive oil.

➤ Don't be afraid to use the **highest heat** your stove can produce.

➤ Use a **large, well-seasoned wok**. Or, a large, deep-sided nonstick skillet—but be aware that you may need a little more oil because of the flat cooking surface.

➤ **Heat the pan before you add the oil**; then heat the oil; then start stir-frying. All this heating prevents sticking.

➤ **Don't skip the egg**—it adds flavor and acts as a binder. Season the egg with a highly flavored oil such as dark sesame oil or garlic oil.

Turn simple rice into a treat by replacing some of the water with unsweetened coconut milk. I like to serve this alongside grilled steak or pork chops seasoned with chili paste.

Coconut rice

Prep: 5 minutes | Cook: 30 minutes | Makes: 6 servings

Be sure to use unsweetened coconut milk here, not the sweetened variety we like in our pina coladas. I like the canned variety sold in the Asian food section of large supermarkets.

2 cups jasmine or long-grain white rice

1²/₃ cups hot water

1 cup unsweetened coconut milk

1 teaspoon salt

¼ cup shredded unsweetened coconut, optional

① Put rice, water, coconut milk and salt in a medium saucepan; heat to a boil. Reduce heat to very low; cover tightly. Simmer until rice is nearly tender, about 15 minutes. Remove from heat; let stand covered (don't stir) 5 minutes. Fluff with a fork.

② If desired, while the rice cooks, saute the coconut in a small nonstick skillet until golden about 2 minutes. Serve rice sprinkled with toasted coconut.

....

Nutrition information per serving: 321 calories, 9 g fat, 7 g saturated fat, 0 mg cholesterol, 55 g carbohydrates, 6 g protein, 394 mg sodium, 1 g fiber

OUSCOUS PROVES A SUPER SPEEDY SIDE DISH THAT PAIRS WELL WITH everything from grilled to roasted meats, fish and poultry. A crunchy, nutty topping keeps it interesting; so does fresh lemon.

Nutty lemon couscous

Prep: 5 minutes | Cook: 5 minutes | Makes: 6 servings

Larger Israeli or pearl couscous can be used here, too. Simmer it about 5 minutes before the 5 minute standing time in step 2.

½ cup (2¼ ounces) slivered blanched almonds

2 tablespoons each: sesame seeds, butter

2 cups low-sodium chicken broth

½ teaspoon salt

1 box (10 ounces) plain couscous

Finely grated rind of 1 lemon

① Combine almonds, sesame seeds and butter in a skillet; heat over medium heat, stirring, until almonds are golden, about 3 minutes. Remove from heat.

② Heat broth and salt to boil in a large saucepan. Stir in couscous and lemon rind. Cover; let stand until broth is absorbed, about 5 minutes. Fluff with a fork; stir in toasted nuts.

....

Nutrition information per serving: 297 calories, 11 g fat, 3 g saturated fat, 10 mg cholesterol, 40 g carbohydrates, 10 g protein, 225 mg sodium, 4 g fiber

QUINOA MAKES A DRAMATIC SIDE, IN LITTLE TIME. THE BACONY QUINOA and black beans that follows just might be the best quinoa recipe ever. I always make a double recipe and enjoy it cold the next day with bits of shredded cooked chicken stirred in along with chopped fresh cilantro.

Bacony black beans and tricolor quinoa

Prep: 10 minutes | Cook: 20 minutes | Makes: 4 to 6 servings

Look for tricolor quinoa at special grocery stores such as Whole Foods and Trader Joe's. Red or regular quinoa works too. Double this recipe if desired; leftovers taste delicious. Serve at room temperature.

1 medium leek or 1 medium sweet onion

¼ cup finely diced smoky bacon

1 large clove garlic, finely chopped

1 or 2 teaspoons olive oil

2 cups low-sodium chicken broth

1 cup tricolor quinoa

1 small orange habanero, left whole, optional

1 can (15 ounces) black beans, drained, rinsed

Salt to taste

Chopped fresh cilantro

① Cut off the tough leaves and dark green portion of the leek; set aside for use in a stock later. Cut the white and pale green section of the leek lengthwise in half. Rinse it well, then cut into ⅛-inch-thick slices.

② Cook bacon, leek and garlic with oil in medium saucepan over medium heat until bacon starts to crisp and brown, about 5 minutes. Stir in broth; heat to a boil while scraping up any browned bits from the bottom of the pan. Stir in the quinoa. Nestle the habanero into the quinoa. Reduce heat to low. Cover pan tightly; cook until quinoa is tender and all the broth has been absorbed, about 15 minutes. Stir in beans and salt to taste, usually about ¼ teaspoon. Remove habanero.

③ Serve warm garnished with cilantro.

....

Nutrition information per serving (for 6 servings): 203 calories, 5 g fat, 1 g saturated fat, 5 mg cholesterol, 30 g carbohydrates, 10 g protein, 318 mg sodium, 5 g fiber

Decades of eating well have caught up with us. Now, our resolu-tion to eat more fiber and veggies and less meat has become a quality of life mandate. No problem when we dine out; today's restaurants often feature creative, satisfying vegetable main courses. At home, we turn to transforming pantry staples such as brown rice and beans into entrees such as this pretty stuffed squash.

First-rate squash choices include the readily available (but somewhat bland) acorn squash. Better yet are the solid, honey-flavored buttercup, or the delicate delicata, the sturdy baby blue hubbard and the richly flavored, dense, not-too-sweet, sweet dumpling.

Choose specimens that weigh about a pound each, then scrub them clean before cutting in half to par-cook. Sweet dumpling squash looks great halved horizontally so the pretty stem stays attached, making a lid. Acorn squash and delicata can be cut in half through the stem end. Use caution when cutting through the tough skin. A serrated grapefruit spoon makes quick work of scooping out the seeds and fibers to create the perfect hollow for the filling.

A steamy environment cooks the halved squash quickly and retains moisture. The microwave oven proves ideal and makes for easy cleanup. The par-cooked squash will keep a couple of days in the refrigerator, so you can work in advance.

Sweet dumpling squash with rice and peas

Prep: 30 minutes | Cook: 55 minutes | Makes: 4 servings

Instead of using the microwave oven, you can bake squash in a 350-degree oven until tender, about 40 minutes. After halving the squash, cut a small slice from the uncut ends so the squash halves sit level.

4 small (about 1 pound each) sweet dumpling or acorn squash, halved, seeds and fibers removed

2 to 3 tablespoons unsalted butter or olive oil

1 small sweet onion, chopped

2 ribs celery, chopped

1 small red bell pepper, seeded, finely chopped

1 cubanelle or anaheim pepper, seeded, finely chopped

2 large cloves garlic, crushed

1 can (15 ounces) pigeon peas (gandules) or black-eyed peas, drained

1½ teaspoons salt

½ teaspoon each: thyme, freshly ground black pepper

⅛ teaspoon freshly ground allspice

1 pouch (8.8 to 10.5 ounces) fully cooked brown rice (or 2 cups cooked)

¾ cup unsweetened coconut milk, optional

3 green onions, trimmed, chopped

Lime wedges

① Put 4 squash halves, cut side down, in a single layer in a microwave-safe baking dish. Add about ½ inch of water to the dish; cover with plastic wrap vented at one corner. Microwave on high (100 percent power), turning dish if needed, until a fork easily can be inserted in the flesh of the squash, 13-15 minutes. Keep covered while you cook the remaining squash halves. (Refrigerate cooked squash halves up to 2 days.)

② For filling, melt butter or heat oil in large skillet. Add onion and celery; saute until tender, about 3 minutes. Stir in red pepper, cubanelle pepper and garlic; cook until almost tender, about 3 minutes. Stir in peas, 1 teaspoon of the salt, thyme, pepper and allspice; heat thoroughly. Stir in rice, coconut milk if using and green onions. Remove from heat. Taste and adjust seasonings.

③ Heat oven to 350 degrees. Arrange cooked squash halves cut side up in oiled baking pan. Sprinkle with remaining ½ teaspoon of the salt and pepper to taste. Spoon about ½ cup of the filling into each squash. Cover with oiled foil (or the lids if using sweet dumpling squash). Bake until thoroughly heated, about 20 minutes (longer if squash has been refrigerated before stuffing). Serve hot with lime wedges.

....

Nutrition information per serving: 433 calories, 7 g fat, 4 g saturated fat, 15 mg cholesterol, 87 g carbohydrates, 11 g protein, 1,236 mg sodium, 19 g fiber

THIS ASPARAGUS IS A DELICIOUS ACCOMPANIMENT TO ANY MEAL, AND THE herb mixture is worth making for more reasons than the asparagus alone. It also works wonders on luxurious burrata cheese for a decadent appetizer any time of the year.

Herb roasted asparagus

Prep: 5 minutes | Cook: 12 minutes | Makes: 4 servings | Pictured on p. 146

This recipe doubles easily — just don't crowd the pan. The griddle should be oily enough to cook a second batch.

1 bunch (about 12 ounces) skinny asparagus, ends trimmed

1 tablespoon olive oil

Coarse salt

2 tablespoons olive and herb mixture (recipe follows)

① Heat oven to 400 degrees. Put asparagus on a large cast-iron griddle or ovenproof skillet in a single layer. Toss with oil and a sprinkle of salt. Roast, turning asparagus occasionally, until tip of a knife goes in easily, 10-12 minutes. Transfer asparagus to a serving dish; toss with the herb marinade.

Nutrition information per serving: 51 calories, 4 g fat, 0 g saturated fat, 0 mg cholesterol, 2 g carbohydrates, 1 g protein, 27 mg sodium, 1 g fiber

Olive and fresh herb mixture

Prep: 20 minutes | Makes: about 2 cups

2 Meyer lemons

1 large regular lemon

½ cup finely chopped pitted oil-cured olives (about half of a 10-ounce jar)

⅓ cup extra-virgin olive oil

1 cup finely sliced fresh chives or 1 bunch green onions, trimmed, white and tender greens chopped

6 large cloves garlic, finely chopped, about 2 tablespoons

½ cup chopped fresh parsley

1½ tablespoons finely chopped fresh oregano

2 teaspoons each, finely chopped, fresh: thyme, rosemary

½ teaspoon each: salt, freshly ground black pepper

① Use a rasp grater to grate zests from all lemons into a medium bowl. Squeeze just the Meyer lemons and add their juice (about ⅓ cup) to the bowl. Stir in olives and olive oil. Stir in remaining ingredients. Refrigerate, covered, up to 2 days.

CHAPTER 8

Holiday Dinner at Home

GOOD NEWS: ROAST BEEF IS EASY. ORDERING IT FROM THE BUTCHER proves the only tricky task. This will be the most expensive entree I cook all year, so I patronize a meat market with expertise. I always ask the butcher for advice and to help calculate the weight of the roast needed. I know I need a couple more ounces per person than when cooking a boneless roast. The butcher recommends 12 ounces per person when serving several side dishes. I order a slightly bigger roast because we relish leftovers.

My father, once a butcher, reminds me to order a first-cut rib roast. The butcher agrees. This roast, cut from near the loin, contains ribs 1 to 3 along with a large, lean rib-eye muscle. A second-cut roast contains ribs 4 to 7 with a smaller rib-eye muscle because it comes from nearer the chuck end. No worries. Both are eminently more tender than the tri-tips and sirloin roasts we cook at less extravagant times of the year.

The butcher beautifully trims away all but a modest covering of fat and does me a solid by separating the eye of the roast from the ribs. Then he ties both back together. The result: a beautiful boneless roast sitting on a rack of ribs. This extra care means the bones will add flavor and moisture during the cooking, yet the carving of the eye will be supereasy. After roasting and presenting the fabulous treat to the guests, I simply snip the strings, lift the boneless roast off the ribs and slice.

Herb-crusted standing rib roast

Prep: 25 minutes | Rest: 3 hours | Cook: 1 hour, 45 minutes | Makes: 8 to 10 servings

If no one wants them, I'll save the roasted bones to use in soup.

1 three-rib standing rib beef roast, usually 7½ to 8½ pounds, trimmed, tied

Traditional herb rub (see recipe on p. 264)

1 cup homemade or low-sodium beef broth

½ cup dry red wine

Salt, freshly ground black pepper

Mascarpone horseradish (recipe follows), for serving

① Put roast into a large shallow roasting pan. Coat generously on all sides with the rub. Position it in the pan fat side up and bone side down. Refrigerate uncovered at least 2 hours and up to 2 days. Remove roast from refrigerator 1 hour before cooking.

② Heat oven to 325 degrees. Cook roast until an instant-read thermometer registers about 130 degrees for medium-rare when inserted in the thickest portion away from the bone, usually 1½ to 1 ¾ hours. Remove roast from oven; tent with foil. Let rest, at least 15 minutes (or up to 30 minutes). The temperature will rise about 10 degrees.

③ To make a sauce, transfer the roast to a cutting board. Pour beef broth and wine into the roasting pan. Boil over high heat, scraping up any bits from the bottom of the pan. Taste and adjust seasonings with salt and pepper. Carve meat into ⅛- to ¼-inch-thick slices. Serve with the pan juices and pass the Mascarpone horseradish.

....

Nutrition information per serving: 424 calories, 25 g fat, 10 g saturated fat, 144 mg cholesterol, 1 g carbohydrates, 49 g protein, 1,323 mg sodium, 1 g fiber

Mascarpone horseradish: Whisk together 1 cup heavy (whipping) cream and ½ cup mascarpone until soft peaks. Whisk in 2 to 3 tablespoons prepared horseradish and 2 tablespoons Dijon mustard. Season to taste with salt and pepper.

ON THE GRILL

➤ It's best to monitor the grill temperature with an **oven thermometer** to prevent overcooking. Instead of the au jus, serve with the simple horseradish-spiked mascarpone for a nice accompaniment.

INDIRECT GRILLING

To grill roast by indirect grilling method (heat source not directly underneath the meat):

➤ Heat a gas grill to medium, and turn off the burners in the center of the grill. For a charcoal grill, heat hardwood charcoal until covered with gray ash, then arrange the coals on two sides of the grill and place a drip pan in the middle.

➤ Set the cooking grate in place, and let it heat for 5 minutes. Place the roast, fat side up, in the center of the grill (not directly over the heat source). If you have an oven thermometer, place it near the meat but not over the heat source. Cover the grill.

➤ Cook, checking the meat every 30 minutes and adding coals if necessary, until a meat thermometer registers about 130 degrees for medium-rare, about 1 hour 45 minutes. Remove from grill and tent with foil. Rest the meat, then carve and serve, as described in the main recipe.

For multigenerational gatherings, such as at Passover, the host's duty includes trying to please everyone.

Serving simple dishes without a lot of culinary trickery requires the best ingredients. For example, choose a lean brisket, make a seasoning rub from fresh spices, and add a delicious beef stock. Add plenty of sweet onions and prunes to melt into the flavorful broth.

While the brisket cooks, add a foil packet of seasoned beets to cook alongside. Then, serve the beets atop a salad of bitter greens dressed with vinaigrette flavored with a little walnut oil. (See recipe on p. 56.) Candied walnuts add a sweet touch everyone enjoys.

Peppered brisket with melted sweet onions and prunes

Preparation time: 25 minutes | Cooking time: 3 to 3½ hours | Yield: 12 servings

A commercial steak seasoning makes a suitable substitute here for the homemade rub.

5 pounds beef brisket, trimmed

2 to 4 tablespoons sea salt and four pepper seasoning, see recipe below

¼ cup safflower or expeller-pressed canola oil

4 large sweet onions, halved, thickly sliced

5 cloves garlic, chopped

2 cans (14½ ounces each) beef broth

1½ cups pitted prunes

¼ cup chopped fresh parsley

Note: For the sea salt and four pepper seasoning, combine 3 tablespoons coarse sea salt with 1 tablespoon freshly ground black pepper, ½ teaspoon each: freshly ground white pepper and sweet paprika, and ¼ teaspoon cayenne pepper.

① Heat oven to 325 degrees. Generously rub brisket on both sides with the seasoning. Heat a Dutch oven or heavy-bottomed roasting pan over medium heat. Add the oil; heat 30 seconds. Add the brisket; cook, without turning, until nicely browned, about 8 minutes. Turn; top with onions and garlic. Add broth; cover with foil and a lid.

② Bake for 2 hours. Add prunes; cover. Bake until the brisket is tender when pierced with a fork, about 1 hour. Uncover; turn the brisket. Bake until brisket lightly browns, about 15 minutes.

③ Transfer the brisket to a cutting board; tent with foil. Let stand 10 minutes before cutting into thin slices. Serve with pan juices, onions and prunes. Garnish with parsley.

Nutrition information per serving: 362 calories, 13 g fat, 4 g saturated fat, 81 mg cholesterol, 18 g carbohydrates, 41 g protein, 865 mg sodium, 2 g fiber

CHRISTMAS DINNER ROTATES IN OUR FAMILY—NOT WHERE WE GATHER but what we serve. Ideas get tossed around early in the season. Family members voice their opinions. Often our local butcher sways the decision. He likes roast pork for universal appeal and moderate cost. Not a fussy, crown roast in which two rib racks contort into a crown. Just a bone-in pork loin roasted flat for even cooking and supereasy carving. We're in!

There are only nine ribs per side of pig. A whole bone-in pork loin roast, with eight or nine ribs, weighs 5 to 6 pounds. Usually a serving is one rib bone with meat. I find it just as easy to cook two roasts when feeding a crowd. Always be sure to use a large enough roasting pan to accommodate the roast comfortably.

Holiday roast pork with Honeycrisp apples

Prep: 45 minutes | **Brine:** 8 hours | **Cook:** 1½ hours | **Makes:** 8 servings

If you wish, while the pork rests on the cutting board, make a quick pan sauce out of the drippings. Start by scooping the apple mixture into a serving bowl and covering it to keep it warm (and to prevent guests from stealing the fantastic apples). Then boil some red wine in the roasting pan while you scrape up the pork drippings; add broth and a little dissolved arrowroot to the pan and cook until thick enough to coat a spoon.

Red wine and rosemary brine:
- ⅓ cup each: coarse (kosher) salt, sugar
- ⅔ cup dry red wine
- ⅓ cup red wine vinegar
- 1 tablespoon juniper berries, optional (or 2-4 bay leaves)
- 1 tablespoon dried rosemary
- 1 teaspoon thyme
- ½ teaspoon crushed black pepper
- 5 to 6 pound bone-in pork loin roast, about 8 bones, chine bone removed, rib bones frenched

Roasting the pork:
- 6 large (2 pounds total) Honeycrisp apples, peeled, quartered, cored
- 1 pound small parsnips, peeled, halved lengthwise
- 6 to 8 cloves garlic
- ¼ cup plus 1 tablespoon olive oil
- 2 teaspoons thyme
- 1 teaspoon each: sage, table salt

Pan gravy:
- ½ cup red wine
- 1 cup chicken broth
- 1 tablespoon arrowroot (or tapioca starch or cornstarch) dissolved in ¼ cup water
- Fresh herbs for garnish

① For brine, dissolve coarse salt and sugar in 2 cups very hot water in a non-aluminum container large enough to hold the pork. Add red wine, vinegar, juniper berries, rosemary, thyme and the pepper. Add the pork; pour in enough cold water to cover the pork by about 1 inch, usually 2 to 2½ quarts. Refrigerate the pork, covered, for at least 8 hours or up to a day.

② To roast the pork, heat oven to 400 degrees. Cut apples into 1-inch-thick wedges. Cut parsnips into ½-inch-thick slices. Put both in the bottom of a large roasting pan. Add garlic, ¼ cup oil, 1 teaspoon thyme and half of the sage. Toss well to mix everything with the oil and herbs. Arrange the apple mixture around the edges of the roasting pan.

③ Remove pork from brine, discarding brine. Place pork in the center of the pan. Drizzle pork with remaining 1 tablespoon oil; sprinkle with remaining 1 teaspoon thyme and ½ teaspoon sage. Sprinkle with the salt. Roast pork, turning pan occasionally and basting meat and apples with accumulating pan juices, until a meat thermometer registers 145 to 150 degrees, 60-75 minutes.

④ Remove pork to a cutting board; cover loosely with foil. (Temperature will rise about 10 degrees.) Use a slotted spoon to transfer apple mixture to a serving bowl. Keep warm.

⑤ For pan gravy, pour wine into the roasting pan; boil hard on the stove-top while scraping up any browned bits. Whisk in broth and then the dissolved arrowroot. Cook, whisking constantly, until it's smooth and thickened. Season to taste with salt and pepper.

⑥ Serve pork by slicing between the bones into chops. Pass the pan gravy and apples. Garnish plates with fresh herbs.

....

Nutrition information per serving: 549 calories, 34 g fat, 10 g saturated fat, 124 mg cholesterol, 24 g carbohydrates, 38 g protein, 769 mg sodium, 3 g fiber

THANKSGIVING MIGHT JUST BE THE ULTIMATE POTLUCK. NEARLY EVERYONE we know loves this food-centric holiday. Long gone are the days of one person cooking the whole Thanksgiving dinner.

When it's my turn to bring a main course, I volunteer a braised turkey. I have the butcher cut the turkey into parts (like a chicken) for maximum flavor and moistness. I rub a spice blend evocative of Moroccan tagines to season the turkey. Then the turkey parts are arranged on a bed of vegetables with broth added to the pan.

You can cook the turkey at home and transport it safely while hot—it should be served within an hour or so out of the oven. Otherwise, cook it in advance, cool it and reheat gently before serving.

The recipe just might be the ultimate turkey to-go for all your holidays.

Braised turkey with Moroccan spices

Prep: 45 minutes | Cook: 2 hours | Makes: 12 to 14 servings | Pictured on p. 183

Most butchers will cut the turkey up for you. Za'atar, a blend of sumac, thyme, oregano, sesame and other seasonings, is available in the spice section of most large supermarkets, Whole Foods and online from thespicehouse.com.

1 turkey, 13 to 15 pounds

2 tablespoons za'atar seasoning blend

1 tablespoon each: ground cinnamon, turmeric

2 teaspoons each: ground cumin, garlic powder

½ teaspoon coarsely ground black pepper

¼ teaspoon cayenne, optional

2 or 3 carrots, diced

1 large onion, diced

1 large bulb fresh fennel, stalks and fronds removed, bulb diced

1 small leek, split, rinsed, diced

6 cloves garlic, crushed

2 teaspoons salt

① Remove the giblets and neck packets from the cavity of the turkey. Rinse turkey well and pat dry. Cut the turkey in portions like you would a chicken: First remove the legs and cut them apart into drumsticks and thighs. Then cut off the wings. Use kitchen shears to cut out the back bone. Use a large knife or kitchen shears to carefully split the turkey breast down the middle into two halves.

② Mix all the spices together in a small bowl. Rub the mixture on all sides of the turkey breast halves, thighs and drumsticks set on a baking sheet in a single layer. Rubbed turkey can be refrigerated, loosely covered, up to several days.

③ Put the giblets (not the liver), neck, wings and backbone into a large pot. Add cold water to cover by 2 inches, usually 3 quarts. Simmer, adding water if needed, 2 to 3 hours. Strain into a bowl, discarding the solids. Refrigerate broth for up to 3 days. You should have about 6 cups.

④ Heat the oven to 350 degrees. Mix carrots, onion, fennel, leek and garlic in the bottom of a large metal baking pan. Nestle the turkey parts into the vegetables in a single uncrowded layer. Sprinkle everything with salt.

⑤ Put the pan in the oven. Carefully pour 3 to 4 cups of the turkey broth into the pan, taking care not to pour it over the rubbed turkey; you don't want to wash off the rub. The broth should come halfway up the sides of the meat. Cook until an instant-read thermometer registers 160 degrees when inserted in the breast and the juices run clear, about 1 hour. Use tongs to remove breasts to a cutting board. Continue cooking the thighs and legs, 15-20 minutes.

⑥ Arrange all the turkey pieces on a platter or cutting board. Let turkey rest about 10 minutes before slicing. Skim off and discard any fat from the pan juices. The juices can be thickened to make a gravy, using a cornstarch slurry (a tablespoon of cornstarch dissolved in a little cold water). Serve the vegetables with the sliced turkey.

....

Nutrition information per serving (for 14 servings): 417 calories, 13 g fat, 4 g saturated fat, 239 mg cholesterol, 6 g carbohydrates, 65 g protein, 500 mg sodium, 2 g fiber

CORNISH HENS HANG OUT IN THE FREEZER CASES OF MOST LARGE SUPER-markets. Plan ahead—they'll take 2 days in the fridge to thaw completely. Occasionally, you'll also find them in the fresh meat case.

A simple curry-based roasting rub adds flavor, as does a pile of sweet onions in the bottom of the pan. Roasting, the easiest cooking technique to master, simply requires a heavy-duty pan and a reliable oven. Use the convection setting if it's an option; the skin will brown beautifully.

Spice-rubbed Cornish hens with sweet onions and rice

Prep: 30 minutes | Cook: 45 minutes | Makes: 8 servings

If sweet onions are not available, substitute large yellow onions and add ¼ to ½ teaspoon sugar or honey.

4 Rock Cornish hens, 1¼ pounds each, rinsed, patted dry

2 tablespoons curry roasting rub, see note

2 large sweet onions, halved, thinly sliced

1 large leek, quartered lengthwise, well rinsed, roughly chopped

1 cup currants or raisins

¼ cup olive oil

2 pouches (about 8 ounces each) fully-cooked brown rice or 4 cups warm cooked rice

Flat leaf parsley sprigs

① Cut the backbone out of the hens with kitchen shears by cutting along either side of it. Then flatten the hens a bit on the cutting board. Use the shears to cut the hens in half through the breast bone. Tuck the wing tip under the wing. Coat the hens on all sides with the curry roasting rub.

② Mix the onions, leek, currants and oil in the bottom of a 13-by-9-inch baking dish. Transfer half of the mixture into a second 13-by-9-inch baking dish. Arrange 4 hen halves in each pan over the onions.

(You can prepare the recipe to this point 1 day in advance; refrigerate tightly covered.)

③ Heat oven to 400 degrees (or 375 degrees if using convection). Roast the hens until skin is nicely browned and juices run clear when the thigh is gently pierced, about 45 minutes. Remove hens to a warm platter; tent with foil.

④ Microwave the rice as directed on pouch, usually about 90 seconds each. Stir the rice into the onion mixture in the bottom of the baking pans. Transfer the rice to a serving bowl. Garnish the hens with parsley; serve with the rice.

Nutrition information per serving: 615 calories, 37 g fat, 9 g saturated fat, 210 mg cholesterol, 32 g carbohydrates, 39 g protein, 545 mg sodium, 3 g fiber

Note: For a curry roasting rub, mix 2 tablespoons curry powder, 1 tablespoon salt and 2 teaspoons dried basil in a bowl.

ROAST DUCK, LIKE BEEF TENDERLOIN AND LOBSTER, DEFINES HOLIDAY MEALS in our family. More than Sunday dinner fare, a duck in the oven warrants celebration—of dining with friends, of indulgent goodness and of the enjoyable act of cooking.

My younger sister's friends surprised me recently when we gathered for an evening of girl talk. When the conversation shifted to food, which happens a lot when I am around, duck talk took center stage. Nearly everyone in the room loved eating it, most had attempted to cook it, and two had great fun boning a duck a la Julia Child. All lamented the excessive richness of most recipes and the fact that duck in this country is nearly always sold whole and frozen solid.

I found fresh duck breasts at a specialty market and boneless duck fillets in the freezer case of several supermarkets. The quick-cooking fillets have an enormous convenience factor. When I have time, I find cutting a thawed whole duck into boneless breasts and easy-to-roast legs easier than cutting up a chicken.

The beauty of cut-up duck? Crisp skin, moist and flavorful meat, moderate richness, quicker cooking, portion control, ease of service, attractive presentation. My holiday dinner just became a no-brainer.

I'll roast the legs until the fat renders out, the skin crisps and the meat is fall-apart tender. For the boneless breasts, just 10 minutes in a hot pan and then a final 10 in a superhot oven will yield medium-pink interiors and stunning flavor.

A blend of sweet spices seasons the duck pieces and fills the house with a great aroma while the duck cooks. Complementing the spices, a ginger glazing sauce finishes the duck beautifully. The glaze simply combines cooked shallots, wine and duck broth along with a generous portion of ginger preserves.

Spiced duck with ginger glaze

Prep: 45 minutes | Cook: 1½ hours | Makes: 8 pieces, serving 6

Ask your butcher to cut up the ducks if you prefer; indicate that you want two boneless breast halves, two whole legs and the carcass for making broth.

2 whole ducks, each about 6 pounds, rinsed
Poultry spice rub (see recipe on p. 274)
Ginger glazing sauce, heated (recipe follows)
Fresh parsley sprigs

① Rinse ducks; pat dry. Remove duck breasts by cutting down the breast bone with a very sharp knife and working the knife along the carcass to free the breast. Repeat to remove the breast on the other side. Use the knife to remove the legs at the joint.

② Lightly coat the duck breasts and the legs with the spice rub, about 1 tablespoon per duck. Place on a rack set in a baking pan. Refrigerate covered, 1 hour or up to 24 hours.

③ Heat oven to 350 degrees. Set duck breasts aside. Roast the legs on the rack in the baking pan until the juices run clear, 1-1¼ hours. Let rest covered with foil while you cook the breasts.

④ Increase oven temperature to 400. Heat a large, well-seasoned cast-iron skillet (or two smaller skillets) over medium-low heat until hot. Add the breasts, skin side down, in a single, uncrowded layer. Cook over low without turning until skin is crisped and nicely browned, about 10 minutes. Flip breasts skin side up; place in oven. Cook until medium rare (breast will be nearly firm at edges but still soft when pressed in the center), 10-12 minutes.

⑤ To serve, thinly slice the duck breasts. Some guests get a leg and a few slices of the duck breast, while others get all breast. Serve with the ginger sauce; garnish with parsley.

....

Nutrition information per serving: 498 calories, 26 g fat, 8 g saturated fat, 195 mg cholesterol, 13 g carbohydrates, 50 g protein, 415 mg sodium, 0 g fiber

Ginger glazing sauce

Makes: about 1½ cups

This ginger glazing sauce finishes a duck dish beautifully. The glaze combines cooked shallots, wine and duck broth along with a generous portion of ginger preserves.

4 shallots, finely chopped

2 tablespoons butter

½ cup dry white wine

2 cups unsalted or low-sodium duck or chicken broth

2 tablespoons cornstarch

¼ cup cold water

½ cup ginger preserves

1 tablespoon balsamic vinegar (or more to taste)

½ teaspoon salt

Freshly ground black pepper, to taste

① Cook the shallots in the butter in a saucepan over medium heat until golden, about 3 minutes. Stir in the wine; boil until reduced to a glaze, about 3 minutes. Stir in the broth; simmer over low, about 20 minutes. Dissolve the cornstarch in the cold water; vigorously whisk mixture into broth. Cook, whisking constantly, until boiling and thickened. Stir in the ginger preserves, balsamic vinegar, salt and pepper. Taste; adjust seasonings.

MOST OF THE YEAR WE ENJOY CULINARY FREEDOM, COOKING AND EATING whatever strikes our fancy, from elaborate ethnic favorites to all-popcorn dinners. Not so much when it comes to Thanksgiving dinner. So every time we roast a turkey, we lovingly re-create a handful of childhood taste memories.

Take turkey stuffing (never call it "dressing" in our house), for example. It stands to reason for the chief cook and bottle washer to make the sausage and apple stuffing of her childhood, but now with whole wheat bread in place of white.

Sausage, apple and whole wheat bread stuffing

Prep: 45 minutes | Cook: 1 hour | Makes: 18 servings

Order bulk pork sausage from the local butcher for the best flavor; in a pinch, use the tubes of pork breakfast sausage (select the lower fat options) from the supermarket meat case. The beaten eggs give the stuffing a super-light texture. Make a simple turkey stock by simmering the neck, giblets and wing tips in water for an hour or so.

1½ pounds sliced hearty whole wheat bread

1 pound lean bulk pork sausage (no casing)

3 ribs celery, finely chopped

1 large sweet onion, diced

3 large eggs, lightly beaten

3 crisp apples, peeled, cored, diced

1 cup raisins or dried cranberries

2 tablespoons each, finely chopped: fresh sage, fresh parsley

2 teaspoons each: salt, dried thyme

1 teaspoon finely chopped fresh tarragon or ½ teaspoon dried

1 teaspoon finely chopped fresh rosemary or ½ teaspoon dried

1 quart turkey stock or chicken broth

① Heat oven to 350 degrees. Lay the bread slices out on 2 or 3 baking sheets in a single layer. Bake, turning bread slices over once, until crisp and lightly toasted, about 20 minutes. Tear bread into bite-size pieces; place in a large bowl or roasting pan.

② Meanwhile, cook the sausage in a large skillet, breaking it into small pieces with a spatula, until cooked through, about 12 minutes. Add celery and onion; cook, stirring, until crisp-tender, about 5 minutes. Add the sausage mixture to the bread. Stir in eggs, apples, raisins and seasonings; mix well. Add the stock; stir until bread is moistened.

③ Transfer the mixture to 2 well-buttered 3-quart baking dishes. Cover with lids or buttered heavy-duty foil. Bake until piping hot in the center and the edges are crispy, about 45 minutes.

....

Nutrition information per serving: 197 calories, 6 g fat, 2 g saturated fat, 43 mg cholesterol, 27 g carbohydrates, 9 g protein, 826 mg sodium, 4 g fiber

NO MATTER WHAT WE'RE COOKING, WE ALWAYS USE THE FRESHEST INGREDIENTS possible. That means real potatoes in the mash and fresh garlic and herbs throughout. We're always looking for more ways to boost flavor. Lately we've been adding whole spices and chunks of garlic to the rice cooker for flavorful rice without calories. So we're taking the same approach with our mashed potatoes by adding garlic and herbs to the cooking water. The results are amazing.

Sage and garlic mashed potatoes

Prep: 20 minutes | Cook: 30 minutes | Makes: 8 to 10 servings

You can peel the potatoes if you wish; I enjoy the look and flavor of the skins. A combination of golden potatoes and russets yield great flavor and texture.

6 or 8 sprigs fresh sage

1 or 2 sprigs fresh rosemary

1½ pounds (about 6 medium) Yukon gold potatoes, scrubbed, cut into 2-inch chunks

1½ pounds (about 3 medium) russet baking potatoes, scrubbed, cut into 2-inch chunks

4 to 6 large cloves garlic, peeled, roughly chopped

2½ teaspoons salt

½ cup each: skim milk, half-and-half

½ cup (1 stick) unsalted butter, softened

Freshly ground black pepper

① Separate sage and rosemary leaves from stems. Slice leaves finely; set aside. Tie stems together with kitchen string.

② Put potatoes, garlic and herb stems into a large pot. Add cold water to cover by 1 inch. Add 1½ teaspoons salt. Heat to a boil; simmer gently with lid slightly askew. Cook, checking potatoes occasionally with a knife, until tender, 15 to 20 minutes. Drain well. Discard herb stems.

③ Return the potatoes and garlic to the pot. Make a well in the center; pour in the milk and half-and-half. Set the heat to medium. When the milk starts to boil, reduce the heat to low; start mashing vigorously using a potato masher. Add about three-fourths of the soft butter; continue mashing until the mixture is fairly smooth. Season to taste, usually about 1 teaspoon salt and ½ teaspoon pepper. Remove from heat.

④ Meanwhile, melt remaining butter in small, nonstick skillet. Add herb leaves; saute until crisped, about 1 minute. Pile hot potatoes into a heated serving dish. Spoon sage butter over potatoes.

Nutrition information per serving (for 10 servings): 226 calories, 11 g fat, 7 g saturated fat, 29 mg cholesterol, 28 g carbohydrates, 4 g protein, 437 mg sodium, 2 g fiber

HOLIDAY SIDE DISH BOOSTS

➤ Use the **freshest ingredients** you can find: The results are worth it. Look for time-saving fresh ingredients such as bags of trimmed fresh green beans, diced root vegetables and squash.

➤ Use **unsalted butter**. It tastes sweeter and fresher and allows the cook to adjust salt to taste.

➤ Splurge on **fresh herbs**. Fresh sage in the stuffing and chives in the mashed potatoes prove worth the expense and effort.

➤ **A mixture of russet and golden potatoes** yields light, fluffy mashed potatoes that have a rich color and flavor.

➤ **To keep mashed potatoes warm**, put a piece of plastic wrap directly over the surface. Cover the pot and wrap it in a heavy towel. Potatoes will stay warm about 30 minutes.

➤ **Green beans** (as well as broccoli, carrots and cauliflower) can be blanched (cooked in boiling water) up to two days in advance; rinse with cold water to stop the cooking. When cool, shake them dry and store in a container in the refrigerator. Then season or sauce shortly before serving.

CHAPTER 9

Breakfast for Dinner

Julia Child taught us everything we know about crepes: They cook in less than a minute, they can be made days ahead and they taste great sweet or savory. She also advocated making the crepe batter in advance so the flour absorbs the liquid, creating tender, lacy thin pancakes every time. In her 1989 book, "The Way to Cook," she advises using instant-blending flour to shorten the waiting time. That works well, but these days, I swap a little of the all-purpose flour with whole wheat for a nutty taste and more healthful profile.

I've also switched from whole milk to skim in the batter. When I cooked crepes side-by-side with skim and with whole, the results showed little difference. So I'm happy to use skim and skip the added fat.

We fussed mightily to properly season our steel crepe pan (carried back from France on an anniversary trip). Now, we simply enlist a small nonstick skillet. Piece of cake to make a thin crepe that slides right out of the pan. More great news from the nonstick world: Zero fat is needed to cook the crepes. Simply use a hot skillet for fewer calories, less stove splatter and easier cleanup.

Two tricky things about cooking crepes—knowing how much heat to use and how much batter per crepe. I work over medium to medium-high heat. I heat the pan pretty thoroughly before adding batter: A drop of water should evaporate upon contact. Keep adjusting the heat so the pan is hot enough to start cooking the batter as soon as it hits the pan but does not burn the delicate pancake. You'll want to practice a bit with just how much batter you need. Pour the batter in, then swirl it around to cover the bottom into a thin crepe. For the thinnest crepes, pour off any excess back into the batter bowl.

Stack cooked crepes on top of each other to keep them warm. Cooked crepes also can be cooled on a wire rack for later use. Store the cooled crepes in a covered container and refrigerate for several days. Leftover crepes make a terrific snack when smeared with a thin coating of cream cheese, cookie butter—a ground cookie spread known as speculoos; fig jam or even softened ice cream. Or, make a lunch rollup by layering smoked ham and cheese and a smear of mayo over the crepe then roll into a cigar shape.

Sweet crepes with lemony grapefruit curd

Prep: 15 minutes | Makes: 4 servings

Use fresh berries mashed with a little sugar when they are in season. Jarred lemon curd can be substituted for the homemade lemony grapefruit curd. I also like to smear the crepes with apple butter or pumpkin butter and garnish with sauteed apples in place of the berries.

3 tablespoons mascarpone or creme fraiche

A little half-and-half or milk

10 warm cooked 7-inch whole wheat crepes (recipe follows)

About ¾ cup Lemony grapefruit curd (see recipe on p. 270), at room temperature

½ cup mixed frozen unsweetened berries (such as raspberries, blueberries, sliced small strawberries), thawed

Powdered sugar

① Whisk the mascarpone and a little half-and-half in a small bowl until light and almost pourable. Place 1 crepe on a serving plate. Smear with about 1 tablespoon curd. Fold into quarters and place on serving plate. Repeat to fill and fold all crepes. Spoon thinned mascarpone over the crepes. Spoon berries over all. Sprinkle with powdered sugar.

Nutrition information per serving: 456 calories, 24 g fat, 13 g saturated fat, 234 mg cholesterol, 211 g carbohydrates, 13 g protein, 164 mg sodium, 1 g fiber

Whole wheat crepes

Prep: 10 minutes | Chill: 1 hour or overnight | Cook: 15 minutes | Makes: 14 to 16 crepes

I suggest you don't skip the melted butter added to the batter after the resting. It helps with flavor and tenderness and to release the pancake from the pan.

1½ cups skim milk

3 large eggs

1⅓ cups unbleached all-purpose flour

⅓ cup whole wheat flour

⅛ teaspoon salt

1 to 2 tablespoons butter

① Measure milk into a blender; add eggs. Process to mix. Add flours and salt. Blend until smooth. Put the batter (I leave it in the blender jar) into the refrigerator, at least 1 hour or preferably overnight. (Batter will keep in the refrigerator for several days. If necessary, thin it with a little milk to bring it back to the consistency of cream soup.)

② After batter has chilled, melt the butter in a small dish in the microwave; stir it into the crepe batter.

③ Heat a 7- or 9-inch nonstick skillet over medium-high heat until a drop of water evaporates on contact. Pour or ladle in about ¼ cup batter. Immediately swirl the pan to distribute batter into a thin, even layer. Tip excess batter back into container. Cook just until golden on the bottom, 20 to 30 seconds. Carefully flip the crepe; cook the second side just long enough to color it, about 15 seconds.

④ Slide the crepe onto a plate. Repeat to cook all the crepes. When cool, the crepes can be wrapped and kept in the refrigerator for several days.

TIPS

➤ The number of crepes that the basic batter yields will depend on the diameter of your pan and how adept you are at making a thin pancake.

➤ If making crepes in advance, separate them with plastic wrap before chilling.

➤ For savory crepes, you can add 2 or 3 tablespoons chopped fresh herbs to the basic batter. For sweet crepes, you can add a tablespoon of sugar.

Nutrition information per crepe (for 16 crepes): 74 calories, 2 g fat, 1 g saturated fat, 37 mg cholesterol, 11 g carbohydrates, 3 g protein, 44 mg sodium, 1 g fiber

DECADES AGO, OUR FAMILY SPENT VACATIONS CAMPING IN ARKANSAS. WE'D eat out twice: once for fried catfish and hush puppies and the other time for a pancake breakfast. Reading the menus in the Mountain Home cafe, my Chicago-born siblings and I would marvel at the odd-sounding options, especially biscuits and gravy. We knew biscuits: Our mom served them for dessert with fresh strawberries and whipped cream. But breakfast? With sausage gravy? Not so much.

I was newly married and a culinary school graduate when I ordered them at a coffee shop in Brown County, Ind. Fluffy white biscuits split open and completely covered in a pale, chunky white sauce. My husband immediately embraced the richness. My conversion proved slower. During three decades of travel together, we've continued to order the dish whenever it appears on menus. A diner in Austin, Texas, filled with antique mixers, toasters and coffee pots, serves my favorite rendition: Crusty, herb-riddled biscuits topped with gravy flavored with rusty red, spicy chorizo sausage.

We incorporate this version into our special occasion weekend breakfasts. So much so that I stock the freezer with chorizo and keep the vegetable shortening chilled. To make the morning prep go faster, I mix all the dry ingredients for the biscuits together in advance. No matter the recipe, warm, fresh-baked biscuits always gratify.

Herbed breakfast biscuits

Prep: 25 minutes | Cook: 12 minutes | Makes: 12 biscuits | Pictured on p. 199-201

The best tip for light, fluffy and delicious biscuits: Do not use excess baking powder. The biscuits will have a bitter, metallic aftertaste (which I always detect in the refrigerated dough versions). That's also my problem with self-rising flour and buttermilk baking mixes—excessive leavening giving an off taste. It's simple enough to mix flour, salt and baking powder anyway.

1½ cups all-purpose flour

½ cup whole wheat flour (or more all-purpose flour)

2½ teaspoons baking powder

2 to 3 teaspoons sugar, to taste

½ teaspoon salt

3 tablespoons cold unsalted butter, diced

3 tablespoons trans fat-free vegetable shortening, very cold

3 to 4 tablespoons chopped fresh cilantro or chives (or a combination)

¾ cup whole milk or half-and-half, very cold

Milk for brushing on top

① Heat oven to 425 degrees. Put flours, baking powder, sugar and salt into a food processor or into a large bowl. Pulse or stir to mix. Drop diced butter and shortening randomly over the flour mixture. Pulse or use two knives to cut the butter and shortening into the flours until the mixture resembles coarse crumbs. Stir in herbs. Sprinkle the milk over the mixture. Pulse or stir until the mixture barely gathers into a ball.

② Transfer to a piece of floured wax paper; gather into a ball. Cover with a second piece of floured wax paper; gently roll or press into an even ½-inch-thick circle.

Use a floured 3-inch round biscuit cutter or drinking glass to cut into circles. Place the circles on a parchment-lined baking sheet. Very gently gather up the scraps; roll into a ½-inch-thick piece and cut more biscuits.

③ Brush the tops with milk; bake until tops are golden, 12-15 minutes. Cool on wire rack. Serve warm.

....

Nutrition information per biscuit: 141 calories, 7 g fat, 3 g saturated fat, 9 mg cholesterol, 17 g carbohydrates, 3 g protein, 219 mg sodium, 1 g fiber

Chorizo and roasted pepper sausage gravy

Prep: 15 minutes | Cook: 15 minutes | Makes: 6 servings | Pictured on p. 200-201

Seasoned pork sausage, crumbled and skillet-browned, flavors the classic milk-based gravy served throughout the South. If the sausage is good, so follows the gravy, since it's based on the sausage drippings.

1 package (12 ounces) pork or beef Mexican
    chorizo sausage, casings removed

1 small onion, finely chopped

3 cups whole milk

6 tablespoons flour

1 small red bell pepper, roasted, peeled, seeded,
    diced (or ½ cup diced bottled roasted red
    bell pepper)

½ teaspoon salt

Freshly ground black pepper

Chopped fresh cilantro

① Crumble chorizo sausage into a cast-iron pan or nonstick skillet. Add onion. Cook until nicely browned, about 10 minutes. Transfer sausage and onion with a slotted spoon to a plate.

② Drain off all but 2 tablespoons of the pan drippings. Mix ½ cup of the milk and the flour in a small bowl until smooth. Stir into pan drippings; stir in remaining milk. Cook, stirring, over medium heat until smooth and thickened, about 5 minutes.

③ Stir in sausage, diced red pepper, salt and black pepper to taste. Heat to warm through, 1-2 minutes. Serve over biscuits; sprinkle generously with cilantro.

....

Nutrition information per serving: 369 calories, 26 g fat, 10 g saturated fat, 62 mg cholesterol, 15 g carbohydrates, 19 g protein, 948 mg sodium, 1 g fiber

No matter the recipe, warm, fresh-baked biscuits always gratify.

Herbed breakfast biscuits (p. 197) and Chorizo and roasted pepper chorizo gravy (p. 198)

RECENTLY, EVEN A PRE-DAWN AIRPORT TRIP LEFT ME EAGER TO COOK (AND EAT): The taxicab driver spoke passionately of the food his Syrian family relishes daily. With the dark and bitter cold outside, the driver had me at "grilled breakfast sandwich." My mouth watered and my brain raced to absorb everything he described. Sure as I was sitting there, I knew I'd be making his recipes.

The ultimate steak and egg sandwich

Prep: 20 minutes | Cook: 10 minutes | Makes: 4 servings

This sandwich can be grilled in a panini press if you have one. Cut in half before grilling if that is easier.

1 loaf ciabatta bread or a wide baguette, about 10 inches long and 3 inches wide

Olive oil

12 to 14 ounces very thin (less than ¼-inch) sliced sandwich beef steak, such as boneless rib-eye or sirloin

Chopped fresh oregano (or dried)

Salt, freshly ground black pepper

2 or 3 large eggs

6 to 8 very thin slices fresh Syrian cheese or fresh mozzarella (about 6 ounces total)

Hot chili paste, optional

① Cut the bread horizontally in half. Drizzle olive oil over the cut sides of the bread.

② Season the steak slices to taste with olive oil, oregano, salt and pepper. Heat a heavy nonstick skillet or seasoned cast-iron skillet over medium-high heat. Add the steak to the skillet in a single, uncrowded layer. Cook until golden and the meat just releases from the pan, about 1 minute. Flip and cook the second side until golden, about 1 minute. Do not overcook. Place steaks on the bottom half of the bread. Drizzle the top half of the bread with any pan juices.

③ Lightly oil the skillet or griddle, then crack the eggs onto it. Cook eggs until almost set, 1 or 2 minutes; flip and cook the second side until eggs are done to your preference, about 30 seconds more for medium. Place eggs over steaks on bread. Sprinkle with salt and pepper; top with the cheese slices. Close the sandwich.

④ Wipe the skillet or griddle clean; heat it until medium hot. Add the sandwich; place a heavy skillet on top of the sandwich to compress it down a bit. (The yolk may break, spreading its gooey richness into the bread; this is good.) Cook until bottom of sandwich is golden, about 2 minutes. Carefully flip the sandwich to crisp and brown the top.

⑤ Set the sandwich right-side up on a cutting board. Use a serrated knife to cut it into 4 sections. Serve hot with a smear of chili paste if desired.

Nutrition information per serving : 725 calories, 24 g fat, 9 g saturated fat, 167 mg cholesterol, 79 g carbohydrates, 47 g protein, 1,384 mg sodium, 4 g fiber

WE HIT THE AUSTIN DINER HARD ON OUR FIRST VISIT TO AUSTIN. We've not stopped wishing for a plate of migas with a side of black beans since.

Fortunately, an anniversary celebration took us back to the Live Music Capital of the World. The Austin Diner did not let us down—an indulgent, filling and slightly spicy plate of eggs scrambled with broken tortillas, aka migas, fulfilled our dreams.

It also fueled a decision—we need to learn to make migas at home. After all, they're just scrambled eggs with tortillas and veggies. The trick: Make them as irresistible as the restaurant's version.

Migas, it turns out, probably arrived in Texas as an import from Spain where they use up leftover bread by frying it in oil and scrambling in a few eggs. Tortillas prove more plentiful than bread in parts of Texas—so it makes sense that this rustic dish would use leftover tortillas. The dish reminds us of our favorite Mexican almuerzo (lunch) dish: chilaquiles (leftover tortilla chips softened in brothy sauce and topped with fresh garnishes).

Think of this recipe as the starting point for creativity. For variations:

- Replace the chorizo with 2 cups shredded cooked beef, pork or chicken (skip the first step and add the shredded meat to the cooked vegetables as directed).
- Switch out the smoky chipotle chili with pickled or fresh jalapeno.
- Try crumbled goat cheese or queso fresco (fresh Mexican cheese) in place of the shredded cheese.
- A handful or two of fresh chopped spinach leaves will make an attractive replacement for the green peppers.

Chipotle migas with chorizo

Prep: 30 minutes | Cook: 20 minutes | Makes: 6 servings

Remember that whenever you are cooking eggs, all the ingredients should be prepped and ready before you turn on the stove.

½ package (from a 12-ounce package) Mexican pork chorizo, removed from casing

2 tablespoons olive oil

½ sweet or Vidalia onion, chopped

1 cup sliced mushrooms

½ each, chopped: red bell pepper, green bell pepper

1 canned chipotle chili, removed from sauce, finely chopped

1 large ripe tomato, halved, seeded, diced

12 large eggs

¼ cup each: half-and-half, water

½ teaspoon salt

2 cups coarsely crumbled tortilla chips (about 4 ounces)

1 cup shredded Mexican cheese blend, optional

Chopped fresh cilantro, diced avocado, optional

Saucy black beans (recipe follows)

① Crumble chorizo into a large (12-inch) nonstick skillet. Cook over medium heat, stirring often, until golden, 8 minutes. Remove from pan to a paper-towel-lined plate. Wipe the skillet clean.

② Heat oil in skillet; add onion and mushrooms. Cook until crisp-tender, about 5 minutes. Stir in bell peppers; cook until tender, about 3 minutes. Stir in chili, tomato and cooked chorizo. Remove from heat. (You can do this up to 30 minutes in advance; divide the mixture between two nonstick skillets if you are not using a 12-inch skillet.)

③ Shortly before serving, whisk together eggs, half-and-half, water and salt in a large bowl. Stir in tortilla chips to moisten them.

④ Heat the chorizo mixture in the skillet(s) over medium heat until sizzling. Add the egg mixture. Reduce the heat to medium-low; gently scramble the eggs. When eggs are nearly set, stir in the cheese. Continue gently moving around the egg curds until set but still moist, for a total cooking time of about 5 minutes.

⑤ Spoon onto serving plates. Garnish with cilantro and avocado. Serve with Saucy black beans.

....

Nutrition information per serving (without cheese or beans): 350 calories, 25 g fat, 8 g saturated fat, 343 mg cholesterol, 13 g carbohydrates, 18 g protein, 645 mg sodium, 2 g fiber

Saucy black beans: Mix 2 cans (15 ounces each) drained and rinsed black beans with 1 jar (16 ounces) salsa in a microwave-safe bowl. Microwave on high, stirring once or twice until hot, about 2 minutes. Serve in small bowls.

On a recent vacation to Austria, I was bombarded with memories of my paternal grandparents. Everywhere we traveled, we encountered the bacons and sausages my grandfather cured in his smokehouse and the sweets my gram made so lovingly in their Chicago bungalow: kuchens and strudels of all flavors.

When we stopped at Manuela's Radlerstation in Hossgang, Austria, for Topflenstrudel (cheese strudel) and Kaiserschmarrn (a pancake), I felt certain my gram was in the kitchen. Manuela's delicious flaky, rich treat comes *thisclose* to gram's legendary strudel. The pancake likewise brought back memories of her home, which often smelled of butter and sugar baking.

Kaiserschmarrn (also Kaiserschmarren), the torn emperor's pancake, just might be the perfect recipe for pancake novices because it's meant to be served torn up and ragged-looking. The only tricky part is separating eggs so the whites can be beaten for a light textured batter. The soft batter simply gets scraped into an oiled skillet. No shaping skills required. After the first side is browned, a metal spatula makes easy work of cutting the pancake into quarters for flipping. The pancake then spends a brief time in the oven while everyone gathers at the table. A generous sprinkling of confectioners' sugar makes it all look great.

Kaiserschmarrn (Emperor's pancakes)

Prep: 25 minutes | Cook: 20 minutes | Makes: 3 to 4 servings

This is also great served with warmed maple syrup.

4 large eggs, separated

1½ cups milk

½ teaspoon vanilla

1¼ cups flour

Grated zest from 1 lemon

⅛ teaspoon salt

¼ cup granulated sugar

Vegetable oil, such as sunflower or safflower oil for high-heat cooking

¼ cup raisins, dried cranberries or diced dried apricots

3 to 4 tablespoons melted butter

Confectioners' sugar

Jammy plums (see recipe on p. 267) or your favorite fruit preserves

① Heat oven to 350 degrees. Have 2 large (10- or 12-inch) ovenproof nonstick skillets or well-seasoned cast-iron skillets ready.

② Separate eggs, putting egg yolks into a large bowl and egg whites into a medium mixing bowl. Add milk and vanilla to yolks. Whisk until smooth; then stir in flour, lemon zest and salt until smooth.

③ With clean beaters in the other bowl, beat egg whites on high speed until frothy. Gradually beat in granulated sugar until soft peaks form. Do not overbeat. Gently fold beaten whites into flour mixture just until streaks of white disappear. Do not overmix.

④ Heat the skillets over medium-high heat. Very lightly film the pans with oil. Reduce heat under skillets to low. Scrape batter evenly into skillets. It'll be about 1 inch deep. Sprinkle each pan with raisins. Cook on low until bottoms are golden, about 3 minutes. Cut the pancakes into quarters; gently flip each piece so the uncooked side is on the bottom. Put the skillets into the oven. Bake until puffed and golden on both sides, about 10 minutes. (Recipe can be made up to 30 minutes in advance to this point.)

⑤ To serve, use two forks to break the pancakes up into random-size, torn pieces. Drizzle with melted butter and sprinkle generously with confectioners' sugar. Return to oven to glaze the pancakes, about 3 to 5 minutes. Serve sprinkled again with confectioners' sugar. Pass fruit to dollop on as desired.

....

Nutrition information per serving (for 4 servings): 478 calories, 23 g fat, 9 g saturated fat, 216 mg cholesterol, 56 g carbohydrates, 14 g protein, 190 mg sodium, 2 g fiber

MY COOKBOOK ASSORTMENT RIVALS MY HUSBAND'S VINYL COLLECTION. Supersturdy shelving houses both obsessions. Fortunately, when something from his collection blasts on the turntable, I retreat to the kitchen with mine.

At last count, I have more than 10 cookbooks on Moroccan cooking, several on Indian, dozens on Italian fare and French pastry, nearly a hundred on American cooking and even one on Lebanese cuisine. So it comes as a surprise that I have nary a volume on traditional Irish cooking. A recent recipe search for Irish boxty, the tender potato pancake we so enjoyed in Dublin, proved fruitless.

A delicious serving of corned beef and sauerkraut-stuffed boxty at an Irish pub in Milwaukee reignited the search. I knew I wanted to make these tender, potato-laced pancakes at home for our St. Patrick's Day celebration.

A couple of basic tools make quick work of the batter: A microwave oven speedily bakes the russet potato. A four-sided box grater, an inexpensive and indispensable tool, quickly shreds the raw potato and grates the onion. A heavy-bottomed nonstick skillet (or well-seasoned griddle) allows the cook to use minimal fat for cooking the cakes.

Batter in hand, you can vary the size of the pancakes to suit. Larger pancakes, spread thinly in the pan, prove dinner worthy. Top one half of each cake with a savory filling, such as a creamy curried chicken and cabbage mixture. Then fold the other half of the pancake over the filling. A sprinkling of fresh herbs turn these humble breads into company fare. Smaller, silver-dollar-size cakes (skip the onion in the batter) beautifully soak up pure maple syrup or a fruity compote.

Irish boxty are so versatile they're sure to be a standard in your repertoire all year long. Hopefully, someone will put an Irish tune on the stereo while you cook.

Irish boxty (potato pancakes)

Prep: 20 minutes | Cook: 20 minutes | Makes: Sixteen 3-inch pancakes, or 8 larger pancakes, serving 4 to 6

Omit the onion if you plan to serve the boxty with maple syrup or fresh fruit. Use a ¼-cup measure to make pancakes about 3 or 4 inches in diameter. For large pancakes that you can fill and fold, use ½ cup of batter and spread it thinly in the pan. If working in advance, re-crisp the pancakes in a hot skillet.

2 large (12 ounces each) Russet potatoes (total 1½ pounds), scrubbed clean

¾ cup flour

¾ teaspoon salt

½ teaspoon baking powder

1 cup skim milk or half-and-half (or a combination)

¼ of a medium red onion

Bacon drippings or olive oil, optional

① Pierce one potato in several places with a fork. Microwave on high (100 percent power) until fork-tender, 5-6 minutes. Cool.

② Mix flour, salt and baking powder in large bowl. Whisk in milk until smooth.

③ Put a four-sided grater in a colander, set inside a large bowl. Use the side with the large holes to grate the onion into the colander. Transfer the onion to the flour mixture. Shred the unpeeled raw potato on the large holes into the colander. Use your hands to squeeze the shredded potato to remove as much liquid as possible. Stir the squeezed potato into the flour mixture until incorporated.

④ Peel the cooked potato; mash the flesh coarsely. Fold into the batter until incorporated.

⑤ Heat a large nonstick skillet or griddle over medium heat. Grease the skillet with a light coating of bacon drippings or oil. Measure batter into skillet, using ¼-cup or ½-cup measure depending on the size you want. Use a spatula or the back of a spoon to spread the batter a scant ¼ inch thick. Cook until bottom is nicely golden, 2 minutes. Flip; cook the second side until golden, about 2 minutes. Transfer to a warm serving platter. Serve as desired.

....

Nutrition information per serving: 203 calories, 3 g fat, 1 g saturated fat, 3 mg cholesterol, 39 g carbohydrates, 6 g protein, 378 mg sodium, 3 g fiber

Stacked boxty with smoked salmon and lemon

Prep: 15 minutes | Makes: 4 servings

For brunch, I like to serve stacks of 3-inch-diameter cakes topped with thinly sliced smoked salmon and sour cream dollops.

1 recipe boxty, cooked into 3-inch cakes

8 ounces thinly sliced smoked salmon

¼ cup sour cream

Fresh dill sprigs or 2 green onions, thinly sliced

Thinly sliced lemons

① For each serving, stack 3 or 4 boxty on a warm plate. Top with curled slices of smoked salmon and a 1 tablespoon dollop of sour cream. Sprinkle with dill or green onions. Garnish with lemon slices. Serve hot.

....

Nutrition information per serving: 404 calories, 9 g fat, 4 g saturated fat, 27 mg cholesterol, 59 g carbohydrates, 20 g protein, 1,017 mg sodium, 5 g fiber

Nothing comforts like warm, tender sweet pancakes after a busy day.

Sweet potato pancakes with praline mascarpone topping (p. 214)

NOTHING COMFORTS LIKE WARM, TENDER SWEET PANCAKES AFTER A BUSY day. These days we lean toward savory toppings such as the Kale and ham skillet (see recipe on p. 122) alongside sweet options. Flavor-packed sweet potatoes enliven our pancake batter. So does the nutty essence of whole wheat flour and a touch of aromatic allspice.

You have options for the sweet potatoes: Microwave 3 medium (total 1¼ pounds) potatoes on high until fork-tender for 10 or 12 minutes. Then, cool, peel and mash. Or, use 1 can (29 ounces) cut sweet potatoes in light syrup, drained and mashed. Truth be told, canned pumpkin makes a great substitute. Either way, the pancakes taste rich and yield a soft, puddinglike interior.

Sweet potato pancakes

Prep: 20 minutes | Cook: 20 minutes | Makes: 12 to 14 pancakes (each 3 inches in diameter), about 4 servings

These are also great served simply with pure maple syrup or a sprinkling of cinnamon sugar and whipped cream. I also like them with chunky homemade applesauce.

2 large eggs

1½ cups low-fat buttermilk

1 cup pureed cooked sweet potatoes (or 1 cup canned sweet potatoes, drained)

4 tablespoons butter, melted

2 tablespoons expeller-pressed canola oil

1 cup all-purpose flour

½ cup whole wheat flour

2 teaspoons baking soda

½ teaspoon salt

¼ teaspoon ground allspice

Expeller-pressed canola oil or rice bran oil for cooking

Praline mascarpone topping (recipe follows), cinnamon-sugar and maple syrup, or Kale and ham skillet (see recipe on p. 122)

① Heat oven to 200 degrees. Whisk the eggs in a large mixing bowl until blended. Add buttermilk, sweet potatoes, melted butter and oil. Whisk briskly until the mixture is blended.

② Stir the flours, baking soda, salt and allspice together in a small bowl until well blended. Stir flour mixture into the buttermilk mixture just enough to moisten the dry ingredients. It's OK to leave some lumps rather than overmix and make tough pancakes.

③ Heat 1 or 2 large nonstick skillet(s) or a nonstick griddle over medium heat until a drop of the pancake batter bubbles furiously. Lightly oil the cooking surface. Spoon out about ¼ cup of batter per pancake. Spread the batter with the back of the spoon so it is thinned out a little. Cook until a few bubbles break on top and the bottom is golden, about 2 minutes. Gently flip pancake over; cook until second side is golden, 1-2 minutes. Keep oiling the cooking surface and adjusting the heat as you go along so pancakes are golden and not overly browned.

④ Transfer cooked pancakes to a wire rack set over a baking sheet. Keep warm in oven until enough are cooked to serve. Serve with one of the toppings or simply sprinkle with cinnamon-sugar and maple syrup.

....

Nutrition information per pancake: 137 calories, 7 g fat, 3 g saturated fat, 37 mg cholesterol, 16 g carbohydrates, 4 g protein, 315 mg sodium, 1 g fiber

A NOTE ON CANOLA OIL

When shopping for canola oil, be sure to use one suited for high heat, otherwise your pancakes could burn and take on a slight smell of fried fish. I prefer organic expeller pressed for its higher smoke point and neutral flavor. Other options include rice bran oil (great for high heat), safflower oil, peanut oil or sunflower oil.

Praline mascarpone topping

Prep: 10 minutes | Cook: 3 minutes | Makes: 6 servings

2 cups (8 ounces) pecan halves

¼ cup packed dark brown sugar

2 tablespoons butter

1 cup plain nonfat Greek yogurt

½ cup (4 ounces) mascarpone

2 to 3 tablespoons honey

Skim milk, if needed

① Put pecans, sugar and butter in a medium-size nonstick skillet set over medium heat. Cook and stir until sugar has melted and pecans start to brown, 2-3 minutes. Scrape out onto a plate; cool.

② Whisk yogurt, mascarpone and honey together lightly in a medium bowl until blended. Drizzle in a little skim milk if mixture is too thick to dollop easily.

③ Dollop the whipped mascarpone on pancakes; sprinkle with the pecans.

....

Nutrition information per serving: 455 calories, 40 g fat, 9 g saturated fat, 31 mg cholesterol, 24 g carbohydrates, 9 g protein, 31 mg sodium, 4 g fiber

*With a breakfast
dish so sweet
and indulgent,
you'll hardly need
syrup—use pure
maple if you must.*

Blueberry-topped French toast casserole
with fresh berry syrup (p. 218)

N THIS RECIPE, PLENTY OF FRESH BLUEBERRIES, MIXED WITH SWEET BUTTER, light brown sugar, cinnamon and flour, nearly melt into the top of the toast casserole. Of course, more blueberries can be stirred into the bread mixture before baking too. A combination of blueberries, red, black and golden raspberries makes a stunning topping.

Blueberry-topped French toast casserole with fresh berry syrup

Prep: 20 minutes | Stand: 30 minutes | Cook: 45 minutes | Makes: 6 servings | Pictured on p. 216–217

Here's a secret: Leftover French toast casserole makes a terrific late-night snack. Enjoy it super-cold topped with a spoonful of cold milk or softened vanilla ice cream after everyone has gone to bed. (Don't ask.)

12 ounces challah bread or egg twist bread, cut into 1½-inch cubes, about 8 generous cups

5 large eggs

1½ cups skim milk

¾ cup half-and-half or whole milk

1½ teaspoons vanilla

Large pinch salt

Berry topping:

6 tablespoons unsalted butter, softened

⅓ cup packed light brown sugar

½ teaspoon ground cinnamon

Large pinch salt

¼ cup flour

2 generous cups blueberries

Confectioners' sugar

Plain yogurt (or whipped creme fraiche) and/or Fresh berry syrup (see recipe on p. 270)

① Butter the bottom and sides of a deep 8-inch square baking pan. Put the bread into a large bowl.

② Put eggs, milk, half-and-half, vanilla and salt into a bowl or blender. Mix well. Pour over the bread. Stir gently to coat the bread. Transfer to the prepared pan. Let stand while the oven heats (or refrigerate covered up to several hours).

③ Heat oven to 350 degrees. Meanwhile, for berry topping, beat butter in medium bowl with a wooden spoon until light and creamy. Stir in sugar, cinnamon and salt until smooth. Stir in flour until well mixed. Gently stir in blueberries to coat them well.

④ Dollop the blueberry mixture evenly over the bread mixture. Bake until top is golden and puffed and berries are soft and tender, about 45 minutes. Cool on wire rack, 5 minutes.

⑤ Use a spatula to cut mixture into squares. Sprinkle generously with confectioners' sugar. Serve with a spoonful of plain yogurt or whipped creme fraiche and Fresh berry syrup.

....

Nutrition information per serving: 478 calories, 23 g fat, 12 g saturated fat, 248 mg cholesterol, 55 g carbohydrates, 15 g protein, 429 mg sodium, 3 g fiber

SWEET CORNCAKES TOPPED WITH HONEY BUTTER MAKE REGULAR SUMMER appearances in our pancake-loving family. Pureeing some fresh corn into the batter yields maximum corn flavor and tender cakes. Served with smoky Canadian bacon and a berry fruit salad, nothing makes a better summer brunch.

For dinner, add chives to the batter and serve the cakes with thick Greek yogurt and a handful of chopped mixed herbs as an accompaniment to grilled fish or pork chops.

Sweet corn and applewood bacon pancakes

Prep: 30 minutes | Cook: 20 minutes | Makes: 24 pancakes, 6 servings

For savory cakes, stir 2 tablespoons chopped fresh chives and 1 tablespoon chopped fresh parsley or tarragon into the batter.

3 cups fresh corn kernels, from about 4 ears

1 cup whole milk

4 large eggs, separated

2 tablespoons melted butter or bacon drippings

1 ¾ cups flour

¼ cup fine stone-ground corn meal

2 teaspoons baking powder

1 teaspoon salt

4 thick slices applewood smoked bacon, cooked crisp, finely crumbled

2 tablespoons sugar

Vegetable oil

Honey butter (recipe follows), plain Greek yogurt or sour cream

① Puree 1 cup of the corn with the milk and egg yolks in a blender until smooth. Transfer to a large bowl; whisk in melted butter. Mix flour, corn meal, baking powder and salt in a small bowl; add to milk mixture. Add remaining corn kernels and bacon; stir just to moisten flour. Do not over mix.

② Beat egg whites and sugar in small mixer bowl on high speed until nearly stiff but not dry. Gently fold egg whites into the batter just until mixed. Do not worry if you see some white streaks.

③ Heat a large well-seasoned griddle or nonstick skillet over medium heat until hot. Add a light spray of vegetable oil. Spoon batter onto the griddle, making 3-inch round cakes; flatten slightly. Cook until the tops start to bubble and bottoms are golden, about 2 minutes. Turn; cook the second side just until golden, about 1 minute. Serve with desired toppings.

Honey butter: Mix 1 stick (½ cup) softened butter with 2 tablespoons wildflower or favorite-flavor honey in a small bowl until smooth. Scrape into a serving bowl. Refrigerate covered up to 2 weeks. Serve at room temperature.

Nutrition information per serving: 382 calories, 11 g fat, 5 g saturated fat, 160 mg cholesterol, 59 g carbohydrates, 14 g protein, 675 mg sodium, 4 g fiber

OUR SPRING ENTERTAINING OFTEN CENTERS ON BRUNCH AFTER AN EARLY morning bike ride or hike in the woods with friends. Hungry, we're looking for strong coffee and an easy to assemble main course. Enter the oven-baked frittata. Fresh eggs, beaten with cream or milk, embrace tender vegetables and fresh herbs.

Fingerling potatoes, cut into 1-inch rounds, can stand in for round new potatoes. Green onions and fresh dill perfume the whole dish.

Asparagus, new potato and fresh mozzarella frittata

Prep: 25 minutes | Cook: 35 minutes | Makes: 6 servings

Frittatas can be cooked completely on the stove top. I prefer to cook them in a low oven where the steady heat prevents excess browning and overcooking.

8 small (1-inch diameter) new potatoes (12 ounces total), scrubbed clean, quartered

1 bunch (12 ounces) asparagus, tough ends trimmed

2 tablespoons olive oil

4 green onions, trimmed, chopped

1 tablespoon chopped fresh dill

10 large eggs

½ cup whole milk or half-and-half

½ teaspoon salt

¼ teaspoon freshly ground black pepper

1 cup diced (4 ounces total) fresh mozzarella or brick cheese

Chopped fresh dill, for garnish

① Heat oven to 325 degrees. Put potatoes into a large microwave-safe bowl. Add water to barely cover potatoes. Cover with a lid or plastic wrap vented at one corner. Microwave on high (100 percent power), stirring once, until nearly fork-tender, 4-5 minutes. Drain.

② Meanwhile, cut asparagus into 1-inch lengths and set tips aside. Heat olive oil in a 12-inch ovenproof well-seasoned or nonstick skillet over medium heat. Add asparagus stalks; cook until nearly fork-tender, about 3 minutes. Stir in asparagus tips and green onions; cook 1 minute. Remove from heat; stir in potatoes and dill. (Mixture can be made ahead up to 2 days; re-warm before continuing.)

③ Whisk together eggs, milk, salt and pepper in a medium bowl.

④ Place skillet with vegetables over medium heat. When hot, sprinkle cheese over vegetables. Reduce heat to low; gently pour egg mixture over vegetables. Cook until bottom is nearly set, about 3 minutes. Transfer to oven; cook until a knife inserted in center comes out clean, about 20 minutes. Serve warm sprinkled with more dill.

Nutrition information per serving: 279 calories, 18 g fat, 6 g saturated fat, 327 mg cholesterol, 14 g carbohydrates, 16 g protein, 337 mg sodium, 2 g fiber

CHAPTER 10

Sweets and Baked Goods

223

ndividual Yorkshire puddings—aka popovers—make a great accompaniment to holiday roasts and special occasion meals. A basketful of hot popovers makes a tasty treat at brunch, too.

They might just be one of the simplest breads to make—no kneading required. Only trick is that popovers should be served the minute they come out of the oven. Good thing the batter keeps well in the refrigerator. I pop the popovers in the oven while the roast rests on the cutting board and the diners are seated at the table working on a fresh salad.

Easy cheesy popovers

Prep: 20 minutes | Cook: 30 minutes | Makes: 12 popovers

I flavor the crusty airy rolls with fresh rosemary and Parmesan when serving alongside a traditionally flavored beef roast. I switch to cilantro and Monterey Jack to serve alongside a grilled beef or lamb roast. Either way adding a pinch of cayenne to the batter helps counter richness.

1 cup flour

½ teaspoon salt

⅛ to ¼ teaspoon cayenne, optional

3 to 4 tablespoons chopped fresh parsley and chives or cilantro

1 teaspoon minced fresh rosemary or ½ teaspoon dried

½ cup finely shredded cheese, such as Parmesan, white cheddar or Monterey Jack

1¼ cups whole milk

2 large eggs

1 tablespoon melted butter

① Whisk together flour, salt and cayenne in a large bowl (or 2-quart glass measuring cup with a pour spout if you have it). Stir in herbs and cheese. Mix milk, eggs and butter in a small bowl. Pour over flour mixture; whisk gently just enough to moisten the flour. Refrigerate the batter while the oven heats, or up to several hours.

② Heat oven to 450 degrees. When oven is hot, generously coat a regular-size 12-cup muffin pan with nonstick cooking spray. (Or generously spray 12 large custard cups and then coat them with flour and set on a baking sheet.)

③ Pour the batter into the prepared cups, filling them three-fourths full. Put into the hot oven. Bake, without opening the oven, 15 minutes. Reduce oven temperature to 350 degrees. (Do not open the door.) Bake until puffed and nicely browned, about 15 minutes. Serve immediately.

Nutrition information per serving: 89 calories, 4 g fat, 2 g saturated fat, 39 mg cholesterol, 9 g carbohydrates, 4 g protein, 171 mg sodium, 0 g fiber

HOMEMADE BREAD GRACED OUR TABLE MOST DAYS WHEN I WAS GROWING up. Huge, fluffy loaves of white bread dominated until the local grocery store began stocking whole wheat and rye flours. Sweet breads, studded with cinnamon, raisins and walnuts disappeared before they had a chance to cool. At Easter, hot cross buns and sweet dinner rolls filled the house with wonderful aromas.

The dough for these rolls begins with quick-rise dry yeast in place of the fresh, perishable yeast of childhood. These envelopes last on the shelf for many months and shorten the rising time considerably—usually by half. The yeast also can be added to the dry ingredients, eliminating one bowl. For tenderness and a pleasingly tangy flavor, plain yogurt can replace some of the milk. A good dose of sugar helps the bread stay fresh for a couple of days.

One batch of the yogurt dough will yield 24 light, no-butter-needed rolls. Add dried apricots, pineapple and a quick glaze to create hot cross buns. Or, add a generous amount of herbs and black pepper to create a special roll that pairs nicely with everything from ham to roast chicken and grilled steaks.

Super-tender yeast rolls

Prep: 30 minutes | Rise: 1½ hours | Cook: 25 minutes | Makes: 2 dozen rolls

Yogurt creates light, airy rolls that are so good served warm you don't need butter. For slightly denser rolls that freeze and reheat well, you can substitute 1 carton (15 ounces) ricotta cheese for the yogurt, and increase the milk to ¾ cup.

4 to 4½ cups bread flour

2 envelopes (¼ ounce each) quick-rise dry yeast

¼ cup sugar

2 teaspoons salt

½ cup milk

¼ cup (½ stick) unsalted butter

2 large eggs, beaten

2 cups low-fat plain yogurt

① Thoroughly combine 3 cups of the flour, yeast, sugar and salt in the large bowl of an electric mixer. Put milk and butter in a microwave-safe bowl; microwave on high, until butter is melted, about 1½ minutes.

② Add the milk mixture, eggs and yogurt to the flour mixture; beat on low speed until smooth. Switch to the dough hook if you have one, or use a wooden spoon, to work in 1 more cup of the flour. Beat on medium speed (or stir vigorously with the spoon) until mixture makes a smooth yet very sticky dough, about 3 minutes. Beat in add-ins (see variations) if using and additional flour as needed to make a soft dough.

③ Scrape the dough into a greased bowl. Cover with a towel; let rise in a warm, draft-free spot until nearly doubled in size, about 1 hour.

④ Use a greased spoon to scoop the mixture evenly into well-greased muffin tins. Cover with a towel; let rise 30 minutes.

⑤ Heat oven to 350 degrees. Bake rolls in center of oven until nicely golden on all sides, 20-23 minutes. Cool 2 minutes in the pan; remove the rolls to a wire rack. Cool until just warm.

Nutrition information per roll (for basic dough): 130 calories, 3 g fat, 2 g saturated fat, 24 mg cholesterol, 21 g carbohydrates, 5 g protein, 217 mg sodium, 1 g fiber

Pineapple-apricot hot cross buns: Mix 2/3 cup each minced dried apricots and dried pineapple into the dough in Step 2. Let rise and bake as directed. Cool until warm. Meanwhile, mix 1 cup confectioners' sugar with about 1 teaspoon milk (or as needed) to make a thick glaze. Spoon glaze over each warm bun in the shape of a cross.

Herbed dinner rolls: Mix 2 tablespoons dried chives, 2 teaspoons mixed dried herbs, such as tarragon, thyme and rosemary, and ½ teaspoon freshly ground black pepper into the dough in Step 2. Let rise and bake as directed. While still hot, generously brush tops generously with melted butter (about 2 tablespoons total); sprinkle with coarse salt.

CORNBREAD PROVES AN EASY ENTRY INTO BREAD BAKING—NO YEAST TO deal with, no kneading. Sprucing up a boxed mix makes it even less demanding. I like to add sweet corn and spicy chipotles for a treat to serve warm with stews, chili and main-course salads.

Cheesy smoky cornbread

Prep: 15 minutes | Cook: 25 minutes | Makes: 8 servings

I like the Krusteaz brand of cornbread mix; it's all natural and perfectly seasoned with sugar and honey to counter the addition of smoky chipotle chilies.

2/3 cup half-and-half

1/3 cup safflower oil or expeller-pressed canola oil, plus 2 tablespoons for the pan

1 large egg

2 tablespoons finely chopped chipotles in adobo with their sauce

1 cup fresh or thawed frozen corn kernels

1 cup shredded Monterey Jack or cheddar cheese

3 to 4 tablespoons chopped fresh cilantro

1 box (15 ounces) natural honey cornbread mix or another cornbread mix

Softened butter, honey

① Put a 9-inch well-seasoned cast-iron skillet (or 9-by-9-inch baking pan) in the center of the oven. Heat oven to 400 degrees.

② Mix half-and-half, 1/3 cup oil, egg and chipotles in a large bowl. Stir in corn, cheese and cilantro. Stir in cornbread mix just until moistened. Do not overmix.

③ Remove pan from oven; carefully swirl 2 tablespoons oil over the bottom of the pan. Scrape the cornbread mixture into the pan; smooth top. Bake until golden on top and a wooden pick inserted in center is withdrawn clean, about 25 minutes. Cool on wire rack, about 5 minutes. Serve warm with butter and honey.

Nutrition information per serving: 370 calories, 18 g fat, 5 g saturated fat, 43 mg cholesterol, 43 g carbohydrates, 11 g protein, 574 mg sodium, 4 g fiber

We make this pie when the stars align. That is, when our garden's first, tender rhubarb stalks peek out from their foliage and the local farmer's sell baskets of super sweet, super juicy, aromatic strawberries. This clearly exemplifies that the best-quality ingredients make all the difference in the final dish—in this case a classic pie.

This pie is best served warm the day it is made. Leftovers (really?) can be cut into serving pieces and warmed briefly in the microwave.

Strawberry-rhubarb deep dish pie

Prep: 45 minutes | Bake: 55 minutes | Makes: One 10-inch pie, serving 8 to 10 | Pictured on p. 230

If desired, serve each piece of warm pie with a dollop of very softly whipped cream or slightly melted premium vanilla ice cream.

1 recipe pie crust for a double-crust 10-inch pie, well chilled (recipe follows)

2 pounds fresh skinny rhubarb stalks, trimmed

1 to 1⅓ cups sugar

⅓ cup quick-cooking tapioca

½ teaspoon salt

6 cups fresh small strawberries, hulled, halved

2 tablespoons half-and-half

Coarse sugar for sprinkling

① Heat oven to 425 degrees. Have a deep 10-inch glass or ceramic pie plate and a baking sheet ready.

② Roll out the larger disk of pie dough between 2 sheets of floured wax paper into a thin circle about 14 inches in diameter. Carefully fold the dough in half, then place it in the pie dish. Unfold it and fit it over the bottom and up the sides of the pie dish. Trim the overhang to leave about ½ inch all around the pie dish. Refrigerate.

③ Roll the other piece of dough between 2 sheets of floured wax paper into an 11-inch circle; place it (still between the wax paper) on the baking sheet and refrigerate it.

④ For the filling, cut the rhubarb into ½-inch pieces. Place in a large bowl. Add the sugar, tapioca and salt. Mix well. Gently stir in the strawberries. Let stand about 10 minutes.

⑤ Spoon the rhubarb mixture and and about half the accumulated juices into the dough-lined pie dish. Carefully place the top crust over the fruit. Use your fingers to press together the top and bottom crusts, trimming as needed. Use a fork to make a decorative edge. Brush the top of the pie and the edges with the half-and-half. Sprinkle everything generously with the coarse sugar. Gently poke steam vents with a fork into the top of the pie in several spots.

⑥ Bake pie in center of the oven at 425 degrees for 25 minutes. Reduce oven temperature to 350 degrees. Now slide the baking sheet under the pie to catch any drips. Continue baking at 350 degrees until the top crust is nicely browned, 30-45 minutes more. Cool on wire rack until barely warm. Serve warm.

Nutrition information per serving (for 10 servings): 463 calories, 20 g fat, 9 g saturated fat, 26 mg cholesterol, 68 g carbohydrates, 5 g protein, 472 mg sodium, 4 g fiber

Our favorite, forgiving pie crust

Prep: 20 minutes | Chill: 1 hour
Makes: Enough for a double-crust 10-inch pie

We use vegetable shortening for easy dough handling and maximum flakiness; unsalted butter adds rich flavor.

2½ cups all-purpose unbleached flour

1 tablespoon sugar

1 teaspoon salt

½ cup (1 stick) unsalted butter, very cold

½ cup trans fat-free vegetable shortening, frozen

① Put flour, sugar and salt into a food processor. Pulse to mix well. Cut butter and shortening into small pieces; sprinkle them over the flour mixture. Use on/off pulses with the food processor to blend the fats into the flour. The mixture will look like coarse crumbs.

② Put ice cubes into about ½ cup water and let the water chill. Remove the ice cubes; drizzle about 6 tablespoons of the ice water over the flour mixture. Briefly pulse the machine just until the mixture gathers into a dough.

③ Dump the mixture out onto a sheet of wax paper. Gather into two balls, one slightly larger than the other. Flatten the balls into thick disks. Wrap in plastic and refrigerate until firm, about 1 hour. (Dough will keep in the refrigerator for several days.)

Bouchon Bakery in Yountville, Calif., sells chocolate bouchons— little cork-shaped, ultramoist cakes. Nibbling on them during my red-eye flight home, I decided to resurrect a family recipe for a chocolate batter that holds in the fridge for up to a week. Armed with a container of the batter, I can serve warm little cakes at any time in about 20 minutes.

The original recipe uses unsweetened chocolate and plenty of sugar. Nowadays, I prefer to cut the sugar and use a rich, dark, high-quality chocolate with at least 60 percent cacao. I also like to add some espresso powder—a trick that makes the chocolate taste richer with a subtle coffee flavor. For a chocolaty crunch, I opt for cacao nibs—those roasted bits of cacao—that won't soften upon sitting in the moist batter.

The microwave oven proves a great helper for melting chocolate. A 2-quart glass measure does double duty for storing the batter. We always use spoons and rubber scrapers labeled "for chocolate only" to avoid adding off flavors that might be hidden in implements used for savory dishes.

My kids like to push a surprise down into the cakes just before they're baked—everything from a few toasted nuts, to chunks of white chocolate or chocolate mint candies. For special occasions, we will ice the little cakes with chocolate or vanilla buttercream. I also like to serve the cakes warm heavily dusted with confectioners' sugar. Or, spoon crushed fresh berries, sweetened with sugar, on a plate then top with a cake and a dollop of whipped cream. For late night snacks, the confectioners' sugar suffices.

Chocolate mocha cakes

Prep: 15 minutes | **Chill:** 1 hour **Cook:** 20 minutes | **Makes:** 6 cups batter, 48 mini cakes

I like to use dark chocolate that is 60 to 65 percent cacao. Use Scharffen Bergers cacao nibs (roasted, shelled cocoa beans) for an extra-chocolatey crunch (or, use their Nibby bar). If you wish, bury a sweet surprise into each cake just before baking.

8 ounces bittersweet chocolate, 60 to 65 percent cacao, chopped

1¼ cups (2½ sticks) unsalted butter, at room temperature

1 tablespoon instant espresso powder

1¾ cups unbleached all-purpose flour

2 cups granulated sugar

6 large eggs

⅓ cup cacao nibs, optional

Add-ins: Pecan or walnut pieces, chunks of semisweet chocolate or white chocolate

Confectioners' sugar

① Put chopped chocolate and butter into a large, microwave-safe bowl. Microwave on medium (50 percent power), stirring every minute, until chocolate is barely melted, 2 to 3 minutes. (Use caution not to overheat the chocolate.) Stir to mix the two ingredients together. Stir in espresso powder until smooth.

② Combine flour and sugar in a large mixer bowl. One at a time, beat in the eggs until smooth. Beat in the melted chocolate mixture just until incorporated. Stir in cacao nibs, if using. Refrigerate batter, covered, at least 1 hour or up to a few days.

③ Heat oven to 350 degrees. Line mini-muffin tins (2 inches across at the widest point) with paper liners (or heavily grease and flour the pans). Use a large spoon or ice cream scooper dipped in water to scoop 2 tablespoon mounds of the batter into the prepared pans. If desired, tuck nuts or pieces of chocolate into the center of each cake. Bake until a wooden pick comes out clean, 20 to 22 minutes. Cool on a wire rack.

④ Serve dusted with confectioners' sugar.

Nutrition information per cake: 124 calories, 7 g fat, 4 g saturated fat, 36 mg cholesterol, 14 g carbohydrates, 2 g protein, 10 mg sodium, 1 g fiber

M Y SON'S FAVORITE BLOND BROWNIE RECIPE IS FROM GREAT-GRANDMA. He personalized the supersweet bar cookie by substituting dark brown sugar for light, white chocolate chunks for butterscotch morsels and macadamias for the standard pecans.

White chocolate macadamia blondies

Prep: 15 minutes | Bake: 35 minutes | Makes: 48 small bars

The recipe makes plenty; fortunately they freeze well. Serve them slightly warm with vanilla frozen yogurt.

2½ cups flour

1 teaspoon baking powder

½ teaspoon salt

1 cup (2 sticks) unsalted butter, softened

1½ cups packed dark brown sugar

1 teaspoon vanilla

2 large eggs

12 ounces best-quality white chocolate, in ½-inch
    chunks, about 2 cups

1 cup chopped macadamia nuts (lightly salted)

① Heat oven to 350 degrees. Mix flour, baking powder and salt in a small bowl.

② Beat butter in large bowl of electric mixer until light, 2-3 minutes. Beat in brown sugar and vanilla until creamy. Beat in eggs, one at a time, until light.

③ On low speed, beat in flour mixture until incorporated. Stir in chocolate chunks and macadamia nuts with a spoon. Scrape into an ungreased 13-by-9-inch baking pan; spread smooth. Bake until edges start to pull away from sides of pan, 30-35 minutes.

④ Cool on wire rack. Cut into small squares.

Nutrition information per bar: 142 calories, 8 g fat, 4 g saturated fat, 20 mg cholesterol, 16 g carbohydrates, 2 g protein, 54 mg sodium, 0 g fiber

W E'RE THINKING ABOUT CHOCOLATE, SPECIFICALLY, BROWNIES. I GREW up in a house that always had the fixings for a pan of brownies. Not a box of brownie mix, mind you, but unsweetened chocolate, real butter, real vanilla, eggs and sugar. Ever the kitchen adventurers, my sisters and I tinkered with add-ins such as toasted nuts, chocolate chips, toffee bits, chopped candy bars and more. To this day, brownies save the day for every event from Sunday supper to summer potlucks and picnics.

Latte brownies

Prep: 25 minutes | Cook: 35 minutes | Makes: about 32 pieces

For the espresso powder, try Starbucks Via packets for fabulous flavor that dissolves beautifully. I add a couple of packets to the brownies and then save a half packet for the latte glaze. I also like to stir a few tablespoonsful of chocolate covered espresso beans into the batter for flavor and crunch.

8 ounces unsweetened chocolate, coarsely chopped

½ cup (1 stick) plus 2 tablespoons unsalted butter

2 cups granulated sugar

4 large eggs, lightly beaten

2 tablespoons instant espresso powder (or 2½ packets Starbucks Via Italian Roast)

1 tablespoon coffee-flavored liqueur or 2 teaspoons vanilla

⅛ teaspoon salt

1 cup flour

1 package (10 ounces) dark chocolate morsels or roughly chunked bittersweet chocolate bars

Mocha latte icing:

1 cup confectioners' sugar

1 teaspoon instant espresso powder (or ½ packet Starbucks Via Italian Roast)

1½ to 2 tablespoons half-and-half or milk

① Heat oven to 350 degrees. Line the inside of a 13-inch-by-9-inch metal baking pan with heavy-duty foil. Lightly grease the foil.

② Put unsweetened chocolate and butter into a large, heavy-bottomed saucepan. Melt over very low heat, stirring constantly with a wooden spoon, until smooth. Remove from heat. Stir in granulated sugar until well mixed; stir in eggs until well mixed. Stir in instant espresso powder, coffee liqueur and salt.

③ Stir in flour just until incorporated. Fold in chocolate morsels. Spread batter in prepared pan. Bake until center is just set, but not at all dry, 35-40 minutes. Cool completely in the pan on a wire rack.

④ For icing, mix confectioners' sugar, espresso powder and half-and-half in a small bowl until smooth and slightly runny. Use the tines of a fork to swirl the icing over the brownies. Let stand until set. Gently lift the brownies out of the pan and remove the foil. Cut into 32 squares.

Nutrition information per serving: 223 calories, 12 g fat, 7 g saturated fat, 33 mg cholesterol, 27 g carbohydrates, 3 g protein, 20 mg sodium, 0 g fiber

APPLE PIE AND MINCEMEAT PIE TOP THE FAMILY'S REQUEST LIST. TROUBLE is, pies and tarts taste best when served within hours of baking. Tough to do when the cook must also make the rest of the meal.

The solution: Make the filling in advance, purchase the pastry dough and assemble the two when the oven frees up for a half-hour the day of the event. Always trying to please everyone, we've devised a simple tart with a filling that combines a variety of apples and bottled mincemeat.

Sweet apple and mincemeat tart

Prep: 30 minutes | Cook: 25 minutes | Makes: 8 servings

Look for frozen all-natural puff pastry for this recipe, if it's available. Dufour Pastry Kitchens brand uses sweet butter. Thaw according to package directions for best results, usually a couple of hours. Use crisp apples, such as a combination of Honey Crisp, Gala, Golden Delicious.

2 pounds (4 to 6) crisp apples

2 tablespoons unsalted butter

½ cup granulated sugar

1 cup bottled mincemeat

Grated rind of ½ orange

1 package (14 ounces) frozen puff pastry, thawed

Half-and-half and sugar for brushing

Confectioners' sugar

① Peel, core and slice apples into ¼-inch thick slices. Melt butter in large skillet. Add apple slices and granulated sugar; cook, covered, over medium heat, 5 minutes. Remove cover. Cook over medium-high heat, stirring gently, until apples are golden and tender, 5 to 10 minutes. Transfer to a large platter to cool.

② Gently stir mincemeat and orange rind into the apples. (Mixture can be made up to 2 days in advance; refrigerate tightly covered.)

③ Heat oven to 400 degrees. Gently roll out thawed puff pastry on a lightly floured work surface to a 14-by-11-inch rectangle. Carefully transfer to a parchment paper-lined baking sheet. Fill center with the apple mixture leaving a 2-inch border. Fold the border over the apples making a rustic edge. Brush border with a little half-and-half; sprinkle generously with sugar.

④ Bake until pastry is golden, 25 to 28 minutes. Cool on wire rack. Serve warm or at room temperature with a sprinkle of confectioners' sugar and a scoop of ice cream.

....

Nutrition information per serving: 477 calories, 22 g fat, 7 g saturated fat, 8 mg cholesterol, 72 g carbohydrates, 4 g protein, 180 mg sodium, 3 g fiber

EVERY SUMMER WHEN THE KIDS WERE LITTLE, WE RENTED A COTTAGE ON Lake Michigan. The sandy beaches entertained the toddlers for hours while the husband explored the country roads on his bike. Exhausted, they all took long naps. Perfect time for me to prepare the mountains of produce I had bought at the local farm stands.

Versatile fruit compote remains a favorite from those times. I'll make a double recipe on Sunday for week-long pleasure—spooned over plain yogurt with granola for breakfast, served over grilled pork chops for dinner and warmed for pancakes. For dessert, it's great over grilled pound cake, meringues, angel food cake, even sweet cornbread.

When it's just too hot to bake, we make this simple Italian-inspired pudding recipe. Panna cotta, literally cooked cream, can be super-light when made with nonfat yogurt and just a hint of mascarpone. The kitchen stays cool, too, since the microwave easily warms the milk and gelatin. The puddings can be made up to 3 days ahead and then topped with the delectable stunning fruit just before serving. We guarantee you'll start making memories of your own.

Lemon mascarpone panna cotta with peach and berry compote

Prep: 20 minutes | Chill: 2 hours | Makes: 6 servings

Look for mascarpone in the dairy and cheese section of most large supermarkets. Creme fraiche and sour cream make nice substitutes but additional yogurt can be used too.

2 teaspoons (1 small envelope) plain powdered gelatin

2 tablespoons cold water

1 cup low fat milk

½ cup sugar

1½ cups plain nonfat Greek yogurt

⅓ cup mascarpone, creme fraiche or sour cream

Finely grated zest (yellow part only) of 1 small lemon

Juice of ½ small lemon

Pinch salt

Peach and berry compote (recipe follows)

Sprigs of fresh mint for garnish

① Sprinkle gelatin over cold water in small bowl. Let stand until softened, about 3 minutes.

② Heat milk and sugar in large microwave-safe bowl on high, stirring once or twice, until sugar dissolves (rub a little between your fingers), about 2 minutes. Stir in softened gelatin until dissolved. Cool to room temperature.

③ Combine yogurt, mascarpone, lemon rind, juice and salt with a whisk or hand mixer in a large bowl until blended. Whisk in cooled milk mixture until smooth. Divide the mixture among six dessert bowls or stemmed wine glasses. Cover; refrigerate until set, usually 2 hours. (Or up to 3 days.)

④ Serve topped with a generous spoonful of the peach and berry compote. Garnish with mint.

....

Nutrition information per serving: 212 calories, 12 g fat, 6 g saturated fat, 34 mg cholesterol, 23 g carbohydrates, 6 g protein, 91 mg sodium, 0.23 g fiber

Peach and berry compote with fresh herbs

Prep: 20 minutes | Cook: 5 minutes | Makes: 6 cups

Use ripe, local peaches that have not been refrigerated for the best flavor and texture. The recipe doubles easily and will keep in the refrigerator up to 1 week.

6 ripe medium-size peaches, about 1½ pounds

¼ cup sugar or to taste

Juice of ½ small lemon

1½ teaspoons cornstarch dissolved in 1 tablespoon water

3 cups mixed seasonal berries, such as raspberries, blueberries, blackberries, sliced strawberries

2 small sprigs fresh herbs, such as lemon verbena, mint, thyme, rosemary, lavender or a combination

① Heat a saucepan of water to a boil. Gently immerse 1 or 2 peaches in the water; leave them just long enough to loosen the skins, about 30 seconds. Remove with a slotted spoon; let cool. Use a paring knife to remove the skins. Repeat to peel all the peaches.

② Working over a saucepan to catch the juices, slice peaches ¼ inch thick. Let the slices fall into the pan. Add sugar and lemon juice. Heat over medium heat until peaches release their juices, about 2 minutes. Stir in dissolved cornstarch. Heat to a boil, stirring constantly, just until the liquid thickens and clears, about 2 minutes. Remove from heat, stir in berries and herb sprigs; let cool.

③ Remove herbs; refrigerate in a covered container.

....

Nutrition information per serving: 105 calories, 0.54 g fat, 0.03 g saturated fat, 0 mg cholesterol, 26 g carbohydrates, 1 g protein, 0.83 mg sodium, 4 g fiber.

When we're planning ahead, I'll transform a few cups of fresh grapefruit juice into an icy, refreshing granita. If grapefruit's not your thing, try tangerine juice or some of the combination fruit juices such as orange-mango. A little wine adds flavor and prevents the mixture from freezing too hard. Skip it if you'd like.

Easy grapefruit granita

Prep: 5 minutes | Freeze: Several hours or overnight | Makes: 4 servings

Serve the ice in small bowls with sections of fresh citrus fruit. Or, serve it in fluted glasses topped with a generous splash of sparkling wine.

2 cups fresh-squeezed grapefruit juice

¼ cup white wine, such as pinot grigio

¼ cup sugar

Fresh grapefruit wedges

① Mix all ingredients except grapefruit wedges in an 8- or 9-inch metal baking dish until the sugar dissolves completely. (Rub a little between your fingers; it shouldn't feel gritty). Put the dish into the freezer. Freeze until solid. Occasionally stir the mixture with a fork to make large, irregular ice chunks.

② Shave the ice with a large fork. (Or break it into chunks and pulse it in a blender or food processor until fluffy.) Scoop the ice into small dishes. Garnish with fresh grapefruit wedges if desired; serve immediately.

Nutrition information per serving: 109 calories, 0 g fat, 0 g saturated fat, 0 mg cholesterol, 24 g carbohydrates, 1 g protein, 1 mg sodium, 0 g fiber

PEOPLE ALWAYS ASK CHEFS TO NAME THEIR FAVORITE DISH. IMPOSSIBLE! But I will tell you this: A ripe peach makes me so happy. Especially a Red Haven peach from Michigan.

I organize my summer around their short season. I plan travel to Michigan to pick them. Closer to home, I buy basketsful of that juicy, aromatic peach, then I pack them into lunches, eat them over the sink and turn them into jam, salads, pie, ice cream, smoothies and all manner of quick desserts.

For this trifle, use large cubes of either pound cake or angel cake and soak them in sugary bourbon before layering them with peach jam and chopped fresh peaches. Take a tip from the trendy restaurants and serve the peaches and cream trifle in flat-bottomed glasses or jam jars.

Peaches and cream trifle with ginger and bourbon

Prep: 30 minutes | Chill: 30 minutes | Makes: 6 servings

Angel cake makes a lighter trifle. Peach nectar or very sweet black tea can be substituted for the bourbon.

4 to 6 thick slices pound cake (about 10 ounces total)

¼ cup bourbon

5 tablespoons confectioners' sugar

½ -inch chunk fresh ginger, peeled

8 ounces mascarpone or creme fraiche

½ cup heavy whipping cream

¾ cup Quick peach jam (see recipe on p. 269) or best-quality peach preserves

2 or 3 medium peaches, halved, pitted, diced or very thinly sliced

1 cup fresh raspberries

Mint sprigs

① Have 6 flat-bottomed rocks glasses or jam jars (8 ounces each) ready. Cut pound cake into ½-inch cubes. Mix bourbon and 2 tablespoons sugar in a small bowl.

② Grate the ginger into a mixing bowl. Add the mascarpone, whipping cream and remaining 3 tablespoons sugar. Beat into soft peaks with a hand mixer or whisk. (Be careful not to overbeat, or mixture will look lumpy.)

③ For each dessert, put a layer of the cake cubes into a glass. Drizzle with a little of the sweetened bourbon. Layer in this order: 1 tablespoon peach jam, a small scoop of the whipped cream, a couple of peach slices and some raspberries. Add more cake cubes and repeat the layers. Make the remaining 5 desserts. Refrigerate until chilled, at least 1 hour. Serve garnished with mint sprigs.

Nutrition information per serving: 568 calories, 33 g fat, 15 g saturated fat, 75 mg cholesterol, 65 g carbohydrates, 7 g protein, 212 mg sodium, 2 g fiber

ANNED UNSWEETENED COCONUT MILK, ALONG WITH A LITTLE CREAM and sugar, makes a terrific coconut ice cream. Pureed fresh mango or banana make it irresistible.

Coconut mango ice cream

Prep: 20 minutes | Cook: 3 minutes | Chill: Several hours | Makes: About 1½ quarts, 12 servings

Substitute 2 large bananas for the mangos for a banana-coconut variation. Light coconut milk can be used; the mixture will be a little less creamy.

1 can (13.5 ounces) unsweetened coconut milk

1 cup heavy whipping cream

½ cup granulated sugar

Generous pinch salt

2 large ripe mangos or 1½-2 cups fresh or frozen mango pulp

Garnishes: Chopped roasted peanuts, toasted coconut shreds, diced fresh mango

① Heat coconut milk, cream and sugar in a small saucepan just long enough to dissolve the sugar. Remove from heat; add the salt. Refrigerate until cold.

② Puree mango pulp in a blender. Add the milk mixture; blend smooth. Chill base until very cold before making ice cream; it can be refrigerated up to 1 day.

③ Freeze the cold base in an ice-cream-maker according to manufacturer's directions. Remove from the maker; transfer to a covered, freezer container. Freeze 20 minutes or up to a couple of days.

④ Serve in small scoops, garnished with roasted peanuts, coconut shreds or diced mango.

Nutrition information per serving: 171 calories, 14 g fat, 11 g saturated fat, 27 mg cholesterol, 11 g carbohydrates, 1 g protein, 12 mg sodium, 1 g fiber.

These CHOCOLATE CHERRY PEANUT BUTTER OATMEAL COOKIES HAVE IT
all going on: oats, nuts, dried fruit and chocolate. The scent of them baking will warm your
house, through and through.

Chocolate cherry peanut butter oatmeal cookies

Prep: 25 minutes | Cook: 12 minutes | Makes: about 90 cookies

These cookies are made without flour. For the best crunch, be sure to use old-fashioned rolled oats, not the finer-textured quick-cooking varieties. I like natural peanut butter for its deep peanut flavor. Store the cookies in a covered container up to several days or freeze up to 2 months.

¼ cup (½ stick) unsalted butter, softened

¾ cup each: granulated sugar, packed dark brown sugar

2 large eggs

1¼ teaspoons baking soda

1 teaspoon vanilla

1 cup extra-crunchy natural peanut butter, at room temperature

3 cups old-fashioned rolled oats

½ cup salted, toasted pumpkin seeds (pepitas), roasted hulled sunflower seeds or roasted peanuts

½ cup dried cherries (chopped if large), dried currants or small dark raisins

8 ounces milk or semisweet chocolate bars, roughly broken into ¼-inch pieces

① Heat oven to 350 degrees. Beat together butter and sugars in large bowl of electric mixer. Beat in eggs, one at a time, until smooth and creamy. Beat in baking soda and vanilla. Beat in peanut butter until incorporated. Use a wooden spoon to stir in oats, pumpkin seeds, cherries and chocolate pieces.

② Use a teaspoon to make balls about 1 inch in diameter. Place on 2 parchment paper-lined baking sheets spacing them about 2 inches apart. Flatten slightly with a spoon. Bake until set and bottoms are slightly golden, about 12 minutes.

③ Cool cookies on pan, 5 minutes. Transfer with a metal spatula to a wire rack to cool completely. (You can reuse the paper-lined baking sheets to bake the remaining cookies.)

Nutrition information per serving: 67 calories, 3 g fat, 1 g saturated fat, 6 mg cholesterol, 8 g carbohydrates, 2 g protein, 34 mg sodium, 1 g fiber

A CLOSE FAMILY FRIEND INTRODUCED US TO GREEK SPICE CAKE MORE THAN three decades ago. It remains a personal favorite. Somewhere along the line, mom added raisins and increased the spices from the original version. Today, we make a version that substitutes some whole wheat flour for white. And we've reduced the sugar a tad. Thick, nonfat Greek yogurt replaces buttermilk for a supertender crumb, and farmers market honey replaces granulated sugar in the soaking syrup.

Serve pieces of the Honey and Greek yogurt spice cake on small plates topped with a dollop of plain yogurt sweetened lightly with honey (or use frozen vanilla yogurt) and a sprinkle of fresh berries.

Honey and Greek yogurt spice cake

Prep: 25 minutes | Cook: 40 minutes | Makes: 24 pieces

This cake is deliciously moist due to the honey syrup.

2 cups all-purpose flour

½ cup whole wheat flour

¾ cup each: granulated sugar, packed light brown sugar

1½ teaspoons each, freshly ground: cinnamon, cloves

1 teaspoon each: baking powder, baking soda, salt

¾ teaspoon ground nutmeg

3 eggs, lightly beaten

1 cup grapeseed or vegetable oil

1⅓ cups plain nonfat Greek yogurt

1 teaspoon almond extract, optional

1 cup each: raisins, finely chopped walnuts

⅔ cup flavorful honey (or dark agave syrup)

¼ cup water

① Heat oven to 350 degrees. Whisk together flours, sugars, cinnamon, cloves, baking powder, baking soda, salt and nutmeg in large mixing bowl. Whisk eggs in medium bowl; whisk in oil, yogurt and almond extract until smooth.

② Gently stir egg mixture into flour mixture; add raisins and walnuts. Mix just until dry ingredients are moistened. Scrape into greased 13-by-9-inch baking pan. Bake until wooden pick inserted in center comes out clean, 35-40 minutes. Cool 5 minutes.

③ Meanwhile, mix honey and water in glass measure. Microwave until hot, about 45 seconds. Remove cake from oven. Cut cake into squares. Slowly pour hot honey mixture over cake, allowing it to soak into cake. Cool completely. Refrigerate up to several days.

Nutrition information per serving: 272 calories, 13 g fat, 1 g saturated fat, 27 mg cholesterol, 38 g carbohydrates, 4 g protein, 185 mg sodium, 1 g fiber

CHAPTER 11

Condiments, Rubs and Sauces

GARDEN-RIPE, JUICY TOMATOES MOTIVATE ME TO CAPTURE THEIR GOODness for the future. The simplest method is to freeze whole tomatoes on baking sheets until solid and then pack them in freezer bags. Thawed, they're no longer suitable for slicing, but will add sweet goodness to sauces, stews and salsas. Grilling the whole tomatoes first enhances their flavor, especially if you add some wood chips to the grill. A puree of these grill-smoked tomatoes makes chili and pasta sauces fantastic.

Oven-roasting small ripe tomatoes with oil, garlic and herbs makes a condiment suited for warm salads and pastas later in the season. A touch of sugar and vinegar turns it into a sweet-sour combination to accompany roasted meats and poultry.

Agrodolce roasted tomatoes

Prep: 20 minutes | Cook: 2 hours | Makes: about 8 cups

For a fantastic bread salad, mix 2 to 4 cups of these sweet and sour tomatoes along with their juices, 6 cups large cubes of toasted hearty bread and a couple of handfuls of baby arugula or spinach.

4 dozen perfectly ripe small round or
    plum tomatoes

1 cup olive oil

¼ cup red wine vinegar

Coarse (kosher) salt

Sugar

8 cloves garlic, very thinly sliced

¾ cup mixed chopped fresh herbs (such as
    parsley, sage, rosemary, thyme, oregano)

① Heat oven to 350 degrees. Cut tomatoes in half through the stem end. Place on two foil-lined rimmed baking sheets. Add half of the oil and vinegar to each pan; turn tomatoes to coat them well. Arrange all the tomatoes cut sides up in a single layer. Sprinkle cut sides with salt and sugar to taste. Sprinkle with garlic and herbs.

② Bake, rotating the pans occasionally, until tomatoes look concentrated and golden browned, about 2 hours. Cool. Transfer to plastic containers with tight-fitting lids, making sure to capture the pan juices. Refrigerate up to a week or freeze for several months.

Nutrition information per ½ cup: 156 calories, 14 g fat, 2 g saturated fat, 0 mg cholesterol, 8 g carbohydrates, 2 g protein, 11 mg sodium, 2 g fiber

LIKE TO SERVE GRILLED LAMB WITH A CONDIMENT MADE OF SHREDDED cucumber and plain yogurt. The combo reminds us of gyros, so we serve it with flatbreads, toasted until warm on the grill.

Cucumber yogurt sauce with garlic and herbs

Prep: 15 minutes | Drain: 30 minutes | Makes: about 2 cups | Pictured on p. 99

Labneh, the Middle Eastern yogurt, tastes especially rich and satisfying.

1 large seedless cucumber

2 to 3 cloves garlic

1 teaspoon salt

2 cups (16 ounces) labneh or plain Greek yogurt

3 tablespoons chopped fresh cilantro, mint or chives (or a combination)

① Peel off and discard about half of the cucumber skin. Put a four-sided grater into a colander. Use the largest holes to shred the cucumber into the colander. Crush the garlic into the cucumber strands; stir in the salt. Let everything drain in the sink or over a bowl, about 30 minutes. Use your hands to squeeze as much water as you can out of the cucumber.

② Put the squeezed cucumber mixture into a bowl. Stir in the labneh and herbs until well mixed. Refrigerate up to 2 days. Stir well before serving.

....

Nutrition information per tablespoon: 20 calories, 1 g fat, 1 g saturated fat, 3 mg cholesterol, 1 g carbohydrates, 1 g protein, 77 mg sodium, 0 g fiber

SET MY DAUGHTER UP AT HER FIRST COLLEGE APARTMENT WITH EXCELLENT cookware, professional knives and a few basic cookbooks. So it surprised me when she called home for help making homemade salad dressing.

Things like balsamic vinaigrette—her specialty at home—suddenly gave her pause when making it on her own. Skype to the rescue—we talked it through with show and tell. Using recipes with options helps the novice cook build confidence and skills. It also helps the budget—enabling the cook to use ingredients on hand or purchase less expensive ones.

Homemade balsamic vinaigrette

Prep: 5 minutes | Makes: about 1 cup

Use grainy brown mustard in place of Dijon and blend a couple of different oils to keep the dressing from tasting "too gourmet."

¼ cup each: balsamic vinegar, red wine (or cider) vinegar

3 tablespoons each: vegetable oil, extra-virgin olive oil

1 or 2 teaspoons Dijon or whole grain mustard

¼ teaspoon each: salt, freshly ground black pepper

¼ teaspoon sugar, honey or agave syrup

Optional flavor add-ins: ½ teaspoon crushed garlic, 1 tablespoon chopped fresh chives or 1 teaspoon dried basil

① Put all ingredients into a jar with a tight-fitting lid. Shake well. Taste and adjust seasonings. Refrigerate covered up to 2 weeks. Use at room temperature.

Nutrition information per tablespoon: 50 calories, 5 g fat, 0 g saturated fat, 0 mg cholesterol, 1 g carbohydrates, 0 g protein, 40 mg sodium, 0 g fiber

Cucumbers just might be the most refreshing vegetable ever. I feel like I'm at a spa when I add a cucumber slice or two to chilled sparkling water. Slice into a cucumber and the whole kitchen smells fresh. Paired with fresh mint or lime, cucumbers simply transform a hot day.

I learned to make bread and butter pickles from my grandmother's bumper crop. Now I want that sweet and crunchy condiment less sweet and more complex. So I'm mixing up paper-thin slices of cucumber, fresh fennel and fresh ginger. Then I'll store these simple pickles in the refrigerator rather than heat up the kitchen with a water bath canner.

Cucumber and ginger pickles

Prep: 30 minutes | Cook: 5 minutes | Makes: about 2 quarts

Use a super-sharp knife or a mandoline to cut everything into paper-thin slices. The vegetables will become softer and more intensely flavored the longer they sit in the refrigerator.

8 medium pickling cucumbers, about 1½ pounds, scrubbed, very thinly sliced

1 fresh fennel bulb, halved, very thinly sliced

1 small red onion, halved, very thinly sliced

2-inch length of fresh ginger, peeled, very thinly sliced

½ cup each: unseasoned rice vinegar, water

¼ cup sugar

1½ teaspoons salt

① Mix the cucumbers, fennel, red onion and ginger in a large bowl. Pack mixture into jars with tight-fitting lids.

② Heat vinegar, water, sugar and salt in small saucepan until boiling and sugar dissolves. Pour evenly over cucumber mixture. Cover jars tightly. Carefully tip jars to distribute the hot liquid. Cool jars completely on counter; refrigerate up to a couple of weeks.

Nutrition information per ¼ cup serving: 12 calories, 0 g fat, 0 g saturated fat, 0 mg cholesterol, 3 g carbohydrates, 0 g protein, 113 mg sodium, 0.5 g fiber

WE KNOW, FARMERS MARKET PEPPERS LOOK JUST LIKE THOSE SOLD AT grocery stores. However, peppers picked within a day or two of cooking sport crisper flesh, more sweetness and better crunch. Also, when roasted, the skin from super-fresh peppers readily separates from the flesh. So take advantage of the harvest and roast a bunch of peppers to have on hand for weeks or months to come.

Olive-oil preserved peppers

Prep: 15 minutes | Makes: 1 quart

The oil left in the jar when the peppers are gone makes a stunning salad dressing.

    8 assorted peppers, such as red, green, yellow,
        cubanelle, banana, grill-roasted, peeled,
        seeded (see "How to")
    1 small hot pepper, optional
    2 to 4 cloves garlic, thinly sliced
    2 or 3 sprigs fresh herbs, such as rosemary,
        thyme, tarragon, parsley
    2 cups extra-virgin olive oil, about

① Layer the peppers, garlic and herbs in a 1-quart glass jar, making attractive layers. Pour olive oil into the jar to completely cover the peppers. Refrigerate covered up to 2 weeks.

HOW TO GRILL-ROAST BELL PEPPERS

Select large evenly shaped bell peppers for this method of cooking.

➤ Prepare a charcoal grill or heat a gas grill to medium-high heat. Wipe the peppers clean. Rub lightly with olive oil. Place on the grill directly over heat source. Cover grill. Cook 5 minutes, turn and continue grilling and turning until peppers are evenly blackened and blistered, about 15 minutes total. Remove to a platter and let cool.

➤ Working over a platter so you collect any juices, gently peel off the charred skin and discard it. Use your hands to pull the stem and seeds out, then tear the peppers into large sections (they'll pull apart naturally at their creases.) Refrigerate covered with their juices for up to a couple of days.

Note: Peppers also can be roasted under the broiler: Put the oiled peppers on a baking sheet positioned 6 inches from the broiler's heat source, turning often, until skin is blistered.

GOCHUJANG, THE RUSTY RED AND STICKY, THICK KOREAN CHILI PASTE, when mixed with brown sugar, vinegar, garlic and sesame oil, perfectly balances sweet, salty, spicy and tangy. Soy sauce adds that fifth taste sensation—umami. Something akin to eating caramel corn and cheddar popcorn in the same handful, the sweet, salty combination keeps you coming back for more.

Sweet and spicy red chili grilling glaze

Prep: 10 minutes | Makes: 2 generous cups

Sriracha hot sauce, sambal oelek, or Chinese chili paste with garlic can be substituted for the Korean chili paste. Heat levels will vary. This glaze is terrific on baby back pork ribs, skirt steak, chicken thighs, skewered shrimp and meaty fish steaks destined for the grill.

¾ cup packed dark brown sugar

½ cup medium-heat Korean chili paste (gochujang)

½ cup distilled white vinegar

¼ cup soy sauce

1 piece (2 inches long) ginger root, peeled (or 2 tablespoons refrigerated ginger puree)

2 tablespoons dark Asian sesame oil

6 large cloves garlic

1 teaspoon salt

① Put all ingredients into a blender. Process until smooth. Transfer to a covered container; use within 2 weeks.

Nutrition information per tablespoon: 33 calories, 1 g fat, 0 g saturated fat, 0 mg cholesterol, 5 g carbohydrates, 0 g protein, 449 mg sodium, 0 g fiber

Rubs

W HICHEVER RUB YOU CHOSE, THE LONGER THE MEAT CAN HANG OUT coated with the rub the better. I like to refrigerate large roasts for two days (but if you don't have that long, allow at least 2 hours); steaks need only an hour or so.

Traditional herb rub

**Makes: Enough for several steaks
or one 8-pound roast**

① In a jar with a tight-fitting lid or a small bowl, mix together 2 tablespoons coarse (kosher) salt, 2 tablespoons dried rosemary, 1 tablespoon sweet paprika, 1 teaspoon each coarsely ground black pepper and dried marjoram, and ½ teaspoon each dried thyme and rubbed sage. Store in cool dry place up to several weeks.

Spicy espresso rub

**Makes: Enough for several steaks
or one 8-pound roast**

① In a jar with a tight-fitting lid or a small bowl, mix together 2 tablespoons coarse (kosher) salt, 1 tablespoon instant espresso powder or 2 dark roast Starbucks Via packets, 1 tablespoon each smoked sweet paprika and dried basil, 2 teaspoons curry powder and ½ teaspoon dried leaf thyme. Store in a cool dry place up to several weeks.

Simple steak rub

Makes: Enough for 4 steaks

① Mix 2 tablespoons chili powder, 1 tablespoon smoked sweet paprika, 1 teaspoon salt and ¼ teaspoon coarsely ground black pepper in a small bowl. Store in a jar up to a couple of weeks.

Poultry spice rub

**Makes: Enough for several chicken breasts
or a whole chicken**

① Grind 1½ tablespoons whole coriander seeds, 1 tablespoon anise seed and 1 teaspoon whole cloves in an electric spice mill or mortar and pestle until a fine powder. Add 1 teaspoon ground cinnamon and 1½ teaspoons salt; mix.

Lemon fennel rub

**Makes: Enough for several chicken breasts,
a whole chicken or roast**

① Heat 1 tablespoon fennel seeds in a small skillet set over medium heat until fragrant, about 1 minute. Grind in a mortar until powdery. Transfer to a bowl; stir in 1 tablespoon salt and 1 teaspoon black pepper. Stir in the grated rind of 2 small lemons.

Fruit Delights

T HE BEST HOLIDAY MEAL PLANNING BEGINS WITH A TIME-TESTED FORMULA: Make the same recipes as last year but add new touches to suit changing tastes. Take cranberry relish. The table looks boring without Grandma's crystal bowl filled with crimson berries. Most years, we fill it with a variation of a chopped raw cranberry and orange relish—sometimes adding apples, sometimes ripe pears.

A few years ago, our daughter, Claire, decided to really change things up. She began with a cooked cranberry sauce recipe from "Joy of Cooking" and added her own touches—vanilla extract one year, chopped pecans another. Her proudest moment: Her version with fresh clementine sections and crystallized ginger. Now she makes double batches so the leftovers can be divided for the holiday doggie bags we send home with the relatives.

Cranberry clementine sauce

Prep: 25 minutes | Cook: 20 minutes | Cool: Overnight | Makes: About 6 cups

Use the cutup fresh pineapple found at supermarket salad bars to help minimize the kitchen prep.

8 seedless clementines, peeled

1 tablespoon grated clementine zest

2 bags (12 ounces each) fresh cranberries, rinsed

4 cups diced fresh pineapple

2 cups sugar

½ cup unfiltered apple cider

¼ cup fresh lemon juice

1 tablespoon finely chopped crystallized ginger

1 teaspoon ground cinnamon

¼ teaspoon each, ground: cloves, allspice

⅛ teaspoon salt

① Separate the sections of the clementines. Cut the sections in half; set aside.

② Mix the zest with the remaining ingredients in a large, heavy saucepan. Heat to a boil over medium-high heat; cover. Cook without stirring until sugar crystals on the side of the pan dissolve, about 5 minutes.

③ Uncover pan; boil gently, stirring often, until thickened, about 10 minutes. Stir in the reserved clementine sections. Pour into a bowl. Refrigerate, covered, overnight or up to 1 week. Serve at room temperature.

....

Nutrition information per ¼ cup serving: 173 calories, 0.1 g fat, 0 g saturated fat, 0 mg cholesterol, 43 g carbohydrates, 0 g protein, 14 mg sodium, 2 g fiber

Dark, juicy Italian prune plums make the perfect cooked fruit accompaniment. It's not quite jam, not quite compote. The plums briefly cook in a light syrup until they're soft and succulent. Italian prune plums were favorites at gram's house, but other firm plums, like greengage, work too. This same simple sugar-syrup cooking method also makes quick jams of peeled, sliced pears, quince, apples, peaches and apricots.

Jammy plums

Prep: 15 minutes | Cook: 15 minutes | Makes: about 1½ cups

This recipe doubles easily and will keep for several weeks in the refrigerator. Stir leftovers into plain yogurt or serve over vanilla ice cream.

1 pound Italian prune plums or greengage plums or a combination

½ cup sugar

1 teaspoon balsamic vinegar

⅛ teaspoon ground allspice

Pinch salt

① Cut plums in half; remove pits. Cut plums into wedges. Pour sugar and ½ cup water into a small saucepan. Boil gently until sugar is dissolved, about 3 minutes.

② Add cut plums to sugar mixture. Heat to a boil. Reduce heat to very low; cook until plums are falling apart and tender, about 10 minutes. Stir in vinegar, allspice and salt. Cool. Serve warm.

Nutrition information per tablespoon: 28 calories, 0 g fat, 0 g saturated fat, 0 mg cholesterol, 7 g carbohydrates, 0 g protein, 6 mg sodium, 1 g fiber

I F YOU'RE LOATH TO MAKE JAM BECAUSE OF THE TIME AND CANNING EQUIP-
ment investment, I urge you to try this recipe. All you need is a saucepan and some covered
containers. The finished jam is simply kept in the refrigerator; it should last a month or more. At
our house it's gobbled up way before then, so I freeze a few containers too.

This speedy, loose, chunky jam makes a great topping for toast, ice cream, plain yogurt or as
the start of some quick summertime desserts such as the Peaches and cream trifle with ginger and
bourbon (see recipe on p. 245).

Quick peach jam

Prep: 20 minutes | **Cook:** 10 minutes
Makes: a generous 2 cups

*This recipe doubles and triples easily if you are lucky
enough to have a surplus of peaches.*

2 pounds ripe small freestone peaches, peeled

½ cup sugar

1 tablespoon quick-cooking tapioca

½ teaspoon bourbon or pure vanilla extract,
  optional

⅛ teaspoon ground cardamom or nutmeg

Pinch salt

① Working over a medium saucepan to capture the
juices, slice the peeled peaches a scant ¼-inch thick,
dropping the slices into the pan. Add remaining
ingredients. Heat to a simmer over medium heat.
Cook, stirring often, until peaches are tender and juices
thickened, 5-10 minutes. Remove from heat; let cool.
Refrigerate in a container with a tight-fitting lid up to
a month or more.

Nutrition information per tablespoon: 24 calories, 0 g fat, 0 g
saturated fat, 0 mg cholesterol, 6 g carbohydrates, 0 g protein,
5 mg sodium, 0 g fiber

HOW TO PEEL A PEACH

Heat a large pot of water to a boil. One at
a time, slip the peaches into the water and
boil just long enough to loosen their skins,
about 20 seconds. Remove to a cutting
board. When they are cool enough to handle, use a paring knife to slip off the skin.

HOW TO FREEZE
SLICED PEACHES

Peaches freeze well for future use if you
slice them first. Peel peaches as directed.
Cut in half. Cut the peaches away from
the pit into ½-inch-thick slices. Toss
the slices with a little lemon juice then
place them in a single layer on a baking
sheet lined with a silicon liner or plastic
wrap. Freeze solid. Carefully remove to
a freezer container. Freeze in a covered
container for up to 6 months.

Lemony grapefruit curd

Prep: 10 minutes | Cook: 5 minutes | Chill: several hours | Makes: a generous 1½ cups

This sweet-tart citrus curd combines grapefruit and lemon but is equally good with all lemon or some tangerine or orange added to the mix.

2 large eggs

2 egg yolks

1 medium grapefruit, washed

1 small lemon, washed

2 tablespoons cornstarch

½ cup sugar

Pinch salt

5 tablespoons unsalted butter, softened

① Beat the eggs and egg yolks in a small bowl. Use a rasp grater to remove the colored part of the grapefruit and lemon rinds (do not grate the bitter white pith) into a small saucepan. Squeeze the juices into a measuring cup. Remove the seeds; pour about ⅔ cup of the juice into the saucepan. (Reserve any remaining juice for another use.)

② Whisk cornstarch into juices in the saucepan until dissolved. Whisk in sugar and salt. Cook, stirring, over medium heat until clear and thickened, 2-3 minutes.

③ Spoon a little of this thickened juice mixture into the beaten eggs to gently warm them. Then stir the egg mixture back into the saucepan. Cook over very low heat, stirring constantly with a wooden spoon, just until the mixture starts to thicken enough to lightly coat the back of the spoon. Do not let it boil or it will curdle. Remove from the heat. Whisk in the butter, a tablespoon at a time, until incorporated. Scrape into a glass jar and refrigerate several hours or up to 2 weeks.

Nutrition information per tablespoon: 55 calories, 3 g fat, 2 g saturated fat, 37 mg cholesterol, 6 g carbohydrates, 1 g protein, 13 mg sodium, 0 g fiber

Fresh berry syrup

Prep: 5 minutes | Cook: 2 minutes | Makes: about 2 cups

You can use one kind of berry or mix several. Serve warm over French toast or chilled over ice cream. For a breakfast parfait, layer it with plain nonfat Greek yogurt, sliced bananas and granola.

2 cups diced strawberries

1 generous cup fresh raspberries, blueberries or
    black raspberries (or a combination)

2 to 3 tablespoons sugar, to taste

Grated lemon zest from ¼ of a lemon

Pinch salt

① Put all ingredients into a microwave-safe dish. Crush gently with a spoon. Cover with lid or plastic wrap vented at one corner. Microwave on high, stirring once, until berries are softened, 2 minutes. Stir well; allow to cool.

Nutrition information per ¼ cup serving: 34 calories, 0 g fat, 0 g saturated fat, 0 mg cholesterol, 8 g carbohydrates, 0 g protein, 19 mg sodium, 2 g fiber

APPENDIX

Outfitting the Kitchen

'VE SPENT A LIFETIME COLLECTING KITCH-
en gadgets from around the world, but to be honest,
it really doesn't take too much equipment to start
your cooking life—especially if you take advantage of
timesaving options such as the precut vegetables and
individual portions of meat and seafood sold in today's
supermarkets. Today, you can get a decent dinner on the
table with nothing more than one good knife, a nonstick
skillet and a saucepan: Cook pasta in the saucepan while
you saute the meat and veggies in the skillet. Garnish
with some chopped fresh herbs.

If you plan on a life of cooking, gradually add to your
kitchen collection over time, investing in quality rather
than quantity. True, you can cook in the lightweight pans
sold in the grocery store or at the flea market—but using
tools you love will mean you want to use them often.

Getting Started

A nesting set of glass mixing bowls (microwave-safe), a wooden spoon, a heatproof rubber scraper, a set of measuring cups, spoons and a glass liquid measure will get you through just about any recipe.

Fill a small canister or a large can with a wooden spoon, a rubber scraper and a heatproof spatula near the stove. You'll use these tools to make batter, flip pancakes and scrape pans and cutting boards.

Invest in a large cutting board and two basic knives—a small, super-sharp paring knife and a medium-size chef's knife (usually an 8-inch blade)—one that fits comfortably in your hand and that you feel confident using.

Kitchen shears are so versatile, and they can prevent common accidents when knives are used inappropriately. I use my shears to cut up chicken, remove elastic bands from produce, cut open pouches and snip herbs.

Having one 8- × 8-inch baking pan means you can roast a couple of chicken breasts or bake a pan of brownies. Ovenproof glass or ceramic prove most versatile because they can be used in the microwave oven to reheat things.

Purchase the best-quality nonstick skillets that you can afford. The heavier the skillet, the less the chance the food in it will scorch. I like a 10-inch skillet for everyday cooking and a small 6-inch skillet for cooking eggs on the weekend. Use both when making pancakes for two.

For other cooking, you should have a large, not-too-heavy pot for boiling water for pasta and vegetables and for making the occasional pot of brothy soup.

Buy a colander that won't tip over in the sink when you drain pasta or blanched green beans.

For electrics, a small rice cooker means foolproof rice and grains every time. An inexpensive blender will be useful for everything from smoothies to pancake batter.

For the Weekday Cook

Spring tongs just might be the tool that elevates a novice cook to a more accomplished level. They're like an extension of my hand: I use them to turn shrimp in the pan, lift asparagus from boiling water to check doneness, flip meat and poultry on the grill, toss salads, remove hot potatoes from the microwave. Test them out in the store for comfort before you buy. Store them in the canister near the stove.

Add a vegetable peeler, garlic press and Microplane grater to the kitchen tool drawer to make fast work of many kitchen tasks. Likewise, a salad spinner takes the chore out of rinsing garden-grown greens and lettuces.

Adding another knife or two, such as a serrated bread/tomato knife and a long slicing knife for carving meat, is a good idea if you cook often. Designating a second cutting board exclusively for raw meat use is wise.

A heavy-duty, enameled cast-iron Dutch oven comes with a hefty price tag, but your stews, braises, pasta sauces and hearty soups will thank you—no more scorched chili or burnt tomato sauce. You can even use it to bake bread or roast chicken.

I recommend investing in a small covered grill (charcoal takes more commitment, but the food you make on it always tastes better than food cooked on a gas grill) for quick-cooking meats and vegetables before adding roasting pans and more skillets or a slow cooker. (Especially if you already have a Dutch oven.) Grilling makes cooking fun, and nearly everyone loves the flavors that come from the grill.

For the Advanced Enthusiast

A santoku knife or a second, larger chef's knife will give you more options. If you don't like chopping, invest in a small food processor to do the work for you (and allow a little extra time for cleanup).

Add some kitchen appliances, such as a powerful blender for super-smooth soups, chili sauces and batters. A stand mixer will make easy work of cookie doughs, breads and stiffly beaten egg whites. I love using my stick blender to puree soups and sauces right in the pot and whip small quantities of cream. I use my larger food processor most in the summer when I want to make fast, tender pie crusts; big batches of pesto; herbed butters and vegetable slaws.

A digital scale helps when I buy vegetables at the farmers market or for measuring bulk flours, grains and rices.

Cast-iron skillets make browning a snap—they're perfect for crispy potatoes, crusty chicken and great cornbread.

Holiday cooks will need heavy duty baking sheets for cookies and flatbreads. Pie plates, Bundt pans, muffin tins, cookie cutters and loaf pans all come in handy and make welcome gifts.

Most kitchens could use a basic cookbook that offers recipes for simple, everyday items like scrambled eggs, meatloaf, salad dressings, simple soups. I am partial to the *Joy of Cooking*, by Irma S. Rombauer, and use it for guidance and inspiration.

ACKNOWLEDGMENTS

As near as I can remember, I fell in love with food in the fourth grade. My teacher, Mrs. Elvin, gave me a taste of her avocado. That rich, buttery, green flavor stirred a passion in me that never wanes.

Thankfully, my family supported all my efforts from that day forward—happily (mostly) tasting all my creations, stopping at every roadside farm stand on the way home from the beach and tolerating my kitchen experiments.

In college, my Foods and Nutrition professor (and now dear friend), Mary Abbott Hess, encouraged me to pursue the culinary arts. She recognized my unbridled preference for rescuing broken hollandaise over devising low-sodium diets.

Suzanne Checchia, the best editor I ever worked with, taught me to write recipes. Our friendship survived a bevy of red pencil marks on my work.

I am sure I had one of the best jobs in the food business in the 1980s, when I was the test kitchen director for the *Chicago Tribune*. Those days were truly the heyday of the newspaper food section. Every chef and cookbook author arrived in our test kitchens to cook with me—including Julia Child, Jacques Pepin, James Beard, Alice Waters, Emeril Lagasse, Craig Claiborne, Paul Bocuse, the Troigros brothers, Georges Blanc and Linda McCartney (and yes, Paul was by her side).

The longtime *Chicago Tribune* food editor Carol Mighton Haddix led our award-winning team of astonishing talent. Together with Joanne Will, Judy Hevrdejs, Carol Rasmussen, Margaret Sheridan, Barbara Sullivan, Paul Camp, Marcia Lythcott, Dodie Hofstetter and columnist Bill Rice, we captured the world's fast-evolving food scene.

During that time, I had the privilege to work with Beverly Vernon, a *Tribune* test kitchen assistant who is the most instinctive cook I know. We collected cookbooks, tested equipment and gadgets and even maintained a kitchen garden to learn from at Cantigny. I remember taking a camp stove into the corn fields to find out whether it's really true that fresher corn is sweeter (it is). Garden writer William Aldrich grew heirloom vegetables, tricolor beets and baby kale and we cooked with them and wrote about them long before Whole Foods stores spread throughout this country.

Through it all, the talented staff of *Tribune* photographers captured food and people alike. Bill Hogan, Bob Fila, Sally Good, Tony Berardi and Ron Bailey taught me to see food through their lens.

Today, Joe Gray leads the *Tribune* Good Eating section with grace. He gently edits my column and suggests topics, and I welcome his input. Jodie Shield's nutrition analysis keeps us real—mostly.

Recipe testers and stylists Joan Moravek, Lisa Schumacher and Corrine Kozlak all make it look so easy. Thank you too to Michael Tercha and Michael Zajakowski for capturing the spirit of my recipes on the cover and in these pages.

Since 1993, the vision of Rick Bayless has affected my food career and my cooking. I've had the privilege of co-authoring three cookbooks with Rick and his wife Deann. With our partners Manny Valdes and Greg Keller, we've built an astonishing food company that puts first-rate Mexican and new American food on home tables every day. We've shared some pretty great meals, too, all in the name of research. Friendships built around the dinner table prove everlasting.

At Frontera, thank you to Renee Ragin, Kelsey Coday, our talented culinary teams and our amazing, dedicated staff—you encourage me every day.

At Agate, my profound thanks to Doug Seibold and Perrin Davis. Thank you to Amy Carr and all the editors over the years at the *Tribune* who've encouraged the staff to push the boundaries; to go the distance.

Thank you to Pat, Roberta, Annie, Bonnie, Lynn, Linda, Mart, Ken, Tim, Dave, Bob, Don and Bill for being the best sisters and brothers in the world. Our annual cookie bake with the nieces and nephews ranks as the sweetest day of my year. Let's keep cooking together.

I owe a world of thanks to my extended family, dear friends and intrepid food colleagues. Especially Shannon Kinsella and Jeanne McInerney Lubeck and my fellow Les Dames d'Escoffier members. I have learned so much from them. May we continue to wine and dine gracefully.

Thank you from the bottom of my heart to my mom and dad, for their unbridled support and countless miles of travel just to eat at some place on my list.

Thank goodness my husband Scott offers to grocery shop and to eat leftovers; we don't waste a morsel. It's been my life's pleasure to share so many meals in so many places with him and our families. Claire and Glen grew up cooking with me. It's truly heaven on earth when I can stand side-by-side with them, cooking dinner in our home.

PHOTO CREDITS

INDEX

ABOUT THE AUTHOR

JeanMarie Brownson was born in Chicago to a family that enjoys cooking. Her grandparents taught her to make Hungarian sausages, to smoke hams and to stretch strudel dough. Spring and summers meant vegetable gardening. August and September always involved canning vegetables, jams and jellies in a steamy hot kitchen.

In high school, she cooked her way through both volumes of Julia Child's *Mastering the Art of French Cooking*. JeanMarie graduated from Mundelein College of Loyola University with a bachelor of science degree in foods and nutrition. She studied cooking at Le Cordon Bleu in Paris and in Mexico with Diana Kennedy. Her family was not surprised when the American Culinary Federation selected her to become the first female chef's apprentice in Chicago.

She completed her chef's apprenticeship in 1978 to take a position as a test kitchen cook for *Cuisine Magazine*. When the *Chicago Tribune* called in 1980, she accepted the position of test kitchen director for the Food Guide, Taste and Sunday Magazine sections. It was a glorious time to be a part of the award-winning food department. During her tenure at the *Tribune*, JeanMarie cooked alongside Julia Child, Jacques Pepin, Anne Willan, Paul Prudhomme and many of the top chefs and cookbook authors in the food business. She was the cooking host for two years on CLTV's "Good Eating" show. JeanMarie received three writing awards from the Association of Food Journalists.

JeanMarie met Rick and Deann Bayless while on assignment for the *Chicago Tribune*. In 1993, Rick asked JeanMarie to work with him on his second cookbook. Over the years, they co-authored three cookbooks including *Rick Bayless's Mexican Kitchen*, winner of the IACP Cookbook of the Year Award, and *Mexico—One Plate at a Time*, winner of the James Beard Foundation's International Cookbook Award.

In 1996, JeanMarie left the *Tribune* to start Frontera Foods with partners Rick Bayless, Manny Valdes, Conchita Valdes and Greg Keller. Today, Frontera Foods is the country's leading gourmet Mexican food company. The group also owns Red Fork Natural Foods, a growing brand of shelf-stable gourmet American products. As culinary director, JeanMarie leads all new product development, plant training, quality control and consumer educational materials. She also is the co-owner and culinary director for Frontera Media Productions, which produces the public television show "Mexico–One Plate at a Time with Rick Bayless."

JeanMarie currently writes a bimonthly *Tribune* newspaper column (the original blog!), titled "Dinner at Home." Since 2007, she has been chronicling a life spent cooking—for work, fun and family. Her column and original recipes can be found online and in *Tribune* newspapers nationwide.

JeanMarie is a member of Les Dames d'Escoffier, the International Association of Culinary Professionals and the James Beard Foundation.

When not cooking or writing, JeanMarie can be found hiking, cycling or culling cookbooks and food magazines for new recipes for her family's annual cookie bake. She lives and cooks in the Chicago area with her family.